Josiah Wedgwood

JOSIAH WEDGWOOD

A BIOGRAPHY

Anthony Burton

STEIN AND DAY/*Publishers*/New York

First published in the United States of America, 1976
Copyright © 1976 by Anthony Burton
Printed in the United States of America
Stein and Day/*Publishers*/Scarborough House,
Briarcliff Manor, N.Y. 10510

Library of Congress Cataloging in Publication Data

Burton, Anthony.
Josiah Wedgwood.

Bibliography: p. 231
Includes index.
1.   Wedgwood, Josiah, 1730-1795.
NK4210.W4B87   738.3′7   [B]   76-6989
ISBN 0-8128-1907-1

Contents

Illustrations

Preface

ANY author involved in a work of this type soon runs up a long list of debts to those who have helped in a variety of ways. I owe a good deal to many individuals and organizations, and especially to Josiah Wedgwood and Sons Ltd, who were generous in allowing access to documents and providing many of the illustrations used in this book. In particular I am grateful to Bruce Tattersall, the curator of the Wedgwood Museum, who was kind enough to read the manuscript and offer much valuable criticism and comment. Needless to say, any errors of fact or interpretation that remain are entirely my own responsibility. I should also like to thank Lynn Daniels for her unfailing patience in dealing with my many requests for photographs and prints.

Two further debts need special mention: first to Ian H. C. Fraser, archivist at the University of Keele, for his good-natured help with the Wedgwood papers; and then to Albert Sternberg who, if he was unable to turn anyone as clumsy as myself into a potter, at least taught me to understand and appreciate something of the nature and quality of clay.

My thanks to them all.

ANTHONY BURTON

Islip, 1975

[1]

The Potter's Field

I saw the field was spacious, and the soil so good, as
to promise an ample recompense to any who should
labour diligently in its cultivation.

JOSIAH WEDGWOOD,
Introduction to his *Experiment Book*

THE Potteries: the name invokes images of a landscape of brick
terraces, rows of back-to-backs from the midst of which the kilns
poke up towards a smoke-streaked sky. Here are the Five Towns of
Arnold Bennett's novels: here is a world we could, until recently,
see for ourselves, but which is now fast disappearing. But it is not
the world into which Josiah Wedgwood was born in 1730. To
attempt to understand that man and his achievements we must
first look at an earlier world, one that he helped to change.

In the early years of the eighteenth century there were no Five
Towns, merely groups of timber-framed thatched cottages and
houses, clustered together into villages and hamlets of which the
most important was Burslem. Potters had settled in this area of
Staffordshire because it met two basic requirements – it had good
clay for fashioning pots and plentiful supplies of coal for firing the
ovens. But it was an area set in the very centre of Britain, connected
to the rest of the country by muddy tracks, deep-rutted lanes in
summer, all but impassable quagmires in winter. These, which passed
by the name of public highways, were made worse by the unsociable
practice of the potters who, if they ran short of clay, were inclined
to make good the deficiencies from the churned up road. The
alternative transport to the waggons of the highways were the

teams of pack horses that could take a higher, narrower way above the clinging mud of the valleys. It was only when the ware could be brought to the navigable Rivers Weaver or Trent that transport became more efficient. Not surprising, then, to find no great industries, but to discover instead a host of small businesses, a community of craftsmen. Instead of the towering bottle kiln there were low, almost hemispherical ovens, seldom rising above a height of eight feet – yet considered quite big enough to take a full week's output. The ware from such ovens went mostly to the crate men, who humped it off to sell at the fairs and markets of the surrounding districts.

The Potteries at the end of the seventeenth century may have been small-scale, serving purely local needs, but the ware that was produced was bold and vigorous in colour and design, and today is appreciated perhaps more than it was by the connoisseurs of that time. And there was no shortage of inventiveness and drive among the Staffordshire potters. In the seventeenth century, slipware – that is, ware decorated by applying a thin mixture of clay and water in a process very like icing a cake – became popular. The best and most famous of the manufacturers of slipware was Thomas Toft, whose designs were usually naïve, frequently idiosyncratic but unfailingly attractive. Elsewhere, delft was manufactured, earthenware covered with a heavy, opaque white tin glaze that could then be decorated with coloured patterns, generally in blue. It was popular throughout Europe but was very prone to chip and break – good business for the potters, less satisfactory for the customers. An alternative, in use in Germany, was the much stronger stoneware with a salt glaze.

Salt glazing was introduced into Britain by John Dwight of Fulham, who produced what was, in effect, a salt-glazed porcelain. He took out a patent – later to be contested by the Elers brothers, who came from Holland to London and finally settled in Staffordshire, bringing salt glazing with them. It was a dramatic process. The ware was packed into special perforated saggars – fire-proof containers that held the ware during firing – and the saggars were loaded into the oven. The potter then climbed a scaffolding on the outside of the heated oven and began tipping salt into the open top. The salt vaporized and filled the inside of the kiln – over-filled it in fact, for the white vapour was soon billowing out from the oven in a quite alarming manner, as a contemporary describes:

> The vast volume of smoke and vapour from the ovens, entering the atmosphere, produced that dense white cloud, which from about eight o'clock till twelve on the Saturday morning (the time of *firing-up*, as it is called) so completely enveloped the whole of the interior of the town, as to cause persons often to run against each other; travellers to mistake the road; and strangers have mentioned it as extremely disagreeable, and not unlike the smoke of Etna and Vesuvius.[1]

Another innovation of the same period, and a most important one in the history of ceramics, came about, according to popular stories, by accident. A potter called Astbury, who for some reason appears to be the central figure in a whole volume of unlikely stories, is said to have discovered that the body of clay could be improved and whitened by the addition of powdered flint. This same Astbury is said to have wrested the secret of salt glazing from the cautious Elers by getting himself employed as odd job man disguised as a gibbering idiot. The discovery of the value of powdered flint was, however, said to be rather fortuitous than devious. Astbury was on his way to London, when his horse started to go blind. He stopped at Dunstable, where the ostler blew powdered flint into the animal's eyes, producing a discharge and, unlikely as it may seem, greatly improving the horse's vision. Astbury noted that the flints were easily ground and gave a white, clayey mixture when wet, and thus hit on the idea of mixing it with clay for pots. True or not, and it is almost certainly not, the story illustrates very clearly that no one was surprised by such a haphazard method of improving technology in the early eighteenth century.

Powdered flint produced a whiter body; and if the flint was mixed with galena (lead sulphide) and dusted on to the ware before it was given its single firing in the oven, the result was a brilliant cream glaze – a highly satisfactory result. Other aspects of the process were less satisfactory, however. Crushing the dry flints gave rise to a form of silicosis in the unfortunate grinders, known as potter's rot, and the galena gave rise to lead poisoning in the equally

unfortunate glazers. The process was improved, as far as the workmen were concerned, by the introduction of wet grinding, in which
the flints were ground under water, and the use of a fluid glaze.
This produced better ware and a more complex manufacturing
process: the pot was fired first unglazed as "biscuit" and then glazed
and refired in the "glost" or "gloss" oven. This largely removed
the scourge of potter's rot, but lead poisoning continued to be a
hazard.

Another innovation of this time deserves special mention. The
Staffordshire area produces a variety of different coloured clays.
Now all clays, before they can be used for pot-making, have to be
"wedged"; that is, they have to be thoroughly mixed and air
bubbles have to be removed. This was usually done by boys who
raised the lumps of clay over their heads and repeatedly banged
them down on the floor. It was discovered that if different clays
were stuck together and repeatedly wedged, being sliced in half
and restuck between wedgings, then a variegated body could be
obtained. Pots from this clay were known, for obvious reasons, as
"tortoiseshell" or "mottled". Another popular coloured effect was
obtained by using a local black clay to produce a black or "basalt"
ware.

These then were some of the wares and processes to be found in
Staffordshire at that time. But what of the individual pot works?
Wedgwood, in later life, became interested in the history of the
district, and worked out the value of an average pottery producing
black and mottled ware in the period 1710–15 as being approximately
£4 5s 0d per week. This included:

> 6 men, 3 @ 4/- a week, 3 @ 6/-   £1 10s
> 4 boys @ 1/3   5s
> 1 cwt. 2 qtrs of lead ore   12s
>
> .
>
> .
>
> .
>
> profit (including 6s for his labour) for master £0 10s

He noted of the area: "Burslem was at that time so much the
principal part of the pottery that there were very few pot works
anywhere else." He calculated the annual value of the ware produced

in the district as £6,417, with individual potter's turnover averaging out at £216 per annum.

The accuracy of such figures is dubious, and Wedgwood himself later made a higher estimate, but they are of the right sort of order. He seems also to have overestimated slightly the importance of Burslem. What is interesting is not so much the small scale of the enterprises – Wedgwood noted no potters with a turnover above £6 a week – but the very slight difference between the earnings of masters and men. It brings us right back to the notion of an industry of individual craftsmen. The potter, once he had completed his apprenticeship, was expected to be able to turn his hand to all branches of the trade – to "throw, stouk, lead and finish", or, in more common language, to throw pots on the wheel, stouk or stick on handles and spouts, glaze and finish the ware. The master was no less, and frequently no more, expert than the men he employed. Indeed, they might all be in the same family; the eldest son, having inherited a pot works, would often take on his younger brothers as workmen.

This is a picture if not of a cottage industry similar to, say, the handloom weavers, then of a small craft industry. Recent research[2] has shown however that to think of it entirely in such terms is to underestimate the changes that had already taken place and were continuing. For example, already in the early eighteenth century we have seen the beginnings of specialization: the preparation of raw materials, such as flint, had been taken away from the potter and given to an expert working a flint mill. And the improved ware was being sold outside the bounds of local Staffordshire markets. Crates were sent down the Weaver to London shopkeepers, and ware even found its way to the overseas markets of Europe and North America.

The world of the potters was clearly on the move and the directions of that move were already clearly laid down, but still the greatest part of the production was of humble ware made for ordinary, everyday use. The rich looked elsewhere for their pottery and in the early eighteenth century one type of ware was prized above all others – porcelain. Brought in at first from China as part of the exotic trade of the East India Companies, porcelain was soon manufactured in Europe. Kings, princes and dukes were the patrons when porcelain started to appear from the Meissen works in Germany. The style was that of the ornate flourish, the style of Baroque, later to become even more ornate. Flourish was added to flourish and no lily was left ungilded as the Rococo of the French royal factory at Sèvres took up the role of leader of fashion. It was very far removed from the plain earthenware of the English Midlands. Far removed perhaps, but at the same time in Staffordshire all the elements were there and waiting to be turned into something quite new that would challenge the manufacturers of Europe. There were the basic raw materials, the necessary skills and there seemed, at that time, to be something in the climate that nurtured growth and change. There was in Britain the stirrings of a breeze of innovation that was to turn into a strong and powerful wind.

The potters of Staffordshire formed a close community, a complex web of interrelated families. Even today, one finds names in the district that were common on the pages of wage books of eighteenth-century pot works. And among the names of the district the name Wedgwood was prominent: "The surname of Wedgwood half fills the parish registers of Burslem through the seventeenth and eighteenth centuries."[3] Indeed it does, and as a glance at the family tree quickly shows, it leads to an extraordinary complexity of intermarriage and connections. It can all be most confusing, particularly as the same Christian names crop up among a whole host of Wedgwoods so that each has to be given an extra title to distinguish him from the next. Nevertheless, one has to make the effort to disentangle the family if only to gain an idea of what it meant to be born into a world of pots and potters with not just the immediate family in the trade but with countless cousins and uncles busily at work all over the district.

The Wedgwoods were originally farmers, but the endless sub-divisions affected their landholdings and, in the seventeenth century, Aaron and Thomas took to pot-making as a way of supplementing the family income. In the seventeenth century, Thomas inherited a pot works and smallholding close to Burslem church, which was known as the "Churchyard" works. This was passed on to his son, also called Thomas; but, just to complicate matters, Aaron's sons also went into the pot business – they were yet another Thomas

(Dr Thomas, to distinguish him from "Churchyard" Thomas), another Aaron and Richard. These three brothers were all involved as co-defendants in the case in which John Dwight sued for breach of his patent. Josiah Wedgwood noted that Dr Thomas was a manufacturer of brown stoneware.

The Churchyard Wedgwoods seem to have been rather a plodding lot. The next generation of Thomas Wedgwoods took over from the first and was apparently content enough to leave the more adventurous work of expansion to the other branch of the family. And over on that side, things were active indeed. Aaron had three sons – the eldest, Richard, left the pot business to set up as a cheese factor in Spen Green, while the other two, yet another Thomas and John, remained to establish themselves as leading figures among the Staffordshire potters. These two brothers were still in the tradition that placed the masters on much the same footing as the men. They worked in partnership, Thomas as thrower and John in charge of the ovens and glazing. They were among the first to introduce the white, salt-glazed stoneware, which they sold far outside the bounds of their particular neighbourhood. They were sufficiently successful to be able to build a brand new pot works in brick, and even a brick house for themselves. Local people came far out of their way to see such a novelty and tut-tut over such conspicuous extravagance. The house became known in Burslem as "the Big House"; things were beginning to move and change in the Wedgwood family.

Change was less rapid, however, over at the Churchyard, where the latest of the Thomas Wedgwoods, grandson of the original owner, settled down to married life. His wife, Mary Stringer, the daughter of a Unitarian minister from Newcastle-under-Lyme, could have had time for very little outside a home life kept busy with almost perpetual pregnancies. The first son to be born was, needless to say, named Thomas. The twelfth and last child to be born to the family was taken to St John's Church, Burslem, on 12 July 1730, and baptized with the name Josiah.

[2]

The Early Years

COMPARATIVELY little is known about the childhood years of Josiah Wedgwood, though, as with most famous men, there is a comparative abundance of unverifiable stories and unlikely anecdotes. Nevertheless, sketchy as it is, the story of those early years contains events that were to be of the greatest importance to the grown man.

The early biographer of Wedgwood, Eliza Meteyard, claimed that the greatest influence on the young boy was his mother, who stressed the value of those two great pillars of non-conformist virtue, hard work and education. The two were certainly inseparable in Wedgwood's case, for when, at about the age of six, he began school he had a walk of some three and a half miles across the fields to Newcastle and the school run in their own home by Mr and Mrs Blunt, followed by the same long walk home at the end of the day. All accounts agree that the young Josiah was a quick learner who was blessed with a teacher of above average abilities. Mr Blunt may have concentrated, in lesson time, on the three Rs, but he was a man of scholarship, who had studied classics and mathematics and had an interest in chemistry and chemical experiments. So from his early days, the boy had contact with a degree of learning not to be met with in many of the schools of that area.

As well as being quick-witted, the boy was lively and good-humoured. Some brief biographical notes[1] describe him as being noted for his "great vivacity and humour" and show him to have been nimble-fingered as well as nimble-witted. "He was very early distinguished for a readiness in imitating in clay whatever object struck his fancy", which seems credible enough in a child brought up surrounded by potters' clay and by busily working modellers and throwers. There is other evidence of the boy's lively curiosity. Eliza Meteyard tells a story passed on from her father, who himself received it as a first-hand account – a tenuous chain, but more verification than most such accounts can boast. It appears that Josiah became interested at a very early age in fossils. He had a special shelf in his father's workroom, and the pack-horse men bringing coals from the pits at Sneyd or Norton Green would bring him specimens turned up by the miners. He also did some digging and scratching about on his own account among the rubbish dumps of the pot works and began a collection of sherds of older ware.

A more dubious story of the schoolboy's ingenuity tells how he used to tear shapes out of his copy book pages, complex scenes of ships or marching armies, which he would then stick on the inside of his desk lid to show to the amusement of his class mates and the indignation of the Blunts. True or untrue, there is a general agreement among the accounts that Josiah Wedgwood was a lively, intelligent and gifted child. But in 1739 the schooldays were abruptly ended. His father died and the works passed to Josiah's elder brother, Thomas. Cash was short – there were legacies to be paid, though many never were – and Josiah had to take his place in the works as his brother's apprentice. He left with this testimonial from his teacher: "a fair arithmetician and master of a capital hand".

Josiah's legacy was the same as that for all the younger children with the exception of the eldest daughter Ann – £20 to be paid on reaching the age of twenty. What Ann had done to get herself debarred from the will, what dreadful crime remained unpardoned, is not known. But then, as the last of the legacies was not paid until 1776, when even the youngest of the children was in his mid-forties, the blow might not have seemed too hard to bear. So the prospect of Josiah coming into money was remote unless, like his brother Richard, he was to get a windfall from another branch of that widespread family tree. In Richard's case the money came to him from Mrs Egerton, once married to another Richard Wedgwood, and a lady of robust health who outlived three husbands. But for Josiah the prospect was of hard work and long hours as he learned the family trade.

Formal apprenticeship was not drawn up until 11 November 1744 – elder brother Thomas appears to have been rather slow at his paper work – but the documents have survived and spell out quite clearly the relationship between master and apprentice. The apprenticeship was for five years. The main requirement laid upon the master was to teach the "art, Mistery, Occupation or Imployment of Throwing and Handleing which the said Thomas Wedgwood now useth". The master was very much in *loco parentis*, entrusted with the moral guardianship of the boy. The rules for the apprenticeship were explicit:

> At Cards, Dice or any other unlawful Games he shall not Play; Taverns or Ale houses he shall not haunt or frequent; Fornication he shall not Commit; Matrimony he shall not Contract; from the Service of his Said Master he shall not at any time depart or absent himself without his said Masters Leave; but in all things as a good and faithfull apprentice shall and Will Demean and behave himself towards his said Master and all his, During the said Term.

For his part, the boy had quite simply to serve the master and "his Lawful Commands Everywhere gladly do". In return he was to be fed and clothed "both linen and Wollen", in sickness and in health.

Behind this archaic formula with its talk of "art" and "misteries" is a tradition that stretches back to the Middle Ages, and it remained the foundation on which the whole business of the Potteries rested. The apprentice learned the different branches of the trade until he was proficient in each – the complete craftsman. The practice often fell some way short of the ideal. It was easy for the unscrupulous to use the apprentices as cheap labour, paying a good deal of attention to the requirement that the apprentice was to obey all lawful commands, rather less to those that spelled out that the boys were to be taught. Here Josiah was fortunate in working in the family business. He was taught thoroughly and taught well, specializing in the early years in mastering the art of throwing pots on the wheel. Anyone who has succeeded, even in the most amateurish way, in throwing a pot will know the immense satisfaction of seeing and feeling the wet clay take form beneath the fingers. It is a satisfaction made doubly pleasurable by the frustrations of first attempts when the clay seems to want to take on a life of its own, waltzing over the turntable before finally collapsing in an undignified wobbling heap. But once learned, and learned to that level of mastery that we have ample evidence Wedgwood possessed, it is an art that gives more than skill to the hands. The potter will have gained an eye for form and symmetry, a feeling for the rightness of a shape. For Wedgwood the eye was to be more valuable even than the skill of the hand.

The death of his father ended the schooldays of Josiah Wedgwood; a threat to his own life brought his apprenticeship to a temporary halt. In the spring of 1742 one of the smallpox epidemics that were the scourge of the time came to Burslem. It was almost inevitable that the family living and working next to the churchyard, where many of the victims were buried with scant precautions against the spread of the infection, should fall to the disease. Josiah did. He was forced to his bed for a long illness and a longer convalescence. The results were serious enough in all conscience: he was gravely ill, in real danger of his life. At the same time, there was a brighter side. The enforced idleness gave the twelve-year-old a second chance to get something more than a rudimentary education. He returned to his books and became an avid reader. But when at last he was able to get back to work, he found that the disease had badly affected his right knee, and he had to hobble about with the aid of crutches. Without the use of his leg he was unable to use the wheel, which was operated by a foot pedal. What might have seemed a disastrous setback proved to have its advantages, however. If he could no longer concentrate on turning, he now had the opportunity to learn other aspects of the craft, especially modelling.

The apprenticeship years were not without their frustrations for Wedgwood. Quick-minded, full of ideas, he was come into a world that was beginning to hum with the sounds of change. In the nearby coalfields, the huge steam engines of Thomas Newcomen were beginning to dominate the landscape, promising new sources of power. The books of the experimental scientists suggested new ways of tackling the problems and intricacies of the natural world. It was an exciting time, but Josiah found in his elder brother an employer quite content with the world as it was. Thomas was specializing in moulded ware, which was then given a white lead glaze – salt glazing by then was proving too expensive because of the recently introduced Salt Duty. So Josiah began his own search for new directions. His distant relative, Dr Thomas Wedgwood, had achieved a reputation for producing small ornamental objects of a very high quality, and Josiah set himself to follow that line. He began developing his own variations on the popular tortoiseshell ware, colouring the natural clays with different oxides to give a variety of colours in imitation of marbles and agates. These became quite popular for small articles such as knife handles and snuff boxes.

If Josiah found his brother rather stuffy and unimaginative, then no doubt Thomas found his youngest brother's inquisitiveness and love of change no less irritating. He wanted a quiet, steady business life and was not getting it. The uneasy association continued for three years after the official end of the apprenticeship, but Thomas did not offer to take Josiah into partnership and in 1752 they parted. Thomas thankfully sank back into comfortable anonymity and Josiah joined the pot works of Harrison and Alders at Cliff Bank, Stoke. Thomas Alders had then retired, leaving the business under the control of John Harrison, who produced a variety of ware including the popular salt and lead glazes and the equally popular "scratch blue". The latter was made by scratching a design into a plain white ware, then dusting with cobalt blue or zoffre to colour the design. They also produced a good deal of mottled and tortoiseshell, which is presumably what brought Wedgwood and Harrison together. Not much is known about the days at Stoke, though we do know Wedgwood lodged with a wealthy draper, Daniel Mayer, who was a leading figure among the local dissenters. In any case, the connection was short-lived. In 1754 Wedgwood entered into partnership with a man who was both one of the leading potters of the day and an innovator, Thomas Whieldon of Fenton Hall.

Whieldon was in a different class altogether from the other potters with whom Wedgwood had been associated. There was little of the crude peasant craftsman about him. His ware was sophisticated and aimed rather higher than the hawked ware of the crate men. And his was no tuppence-halfpenny concern. Wedgwood kept a note of the trade at Fenton during eight months in 1757. In that time, slightly over £600 worth of ware was sold and, significantly, the wage bill rose as high as £20 a month, which represented quite a considerable work force.

But what was most significant was the terms under which the young man was taken into the partnership. For in Whieldon Wedgwood found a man who appreciated his love of experiment and was prepared to foster and encourage it. The very reasonable condition was made that the results of experiments should be used for the good of the concern, but Whieldon generously made public recognition of his assessment of Wedgwood's value as an experimenter and probity as an individual – it was specifically stated that Wedgwood need not divulge details of his methods to his partner. It is not difficult to imagine the enthusiasm with which Wedgwood went into the new business, an enthusiasm well justified by results.

There must have been a very special atmosphere at the works of Thomas Whieldon, for it grew some exotic blooms – not just Wedgwood, but Josiah Spode and Aaron Wood were both there and a man who was to play an important part in the history of Wedgwood's, William Greatbatch. The business gave Wedgwood another opportunity – a chance to step outside the Potteries to visit some of the other centres where change was coming fast. Of these, far and away the most important was the bustling, burgeoning town of Birmingham, where he made regular visits, taking snuff boxes to be set in metal. Already in Birmingham, the great printing house of Baskerville had been established, Matthew Boulton had begun to manufacture in metal: books and pamphlets were on sale, pictures were displayed and pottery from Europe could be seen, the exuberant twists and twirls of Rococo in such marked contrast to the humbler scratchware of Staffordshire – though even Staffordshire was not unaffected by the style, as Longton Hall pottery was producing its own mild version. It needed no great powers of observation to see that the times were changing, and taste was changing with time.

Wedgwood was again troubled by the pains in his knee and was again forced to abandon the pot works for his sick bed. It must have been a blow to have to leave the exciting atmosphere of Whieldon's, but he found new excitements to occupy him – intellectual excitements, the excitements of speculation and discovery. He read avidly and he had an unofficial director of studies in the person of a local dissenting minister, Rev. William Willett, who had married Wedgwood's sister Catherine. He encouraged the invalid to read science, and Wedgwood became so absorbed in his studies that he later declared that he would have cheerfully abandoned pots and devoted himself to science. That could never be more than a wishful fantasy, for there was no money to keep the would-be scientist while he worked. But the study was not wasted. He kept his love of science, and soon began to apply what he had learned of scientific method to pot manufacture.

Another frequent visitor to the sick room, who brought stimulating ideas in place of fruit and flowers, was a neighbour, Mr Broad. He gave another line of thought to Wedgwood, for Broad was a great enthusiast for transport improvement, full of ideas for bettering the facilities in the area. His favourite scheme was a plan for linking the area to the two main navigable rivers of the region, the Trent and the Mersey, by means of an artificial waterway. But the bulk of Harecastle Hill to the north of Burslem seemed an insurmountable obstacle. Nevertheless, something of his enthusiasm for transport improvement communicated itself to the young potter.

So the days of illness were not all wasted. Eventually, in spite of rather than because of the doctors, who alternately bled him and purged him until he all but wasted away, Wedgwood was able to get back to the pottery. There he began by putting his experiments on to a more systematic base. He wrote this description of the process:[2]

This suite of experiments was begun at Fenton Hall, in the parish of Stoke upon Trent, about the beginning of the year, 1759, in my partnership with Mr. Whieldon, for the improvement of our manufacture of earthen ware, which at that time stood in great need of it, the demands for our goods decreasing daily, and the trade universally complained of as being bad & in a declining condition.

White stone ware was the principal article of our manufacture. But this had been made for a long time, and the prices were now reduced so low that the potters could not afford to bestow much expence upon it, or to make it so good in any respect as the ware would otherwise admit of. And with regard to Elegance of form, that was an object very little attended to.

The article next in consequence to Stone ware was an imitation of Tortoiseshell. But as no improvement had been made in this branch for several years, the country was grown weary of it: and though the price had been lowered from time to time, in order to increase the sale, the goods did not answer, and something new was wanted, to give a high spirit to the business.

I had already made an imitation of Agate: which was esteemed beautiful & a considerable improvement: but people were surfeited with wares of these variegated colours. These considerations induced me to try for some more solid improvement, as well in the *Body*, as the *Glazes*, the *Colour*, & the *Forms* of the articles of our manufacture.

The experiment books and the information they contain are of the very greatest importance in the career of Josiah Wedgwood. Potters had experimented before, had done so for centuries, but seldom quite like this. They had been mostly content to work on a hit-or-miss, try a pinch of this, try a spoonful of that, basis. No one would ever be able to say that Wedgwood found a new process because his horse had a bad eye or through any other accident: what he discovered was to be the result of careful, planned experimental work, meticulously recorded. It is worth stressing again: Wedgwood was doing something quite new, something fundamental to the whole development of the Potteries: he was applying science to a mass industry.

He carefully measured and listed the ingredients for each trial, whether for a new glaze, body or colouring, and to record them he used a numbered code of his own. The numbers made a useful shorthand and, as he noted, "They have likewise an advantage of not being intelligible without the key." At times Wedgwood could be almost paranoid about the need for secrecy, whereas at other times he would talk of making a grand, eloquent gesture, handing over all his work for the benefit of mankind. Secrecy invariably won – the experiment books remained coded.

It was not enough, however, simply to know quantities and ingredients if an experiment was to be repeatable – the first and most important essential of scientific work: it was also necessary to know the temperature at which they had been fired. Here he hit a snag, for there was no thermometer in existence that could record the high temperatures of the oven. So Wedgwood had to invent his own system based on the type of oven used, the position in the oven and the place of the individual saggar in the pile. He listed three types of oven: biscuit (BO), where unglazed ware was fired, gloss (GO), for glazed ware, and white oven (WO), added later for his white ware. The positions were simply listed as top (T), middle (M) and bottom (B). So a reference given as TTBO would mean that the sample had been fired in the top saggar at the top of the biscuit oven. As a system it was rough and ready, and the results were not applicable to different ovens, though that would hardly worry a man of secretive bent.

So Wedgwood began the series of trials and experiments that was to continue throughout his life. Among his first successes were new green and yellow glazes – success with the green is noted as early as experiment 7. These glazes were used, in conjunction with a Wedgwood design, for teapots and coffeepots patterned on vegetables. They were much admired and much in demand, though to one pair of modern eyes at least they seem both ugly and ludicrous. The idea of pouring coffee out of a rather violently coloured cauliflower simply does not attract. But they continued to be made and continued to sell long after Wedgwood had established a reputation for a very different type of design.

Inevitably, Wedgwood wanted more and more to become his own master, to use his own ideas in his own way and for his own advantage. On 1 May 1759, at the age of twenty-nine, he took out a lease on the Ivy House and adjoining pot works in Burslem. He was on his own.

$\begin{bmatrix}3\end{bmatrix}$

Mr Wedgwood's Works

WEDGWOOD's first works were leased from Thomas and John Wedgwood of the Big House. The two brothers were contemplating retirement and were quite happy to lease part of their extensive works in Burslem to a young relative. So for a rent of £10 a year, Wedgwood took over the two kilns, workshops and cottages that made up the Ivy House site. He brought with him his second cousin – yet another Thomas Wedgwood – who had signed on as journeyman at a salary of £22 a year. Thomas was to remain with his cousin as colleague and later as partner.

Wedgwood also drew on the skill and expertise of another craftsman, William Greatbatch, who had been with him at Whieldon's. Greatbatch had also set up on his own in 1759, at Lower Lane, Fenton, and Wedgwood was one of his best customers. He supplied biscuit, which Wedgwood could glaze and decorate, and from the numerous bills that still exist it is clear that he supplied it in a bewildering variety – teapots and candlesticks, coffeepots and dishes, and so many different vegetable shapes – cauliflowers, cabbages, pineapples, pears – that some of the bills might have come from a greengrocer. He was also one of the area's best known block-makers. Greatbatch, sadly for himself, was a better potter than he was a businessman, but the arrangement was ideal for Wedgwood, who could always rely on his own orders being promptly met.

With the main personnel ready – Thomas at Burslem, Greatbatch at Fenton – work could begin. They were grossly understaffed at the Ivy House and Wedgwood was forced to take a hand in every part of the business, selecting clays and body materials, modelling, glazing and supervising the ovens. On top of all this, he had the business side to look after: selling the ware, and what frequently proved the most troublesome part, collecting payment. Any time left over was used for experiments. There was never enough time, though, and such time as could be taken was usually borrowed from the business side. "He knew by want of attention to accounts he lost very large sums annually, but he believed that if he had suffered his mind to be deviated from attending the progress of his works of innovation he should have lost a great deal more."[1] A notably sane judgement.

One of the sadnesses for a biographer is to come to a crucial period in the subject's life, about which one wants to know everything, and to find very little information about it. This is certainly true of the early years at Ivy House. Yet although we have little documentary evidence, Wedgwood the potter left the evidence of what was made at that time. The two types of evidence can be wedged together and shaped into something recognizable. The outline is clear, even if the detail is lacking.

Among the profitable lines that Wedgwood took up at that time was one that might seem beneath the dignity of an ambitious and newly independent potter. He began repairing broken pots. In fact, it was a very instructive occupation, and one that fitted in well with his long-term ambitions, for it brought him into contact with the gentry and gave him an insight into their tastes. For he was not being asked to repair local ware, but the imported pieces from Europe or, more exotically, from China – the only pieces considered appropriate for the aristocratic board. So he handled Sèvres and Meissen, Chinese porcelain or the only slightly humbler Bow and Chelsea. And there was not just repair work, for if a piece was completely smashed it might have to be replaced to complete the set. An anecdote illustrates his mastery of this difficult, albeit second-hand craft. A local family had broken a favourite eighteen-inch delft dish which Wedgwood had to copy. The replacement was so popular that the workman who had delivered the dish was fêted by the family and wined and dined for a whole week. It was all good practical experience and all helped in forming some useful connections.[2]

Wedgwood's own ware was at first a continuation of his work at Whieldon's. He continued with the green glaze and went on producing knife handles and snuff boxes with a mottled glaze. This last was not quite the same as the tortoiseshell, for now, instead of mixing coloured clays, he dusted the ware with oxides, which in the firing melted and ran together in swirls and stripes. But, as he had already noted, taste was a notoriously fickle commodity, and mottled ware lacked novelty. He concentrated, instead, on creamware.

Wedgwood creamware made Wedgwood famous, but the production of creamware did not begin with him. Essentially, it consists of an earthenware body covered by a thin, white glaze. Like many developments it has no real starting point; one cannot point a finger and say: "Here is the first creamware." It made no startling new appearance in the world, but rather evolved slowly throughout the first half of the eighteenth century. Its earliest ancestors were the rather cumbersome pots made from the dark local clay, which were then disguised under a heavy coating of paler slip. The body was then lightened by using flint, and a really major step forward came when the Staffordshire potters turned from the local clays to the white clays of the West Country – the pipe clay or ball clay of Dorset and Devon. Quite when the ball clay was introduced is uncertain, but what we do know, quite definitely, is that it was used by Whieldon throughout the period that Wedgwood was there.

All the ingredients of a good creamware were known before Wedgwood had begun working for himself, so what exactly was his special contribution that made the terms "creamware" and "Wedgwood" all but synonymous for a time? The answer lies partly in the process of manufacture and partly in a brilliant publicity coup. But for the moment we shall concentrate on the practical developments that made the publicity possible.

The main difficulty Wedgwood faced was not how to make creamware; there were many who knew that secret. No, the problem was how to make it consistent. Customers were inclined to complain, with some justification, if their new dinner service covered a whole range of hues from a rich, yellowy cream to an almost pure white. The potters simply could not be sure what they were going to get from any particular firing. Another difficulty could be traced back to the same problem of control – cracking and crazing of the glaze. This was caused by the different rates of shrinkage and expansion of the materials in the kiln. It now seems to us to be a simple matter to tackle such a problem: carry out systematic tests until you have found the right mixture and the right temperature, carefully recording your results as you go. It seems obvious to us, but it was not at all obvious to the Staffordshire potters. They were craftsmen raised on the old, traditional methods – with the exception of the enthusiastic scientist, Josiah Wedgwood. Here, in fact, was a situation ideally suited to the application of his scientific approach.

Wedgwood began systematically improving the creamware body, making it thinner yet stronger, while also working towards a standardized colour. He was successful, and successful at just the right time. He came up with a new product exactly suited to the developing taste of aristocratic Europe. For by the middle of the century taste was going through one of its periods of rather rapid change. The elaboration of Baroque had passed into the excesses of Rococo, and people were beginning to get heartily sick of both. They were looking for something new, a contrast, and they found it in the style we now call "Neoclassicism". And what a contrast it proved to be.

One of the earliest apostles of the new canons of beauty was the Abbé Winckelmann. It is one of the ironies of the age that this prophet, who preached the admiration of pure beauty, all but untouched by emotion, should himself have been a wild-minded homosexual who met a violent end, stabbed to death by a casual friend picked up in a hotel in Trieste. Winckelmann found something very sensual in the contemplation of pure uncluttered form – he would have made an admirable advocate for the abstractions of an Arp or a Moore. In his admiration for purity of form, he was drawn towards an idealization of the human figure – sexless, emotionless, flawless. He wrote in *Die Morgenröte von der Wollust*: "In antique figures, pleasure is not shown through laughter, it is shown through the serenity of an inner content." Colour was a needless distraction in this contemplation of pure beauty. He wanted to teach the world to admire clean, uncluttered lines, simple forms and the freshness of white, which, as Winckelmann pointed out, is not an absence of colour but a harmonious blending of all colours. And for his ideal Winckelmann always looked back towards the ancient world – the statues, ceramics and paintings of Greece and Rome. In his day he had as much influence in swinging taste towards classicism as Ruskin had a century later in the establishment of Gothic. At first the Classical movement may have been only tentatively pushing forward into some of the spaces occupied by Rococo, but the change had begun and it was Wedgwood's great good fortune to be working on a style of pottery ideally suited to meet the demands of the new fashion.

The rigorous, tightly controlled working methods of Wedgwood seem very much in keeping with the rigorous, tightly controlled art of Neoclassicism. But Wedgwood had a struggle to bring his new methods to an industry that was more chaotic than organized, where processes tended to be more haphazard than controlled. He might be able to solve many problems by systematic experiment, but in the works he was faced with a less tractable element: those awkward, capricious, idiosyncratic but essential parts of the process, the human beings.

Wedgwood often gave the impression that he found the human side of his works an unpleasant nuisance that he would gladly get rid of altogether if only it were possible. In his ideal world machines would have replaced men, but in the meantime, in his own famous dictum, he had to attempt to "make such machines of men as cannot err". Throughout his working life he fretted over this inability to make people fit to his patterns: they would insist on arguing over pay and working conditions, they were liable to be bribed away, taking his hard-won secrets with them and, most annoyingly of all, they consistently failed to fit his standards of perfection. Meteyard describes his early years at Ivy House in these terms:

> At first he met with much sullen opposition, often amounting to an insubordination that necessitated immediate dismissal; but by firmness, patience and great kindness he succeeded, in a comparatively short time, in bringing his manufactory into efficient order. His men found that it was much better to obey than to

oppose: and that the regulations that they had at first clamoured against facilitated their labour to a surprising degree.

What were the new regulations? In brief, what Wedgwood was aiming for was a breakdown of the old system of journeymen and apprentices, where each journeyman was expected to work at many different branches of the trade, and the establishment of a new system of specialization. Under the new arrangement, a turner would work just as a turner, a fireman as a fireman: a stewker would spend all his day making and applying handles, and so on through all the different occupations. But specialization was only part of the story: Wedgwood was setting new limits of accuracy to the work and trying to exact ever higher standards. And there was yet one other aspect that jarred with the old ways. In the specialist method of working, the rate of each department had to be regulated by that of the others if there was not to be a bottleneck in one part of the works and idleness in another. What had once been a craft was beginning to look more and more like a factory production line.

Wedgwood was not alone in trying to introduce specialization into the Potteries, but he was the most inflexible in his demands. In the old days a workman's time had been more or less his own, to organize as he chose. There was a time-honoured tradition among many British workers of paying homage to Saint Monday on that weekly holy day. It did not matter to them if they had to work doubly hard for the rest of the week to make up the lost time, for that seemed small enough price to pay for the luxury of a day in the ale house, playing quoits or bull-baiting, or following any of the popular pastimes of the area. Not, however, at Wedgwood's: there was no place for Saint Monday in *his* calendar.

There were many manufacturers in a whole range of industries who were faced with the same problem of breaking centuries-old habits in order to mould workmen to the new patterns of production. In the textile industry, just entering into its great period of growth, the problem had a comparatively simple solution. The new machines could, quite literally, be worked by a child – so malleable children were brought in to take over jobs formerly performed by inflexible adults. Children were both obedient and cheap, great

top Some examples of the kind of ware being
produced in Staffordshire when Wedgwood began
his career: right, a salt glazed tankard of 1723; above,
a loving cup in scratched blue ware, 1754.

bottom One of Wedgwood's early successes came
with his experiments in variegated ware. This agate
teapot is of the type made at the Whieldon
pottery in about 1750.

The Churchyard House and works where Josiah Wedgwood was born in 1730.
The Ivy House works, where Wedgwood first set up on his own in 1759.

advantages to a manufacturer. But pot works were not textile mills. There skill, individual skill, was still needed. There the new breed of employer needed to act much as Meteyard described: he had to cajole and threaten, he had to reason, argue and persuade.

Contemporary observers tended to be mystified by the workers' reluctance to fit into the new regime. They pointed out, quite rightly, that with specialization work could become much easier. They also saw that the new methods could lead to increased production, increased wealth. How could sane men fight against that? It was not then obvious that men would not willingly give up their independence; that, in a period where they worked long, long hours, the way in which those hours were spent was of great significance. The old worker had his range of skills to use – the new was offered only greater monotony in the name of an efficiency that brought very little benefit to the individual's own life. So those early years saw a struggle between the old and the new, which the new was steadily winning. But it was not an easy struggle, and it was to break out many times again over the next decades.

Wedgwood, however, succeeded in organizing both materials and men so that he could produce – and reproduce at will – a fine creamware. He was starting to prosper. In 1760 he was wealthy enough to subscribe £10 – a full year's rent for the Ivy House – towards a school for the poor children of Burslem. The school was, in fact, never built, and the space was later used for a new town hall, but it was a mark of prosperity to subscribe. He was now able to join the company at the Big House on reasonably level terms – that is, when he had time to spare for such frivolities, for it was a period of rapid expansion and days were hectic for the potter. The business was now spread far beyond the Midlands, and he was fortunate in having his brother John living a bachelor existence near Guildhall in London. John had spare time on his hands and was happy to promote his younger brother's interests, helping to sell ware and sending back reports on the fluctuating taste of the capital.

Wedgwood at this time was kept busy at Burslem with improving the works, rebuilding kilns, experimenting and trying new machines. He was still paying regular visits to Birmingham, where he saw the metal-working lathe in regular use. Encouraged by a local man, John Taylor, he began planning a machine lathe that could be used for turning pots. It was on one of these trips to Birmingham around 1761 that he first met Matthew Boulton.

More frequent than the trips to Birmingham were the visits to Liverpool. Here was the port through which he brought in his ball clay, shipped round the coast from Dorset or Devon, and it was from here that he planned to send his ware around the world. The journey to Liverpool was no easy jaunt, and it was especially tiring for a man who still suffered pains in the knee that had been infected in childhood. But Wedgwood was not a man to give in before that kind of physical adversity. He was a worrier over his health in many ways and suffered severely from psychoneurotic illness at various times in his life. But, like many others who suffer from stress symptoms, he was remarkably stoic when it came to coping with a genuine organic illness. He was also something of a health fetishist, subjecting himself to some truly terrifying bouts of exercise and physic. Here is a Wedgwood fitness recipe: "riding on horseback for 10 to 20 miles a day, & by way of food & Physick, I take whey, & yolks of Egg in abundance, with a mixture of Rhubarb & soap, & I find the regimen to agree with me very well".[3]

Early in 1762, even the agreeable regimen was not enough to keep Wedgwood going and he was forced, reluctantly, to take himself to his bed, stranded in Liverpool by a particularly severe return of the knee pains and inflammation. His doctor, Matthew Turner, faced with an irritable, anxiously fretting patient, showed his good sense by prescribing agreeable company. He brought along a friend to amuse and calm the potter, the Liverpool merchant, Thomas Bentley.

[4]

Bentley

WHEN Wedgwood had been forced to his bed during his years at Fenton Hall, he had made good use of his time by studying. Now, in Liverpool, he occupied the time in making friends with Thomas Bentley. The meeting represents a great turning point in both their lives, for the collaboration of Wedgwood and Bentley together was to add up to something greater than a simple sum of their two separate selves.

Bentley was the same age as Wedgwood but his background was very different. Born in Scropton in Derbyshire in 1730, he had received the benefits of the full classical education at the Presbyterian Collegiate Academy of Findene, Derbyshire. At the age of sixteen, he left school and was indentured to a wholesale merchant in the textile trade in Manchester. There he received a training in business to go with his instruction in Latin and Greek, and in 1753 he was able to put his modern languages to the test when he was sent to tour France and Italy. Back from Europe, his commercial education complete, Bentley left Manchester to set up in business in Liverpool. There, in 1754, he was married to Hannah Oates. The marriage was a short one, for Hannah died in 1759, and her sister Elizabeth came to Liverpool to keep house for the widower.

Liverpool was the ideal centre for a merchant: it prospered on those two connected trades of slaves and cotton. As well as being the port through which the clays for Staffordshire passed, it had its own pottery industry, which was in a fine, flourishing state. It was here too that the partnership of John Sadler and Guy Green was established. They had perfected a method of transfer printing from engravings on to pottery, which was a very popular form of decoration. Wedgwood was, for a long time, one of their customers. Although Liverpool was growing fast – from a population of about 8,000 in 1700 to some 26,000 in the 1760s – it suffered from many of the disadvantages that beset other provincial towns. Roads, for example, were all but non-existent; the nearest of anything like a decent standard came no closer than Warrington. But the town was new and lively, having something of that cosmopolitan atmosphere common to all major seaports. There were the riverside taverns and cockpits; but there was also a more genteel Liverpool. The merchants could stroll through the newly laid out public walks, visit the New Theatre in Drury Lane or listen to Handel performed in the Assembly Rooms at the Exchange. It was a very different world from that of Burslem, and in the areas of fashionable taste and learning, Thomas Bentley was one of its leaders.

Bentley was a bustling figure in Liverpool's public life. He was a member of the Philosophical Society, one of the founders of the Public Library in 1758, of the Nonconformist Academy in 1759, and when Wedgwood first met him he was busily at work establishing the Octagon Chapel.

Bentley's friends were drawn from the arts and science as well as commerce and included one of the greatest scientists of the age, Dr Joseph Priestley. Priestley was a dissenting minister who at that time was teaching at the nearby Warrington Academy. His fame rests on his work as a chemist, most especially on his isolation and identification of a number of gases, including oxygen. It is a curiosity of Priestley's life that the discoverer of oxygen should have remained, throughout his life, a firm believer in the phlogiston theory of combustion – a theory that was demolished largely through Priestley's own work on oxygen. But Priestley was theologian as well as scientist: nonconformist in his religion, radical in his politics. He was outspoken and firm in his beliefs, a position that did nothing to secure him the general prestige he undoubtedly deserved. He was a frequent visitor to Liverpool and noted in his memoirs: "At Liverpool I was always received by Mr. Bentley, afterwards partner with Mr. Wedgwood, a man of excellent taste, improved understanding, but an unbeliever in Christianity, which was therefore often the subject of our conversation. He was then a widower, and we generally, and contrary to my usual custom, sat up late."[1]

Priestley's definition of "Christian" was somewhat limited, and Bentley would certainly not have classed himself as atheist or pagan, though his Christianity was never orthodox and in later years he began to move towards the idea of a creed that would embrace all religions. He was, in fact, one of the leaders of a small and curious sect that occupied an uncomfortable halfway house between the established church and the various nonconformist churches. The Octagon Chapel was being built by the new sect to house their services. They accepted the need for a formal liturgy, having little taste for the semi-hysterical public confessions and the ramblings of personal prayer among many dissenters, but they had some obscure theological doubts about certain parts of the prayer book and the Athanasian Creed. Yet in many ways, Bentley was closer to the radical dissenters than to the established church: the bell of the Octagon Chapel would not join with that of St Nicholas Church in welcoming the slavers back to port. Bentley was anti-slavery, and among the friends he welcomed to Liverpool was the American scientist and later statesman, Benjamin Franklin.

Through Bentley, Wedgwood was thus introduced to a whole new circle of intellectuals and intellectual ideas. The world of the arts was brought to him. Bentley acted as guide to literature and music, painting and sculpture. His taste might sometimes be questionable, but it was a taste delicately tuned to every shift of fashion. For Wedgwood it added up to an all but overwhelming experience. Brought up in a society preoccupied with trade and the more stolid virtues of industry and application, he positively revelled in these newly discovered delights.

As soon as he was well enough to travel, Wedgwood was forced to return to Burslem and business, but at once wrote to his new friend. In this first letter[2] all the enthusiasm, all the affection flow as though the thoughts had travelled direct from brain to paper without having to pass through the tedious business of applying pen and ink. It is the first of many, many letters between the two in which the personality of Wedgwood is revealed, his thoughts and emotions displayed. It is worth quoting at some length, if only to show the wide range of interests they shared.

My much esteemed Friend

If you will give me leave to call you so, & will not think the address too free, I shall not care how Quakerish or otherwise antique it may sound, as it perfectly corresponds with the sentiments I have & wish to continue towards you: nor is there a day passes, but I reflect with a pleasing gratitude upon the many kind offices I received in my Confinement at your hospitable Town. My good Doctor, & you, in particular have my warmest gratitude for the share you *both* had in promoting my recovery, & I know he is too well acquainted with the influence of a good flow of spirits (whatever they are) upon the whole Animal Oeconomy to refuse you your share of merit in this instance. Believe me I could with pleasure dwell much longer upon this subject, & may a great deal more without offending your excellent rule in your MS upon the article of Letter-writeing, which teacheth not to belye our own feelings in *writeing better things of any Person &c than we think is strictly true*, but I know your delicacy in this point, & have done. I find by the papers that the subscription for Thompson's Works is opened again, & intend to add my name to the list, or at least become a purchaser. . . .

The letter continues with an attempt to persuade Bentley to publish a manuscript he has written on female education. Why, asks Wedgwood, will he not publish?

"It is not perfect" – Why should *you* or the Publick expect it should be so. do you know any publication, *on this side Rome*, that is so in every respect? . . . . in behalf of myself & many others, his Majesty's good improveable subjects, as well male as female, who are daily lamenting the want of a proper education, & would gladly make use of such an help as you have prepared, I say in behalf of myself and 10,000 fellow sufferers, I do now call upon you to publish the above mentioned book.

Wedgwood ends with a brief mention of his own work, which he declines to describe to Bentley. "You have perhaps this time escaped reading a tedious account of Acids & Alcalies. Precipitation, Saturation, &c."

It is hard to think of this as the beginning of a correspondence between two men of business who had only recently met. Many of the letters of this period are lost, but we later find Wedgwood continuing his correspondence course in literature and the arts. He had been reading Bentley's favourite author, James Thomson, a poet long since descended to a richly earned obscurity. Wedgwood, however, was still in full flood of enthusiasm: "his descriptions of ancient Greece and Rome are truly grand, & place these theatres of liberty and publick virtue in the strongest light of anything I ever met with."[3] As Thomson was such a favourite of Bentley's, and Wedgwood was keen to join the choruses of praise, it is worth looking at the works as an indication of the literary taste of the two men. What one finds is a good deal of turgid rhetoric, seen at its worst in verse dramas such as *Coriolanus* but seldom absent from any of the works. A great favourite of Wedgwood and Bentley was a 5,000-line long poem, *The Seasons*, of which the following is a reasonably representative sample:

> See, Winter comes, to rule the varied year,
> Sullen and sad, with all his rising train;
> *Vapours*, and *Clouds* and *Storms*. Be these my theme,
> These! that exalt the soul to solemn thought,
> And heavenly musing. Welcome, kindred glooms!
> Congenial horrors, hail!

Impossible not to catch the echoes of Milton's *Il Penseroso*, impossible too not to see how far Thomson falls below the standard set by his famous predecessor. Another aspect of the work, much admired by Bentley, was the poet's penchant for a variety of high-minded patriotism seen in a dire poem, *Liberty*:

> By those Three Virtues be the frame sustain'd
> Of British Freedom: Independent Life;
> Integrity in Office; and o'er all
> Supreme, a Passion for the Common-weal.

That intelligent, lively minds could find pleasure in such stuff seems at first very mysterious, yet in a way it fitted in well enough with one side of Wedgwood's nature. However lively he might be with Bentley, he was by no means a stranger to the high moral tone. He was by no means alone in admiring poetry that combined "elegant verse" with preaching or even instruction. Another favourite poem was John Dyer's *The Fleece*, which combined classical allusions with a practical course on wool and woollen manufacture. Classicism was the accepted language of verse, and there seemed to be little odd about the idea of using such a language to describe the everyday business of trade.

The question of Bentley's taste is more important than might seem at first to be obvious. That he acted as artistic mentor to Wedgwood the individual makes it of interest; when we find that taste affecting Wedgwood the potter it is clearly crucial. Literary taste might be less important than, say, taste in sculpture, but it does have relevance. The point to be stressed is that Bentley was not a great and perceptive critic: his taste might be more accurately described as that of the better informed gentleman. And, for commercial purposes, that was precisely what Wedgwood required. He was looking for ways to spread his ware to a more aristocratic public and what he needed, and found in Bentley, was a man always in the forefront of public taste, but never too far ahead and never lagging behind. Bentley was never more than mildly *avant-garde*, and from the first Wedgwood sought his advice in the arts – and followed it.

There remained one other area where one might expect Bentley to exert an influence – politics. In fact, Wedgwood never at any time attached himself to a political party. He was aligned, roughly, with the radical, dissenting group of which Bentley was a member and Priestley a more extreme leader. Wedgwood was in favour of the generalized libertarian sentiment found in Thomson. In practice this libertarianism stopped short at the pot works gate. In his own factory, Wedgwood was absolute ruler. His attitude was by no means uncommon at the time. The early industrialists were busily changing work patterns established for centuries, and as the new work methods would lead to greater prosperity, it seemed only reasonable that those methods should be rigorously enforced. Whether a despotism is seen as benevolent or not depends very much on where you happen to be standing at the time. Wedgwood's particular brand was certainly far milder than many – but despotism it was, none the less.

It is easy to see what Wedgwood gained from the friendship with Bentley. He gained a guide to the world of the intellect. In practical terms, he gained a weather vane, sensitive to every shift in the winds and currents of fashion. Perhaps, more importantly, he gained a correspondent in whom he could confide with absolute candour, someone with whom he could discuss plans and ambitions with no fear that his secrets would be betrayed. But what was the attraction for Bentley? On the face of it, it seems odd that a man respected and honoured in his own society should strike up such an immediate and firm friendship with a comparatively unknown earthenware manufacturer from Burslem. Perhaps at first it flattered Bentley to have such an obviously talented and naturally gifted man so avidly seeking his opinion, so eager to learn whatever he had to teach. It might be tempting, given the highly emotional language of Wedgwood's letters to his friend – language used with no other correspondent – to contemplate a homosexual liaison, but there is absolutely no evidence that such a relationship ever did exist, and considerable evidence to suggest the contrary. Unfortunately, we have so few of Bentley's letters that our view of the relationship is necessarily one-sided and incomplete. Whatever Bentley's motives, however, it says a good deal for the force of Wedgwood's personality that he could so quickly gain and hold the affections of such a man as Bentley. The accident that brought them together began an enduring friendship that was to dominate both their lives.

The meeting with Bentley marked the beginning of a period of great activity for Wedgwood. His was still a small business at that time as, indeed, were those of most of the potters. A petition to Parliament for a new turnpike road in 1763 quotes the area as containing 150 potteries finding "constant employment and support for nearly 7,000 people". This is rather vague, as the term "support" could include those such as carriers not employed directly in the pot works. Even if we do take it as meaning only those directly employed, this gives an average of forty-five workers for each concern. A wage book for Wedgwood's for 1762 lists only sixteen employees, working at rates varying from Thomas Jones at 1s 2d a day to Jane Reed at 2½d. As well as these there were the piece workers, such as Daniel Greatbatch and Joseph Unwin, who received a set wage as well as the piece rate. They made a whole range of ware and here, as an example, is Greatbatch's bill for April of that year:

8 doz.	milk pots	0 – 4 – 0
3 ,,	candlesticks	1 – 3
6 ,,	basons	1 – 6
3 ,,	teapots	2 – 0
6 ,,	sugar boxes	2 – 0

His daily wage was 1s 4d.

If not a large concern, it was an expanding one. During 1762, Wedgwood decided that he had outgrown the Ivy Works and moved to the Brick House works, which had been owned by the Adams family. In an attempt to bring order to the chaos of working conditions and arbitrary time-keeping, he installed a bell to summon the workers and give notice that work was ended for the day. Inevitably, the new factory was christened the Bell Works. Then, in 1763, he brought William Cox from Birmingham to act as bookkeeper – an important post, given Wedgwood's own short-comings in this department, and one that he filled for a great many years. In Cox's letter of acceptance, he mentioned another matter that was preoccupying Wedgwood at that time – engine lathe-turning. The lathe works in much the same way as would a potter's wheel turned on its side – the clay rotates and cutters give shape. It has certain special advantages, for it makes it possible to incise quite intricate patterns of circles, which can emphasize the shape of the piece, with great accuracy. The machine itself was not new, having long been in use in metal and wood working, but it had been greatly improved in the middle of the eighteenth century and its application to the Potteries was new. Cox wrote of the lathe: "I have not been able to get a sight of one nor dont find I well can unless under some particular agreement. I have been recommended to one Richards whom I have waited upon twice he agrees that he will make one that shall well answer your purpose, and instruct me in the art of it for £25 or Guineas, and to have it and me compleat in two months time."[4] The experiments were successful and, as a note in Wedgwood's *Commonplace Book* proudly announces: "Engine lathe turning – first introduced into the pottery by Mr. Wedgwood in 1763."

1763 was a busy year in many ways, and one important piece of business included the promotion of a decent road system for Burslem. This was a period when many independent turnpike trusts were being formed which, if they could receive the appropriate Act of Parliament, were permitted to build roads and recover the costs by charging tolls. Turnpikes already existed in the area, but none came to Burslem, which was still served by muddy wallows. It seemed common sense to the potters of Burslem that they too should have a new road, but they met strong opposition in the person of the Newcastle turnpike proprietors. They contemplated, with outraged horror, a scheme which, if brought to a conclusion, might divert profitable loads away from their own toll-collectors. The general good of the public did not rank very high in the proprietors' consideration. The result was a good deal of ill-natured skirmishing among the interested parties, with Wedgwood in the thick of it. He solicited the support of the influential nobleman, Lord Gower, helped pen a petition to Parliament and in March set out for London to help further the Turnpike Bill in its passage through Parliament.

The time in London was not all taken up with turnpike business. Wedgwood was able to spend some time in collecting new orders and in listening to some of the other debates at Westminster. Lord Bute's Cider Bill, which would have put a tax on cider for the first time, was being debated, and Wedgwood waxed fierce in his denunciations of the proceedings in a letter to Bentley.[5] He wrote with disgust that the "odious" Cider Bill had received the Royal Assent, he was mortified at this "Extension of the Excise laws", which, he claimed, "gives universal disgust here & is the general topic of every Political Club in Town". However, he rather spoiled the effect of his brave words by cautioning Bentley not to show the letter to anyone "unless their Candour is Equall to your own".

Wedgwood, if not a party man, had strong views on political topics and was happy to argue them with his friends. He did not, however, make any public display of his opinions. He believed in putting his business interests before politics. Wedgwood was setting out to woo the aristocracy and other men of influence and considered it imprudent to antagonize politically those he was trying to court commercially. On this occasion, having made his private views known, he had the satisfaction of seeing Bute toppled by the protests over the Cider Bill. He had less satisfaction over the outcome of the Burslem Turnpike Bill. At the end of the wrangling, they got half a turnpike only: instead of connecting two existing roads, at Stoke and Lawton, it was only to join the Lawton turnpike. It was a compromise that satisfied the Newcastle proprietors, and the Burslem interest at least had a road connection of sorts.

In all this hectic period of commercial expansion, road promotion and experimentation, Wedgwood must have found some time for a social life and a highly interesting one at that. For, quite suddenly, into the correspondence of January 1764 there pops a wife, wooed and won, if not actually bestowed. The lady in question was, not surprisingly, another member of the sprawling Wedgwood family. Sarah Wedgwood, usually known as Sally, was four years younger than Josiah. She was the daughter of Richard Wedgwood, the brother of the Big House Wedgwoods, who had left potting to set up as a cheese factor in Spen Green. This was, in general, the more prosperous side of the family, and it was cash that looked like proving the one obstacle to the uniting of the two branches. Wedgwood managed to keep his good humour through what must have been wearisome haggling sessions – he gave progress reports to Bentley:

> I had acknowledged the receipt of your very kind Letter before now, but hoped by waiting a post or two to be able either to tell you of my happiness, or at least the time I expected to be made so. But "O Grief of Griefs" that pleasure is still deny'd me, & I cannot bear to keep my friend in suspence any longer, though I own myself somewhat ashamed, and greatly mortified, to be still kept at bay from those exalted pleasures you have often told me (& I am very willing to believe) attend the Married state. If you knew my temper & sentiments on these affairs, you will be sensible how I am mortified when I tell you I have gone through a long series of bargain makeing – of settlements, Reversions, Provision &c:&c: Gone through it, did I say: would to Hymen I had. No, I am still in the Attorney's hands, from which I hope it is no harm to pray "*good Lord deliver me*" Miss W. & I are perfectly agreed, & could settle the whole affair in three lines & so many minutes, but our

Pappa, over carefull of his Daughter's interest, would by some demands, which I cannot comply with, go near to seperate us if we were not better determined. On Friday next Mr. W. & I are to meet in great form, with each of us our Attorney which I hope will be conclusive.[6]

The meeting went well, and Wedgwood was able to write in triumph only two weeks later:

All matters being amicably settled betwixt my Pappa (Elect) & myself, I yesterday prevailed upon my dear Girl to name the day, the blissful day! when she will reward all my faithfull services, & take me to her Arms to her Nuptial bed! to – pleasures which I am yet ignorant of, and you, my dear friend, can much better conceive than I shall ever be able to express. In three words, we are to be married on Wednesday next. On that auspicious day think it no sin to wash your Philosophic evening pipe with a glass or two extraordinary, to hail your friend & wish him good speed into the realms of Matrimony. Adieu, my good friend, I am very busy today, that no business may intrude on my pleasure for the rest of the week.[7]

Wedgwood was never quite so frank and open about such subjects as sex and marriage again; if anything he became more inclined to prudery in his later years. But, having taken the step into matrimony, he never stopped recommending it to unmarried friends. The couple were in their thirties when they married, and they lost no time in starting with the serious business of getting and raising a family. Sally was very soon embarked on what was to prove almost an annual event – pregnancy.

What sort of woman was Sally, and what kind of life did she have with her husband? Not easy questions to answer. Certainly there seems to be little obvious physical attraction. In contrast to Josiah's broad, friendly face, Sally's portraits all show a certain severity: in appearance, she took very much after her father, and as we have just seen, he could be a very severe man when he felt severity was justified. Sally was certainly a competent and able woman, who could and did take an active part in the running of her husband's business – that is, in the intervals between her regular confinements.

It is a curiosity, though, that in the letters that exist written to her by Wedgwood there is none of that casual intimacy we find in the letters to Bentley. Perhaps the more personal letters have not survived, perhaps Wedgwood kept such things to the times when they were alone together. We cannot tell. There is, though, no reason to believe that the home life of the Wedgwood's was other than happy. As the years passed, indeed, we find Wedgwood placing more and more reliance on the placid comforts of the home as an antidote to the pressures of success.

The marriage also brought fresh capital to the business, a fact that goes some way to explain the lengthy negotiations that preceded the marriage. Not that that need suggest an unduly mercenary attitude on the part of either party: wedding settlements were a matter of great and serious concern to the wealthier citizens of Georgian Britain. The lack of a suitable fortune was the basis of the plot for many a novel of the period, as any reader of Jane Austen can testify. Wedgwood very rarely made direct comments about their relationship but in a letter to Bentley[8] he described himself and Sally, with no hint of self-consciousness, as "two married Lovers, happy as this world can make them".

Wedgwood did not use his marriage as an excuse to neglect his business. Having taken his few days off for the honeymoon, he was back at work as busy as ever. His letters to Bentley began to take on a more serious tone, and he began to make use of his friend's education. He set Bentley to work, for example, in translating a treatise on lathes, Plumier's *L'Art du Tourneur*, commenting that he had a young nephew on hand, Tom Byerley, who was learning French, but he could hardly wait for the completion of those studies. Wedgwood was hoping that Byerley would "make a usefull member of society" – a hope that was some way from realization. Young Tom Byerley had a good many wild and varied oats to sow before he achieved that respectable end. Wedgwood was already becoming aware of the existence of a few of those oats including a dangerous taste for writing: he was "terribly infected with the caoethus scribendi". Later he was to try, unsuccessfully, for a career on the stage, to go to America to attempt a new start, and generally to prove a trial to his family.

If 1764 was notable as the year of Wedgwood's marriage, the

following year was notable as the year of the first major business success. The year began with a suitably favourable omen, the birth on the third of January of the first child, Susannah or Sukey. She was a source of immense pride to her father. His comments about her tended to be rather humorous, as though he was embarrassed by too open a show of affection. But the feelings break through time and again, especially in letters to his brother, John. "The finest girl," he crowed. "So like her father! I wish you could see her." But there was little enough time for family pleasantries: sterner matters soon took over.

> We have now got such pretty employment for you. Sukey is a fine, sprightly lass, & will bear a good deal of dandleing & you can sing – lulaby Baby – whilst I rock the Cradle, but I shall hardly find time for nursing as we have another Turnpike broke out amongst us here betwixt Leek & Newcastle & they have *vi et Armis* – mounted me upon my hobby-horse again, & a prancing rouge he is at present, but hope he will not take the route of London again.[9]

Such intimate moments seem few enough in this busiest of busy years, as we find Wedgwood occupied with the plans for the turnpike to join the Burslem and Uttoxeter roads. We get some idea now of the wealth of the Wedgwoods: "My Uncles Thomas and John have – I am quite serious – at the first asking subscribed – I know you will not believe me, but it is a certain fact – *five hundred pounds*!!!" Not to be outdone, Wedgwood then went on to ask John if he would join him in putting up a further five hundred. Business was clearly not slack, and Wedgwood had already begun on one of the activities that was to form a main support of his trade – the accumulation of important patrons. The first we meet is Sir William Meredith, the Member of Parliament for Liverpool, and in Wedgwood's letter we glimpse something of the effusiveness the patron expected from the patronized.

> You have heaped your favours on me so abundantly that though my heart is overflowing with sentiments of gratitude and thankfullness I am at a loss where to begin my acknowledgements. Your goodness for leading me into improvements of

the manufacture I am ingaged in, and patronising those improvements you have encouraged me to attempt, demand my utmost
attention with such inducements to industry in my calling;
if I do not outstrip my fellows, it must be oweing either to
great want of Genius, or application; the first your Candour
would lead you to excuse, as it might be less my fault than my
misfortune; the latter is in my own power, and I should be
utterly unworthy of Your farther notice if I did not double my
diligence in prosecuting any plan you are so kind as to lay out
for me.[10]

The main purpose of this particular letter was to lobby Meredith
the MP over the establishment of a pottery in South Carolina. A
good deal of trade was done between Staffordshire and America,
but what worried the potters was less the threat to their exports
than the possibility of local workers being lured away by the
promise of higher wages. It is a recurring theme and a classic case of
the ambivalent attitude, not just of Wedgwood, but of the great
majority of eighteenth-century traders. He was indignant over
changes in the rates of excise duty and other attempts to "abridge
the liberty of the subject". He bitterly resented any attempts of
Government to interfere with his trade in goods, but was equally
bitter in his condemnation of workers who attempted to secure a
free trade for their services.

During this hectic period Wedgwood made the mistake of letting
Tom Byerley go to London, where he was soon caught up in the
"giddy Town set". He discovered, however, that he had a new
helper close at hand. Sally, after one year of marriage and one child,
found her spinning wheel carted off to the lumber room and herself
sat down with pen and paper to help her husband. Business was
improving all the time, and Wedgwood was beginning to think of
the possibility of moving to still larger works, when this steady
expansion was given a sudden and powerful boost. Wedgwood's
aim had always been to produce for the new, steadily growing
middle-class market, and he knew that if he could only establish
himself with the aristocracy, the rest would follow where their
social superiors led. Thus, it was important to be supplying ware
to Sir William Meredith, but now a new and far more influential

Thomas Bentley, by Joseph Wright of Derby.

Sarah Wedgwood by Reynolds.

Wedgwood and Bentley's signatures to that most important document,
the partnership agreement of 1769.

A cameo portrait of Queen Charlotte, who permitted Wedgwood to rename his cream-coloured earthenware "Queen's ware"

Decorated Queen's ware. It was ware such as this that formed the foundation of Wedgwood's success.

A page from the Queen's ware pattern book.

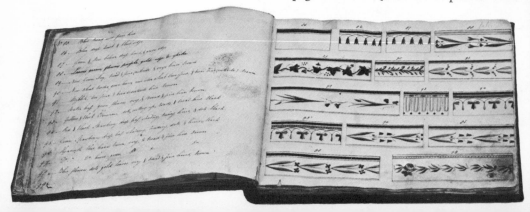

patron appeared on the horizon. Wedgwood received an order from the Court, and gleefully sent a letter off to brother John in London.

> I'll teach you to find fault, and scold, and grumble at my not writing, I warrant you, and as to your going to France, I do not believe I can spare you out of London this summer, if business comes in at this rate, for instance – An order from St. James's for a service of Staffordshire ware, about which I want to ask an hundred questions, and have never a mouth but yours in town worth opening upon the subject.
>
> The order came from Miss Deborah alias Deb. Chetwynd, sempstress and Laundress to the Queen, to Mr. Smallwood of Newcastle, who brought it to me (I believe because nobody else would undertake it) and is as follows.
>
> A complete sett of tea things, with a gold ground and raised flowers upon it in green, in the same manner of the green flowers that are raised upon the *mehons*, so it is wrote but I suppose it should be melons. The articles are 12 Cups for Tea and 12 Saucers, a slop basin, sugar dish with cover and stand, spoon-tray, Coffeepot, 12 Coffee cups, 6 pair of hand candle-sticks and 6 mellons with leaves, 6 green fruit baskets and Stands edged with gold.[11]

A few months before, Wedgwood had been pleading with John to leave the capital – "I do not think that close, smoky place will ever agree with your constitution," an odd sentiment from one living next to a pot works. Now, all that was forgotten before the lure of royal patronage. It was to be all bustle and rush: "*Pray put on the best suit of Cloaths you ever had in your life* and take the first opportunity of going to Court." And the effort proved well worth the trouble, for less than a month later he was again writing to John:

> I shall be very proud of the honour of sending a box of patterns to the Queen, amongst which I intend sending two setts of Vases, Cream-colour, engine-turned and printed, for which purpose nothing could be more suitable than some copper-plates I have by me. I can adapt the Vases so that the designs and they will appear to be made for each other, and intended for Royalty, nor must you hint to the contrary: but I am one

group or design short which I have sketched out and inclos'd
and desire you'l get it done by Wale unless you know a better
hand.[12]

It was the decision to show creamware as well as the green and
gilt that the Queen had requested that was to prove of the first
importance. In the event, the making of the services was not
entirely straightforward – there were, for example, some difficulties
over the gilding – but all the main problems of producing consistent
creamware were solved. The crazing and cracking had been elimin-
ated by using some kaolin in the glaze, which prevented it contract-
ing away from the body. Now the news that creamware was being
made for the Queen attracted a good deal of attention. Wedgwood
could scarcely keep the note of smugness out of his letters to John:
"Dr. Swan dined with Lord Gower this week; after dinner your
Brother Josiah's Pottworks were the subject of conversation for
some time, the Cream colour Table services in particular. I believe
it was his Lordship said that nothing could exceed them for a fine
glaze &c."[13] "I have just had the honour of the Duke of
Marlborough, Lord Gower, Lord Spencer and others at my works.
They have bought some things and seemed much entertained and
pleased."[14]

Wedgwood, encouraged by such a response, began to plan new
and more ambitious ways to sell his goods – and to collect the cash
for the goods already sold. John must, at times, have cursed his
younger brother's enthusiasm.

> Pray how are you for business, or schemes of pleasure? For I
> would by no means break into the latter. But if it would be
> consistent with both and you should choose it, would send a
> pattern or two, a list of my Chaps, and more bills if you choose
> such employment till a *better place* offers. I have this year sent
> goods to an amount of about £1000 to London all of which is
> oweing for and I should not care how soon I was counting some
> of the money.
>
> You know I have often mentioned having a man the greatest
> part of the year, shewing patterns, taking orders, settling
> accounts &c, &c. and as I increase my work, and throw it still
> more into the ornamental way, I shall have the greater need of

such assistance and should be glad to have your advice upon it. Would £50 a year keep such a Person in London and pay rent for 2 Rooms? (both back rooms, and St. Giles's would be as good as St. James's). About so much I think it might answer for me to give.[15]

By the autumn of 1765 he was ready to deliver the service to the Queen. A modern PR agency might have managed a good deal of publicity out of such an event, but they would have been hard pressed to squeeze more out than did Josiah Wedgwood. The ware was no longer plain Staffordshire creamware, it was rechristened Queen's ware, and soon official patronage was officially confirmed. Letter heads and bills could now proclaim the bold title, "Josiah Wedgwood, Potter to Her Majesty". It was a personal triumph, and the realization of an ambition. Now there was none who need feel ashamed if their dinner service came from humble Staffordshire rather than royal Meissen.

⌈5⌉

The Grand Trunk

MAKING a creamware service for the Queen was only one of Wedgwood's major preoccupations in 1765, for that was also the year in which he became involved in a scheme as important to him as the royal order, and probably more important for the development of the Potteries as a whole. He became a canal promoter.

The idea of canal building was not especially new, and the advantages of canals were well known. A group of eighteenth-century engineers were later to spell it out very clearly when they conducted experiments to find the maximum load a single horse could shift by different methods. Overland, the load varied from $\frac{1}{8}$ ton for a pack-horse to 2 tons by waggon on a hard-surfaced road. But once the load was put on to water, the difference was dramatic: 30 tons on a river and an astonishing 50 tons on the still waters of a canal. The advantages were plain enough; all that was lacking – and it was a giant all – was the necessary skills, the engineering experience, the cash and, most important, the courage to attempt something new.

The first canal to take a line quite independent of any natural waterway was built not by one of the rising class of industrialists but by a young nobleman, Francis Egerton, Third Duke of Bridgewater. Frustrated in love, the Duke, still only twenty-three years old, retired to his estates near Manchester in 1759 where, rather than pining, he began to plan a canal that would take coal from his mines at Worsley into Manchester. The plans were successful and the Bridgewater Canal opened in 1761, to the amazement of the public, who came in crowds to gaze at the aqueduct that carried the waterway across the River Irwell at Barton, astonished at the sight of barges passing high above their heads. What had been dismissed by sceptics as a "castle in the air" proved to be a busy and successful river in the air. But if Barton aqueduct was the focus of attention for the general public, it was the Duke of Bridgewater's balance sheets that attracted the gaze of industrialists. What impressed them was the fact that the Duke had halved the price of coal he sold in Manchester.

With the first canal opened so successfully, it was inevitable that other schemes should soon follow and equally inevitable that the potters of Staffordshire, Josiah Wedgwood especially, should take an interest. Creamware manufacture required the import of special clays from the South West. These came by the coastal route to Liverpool and were then taken on by river up the Mersey and Weaver to Winsford in Cheshire. The rest of the journey was overland by lumbering stage waggons. Similarly, the flints that came from the south coast and East Anglia were brought by sea to Hull, then up the Trent as far as Willington, completing the journey by waggon. If a canal could be built through the Potteries that would join the Trent to the Mersey, then the potters would save a fortune in transport costs, and be sure of obtaining regular bulk supplies of raw materials. It would also reduce the cost of sending out ware for export from Liverpool or for coastal shipping to London.

Wedgwood already had some connection with the building of the Bridgewater Canal. The engineer employed by the Duke was James Brindley, a scarcely literate millwright, but a man of great talents. The stories surrounding Brindley are legion. It was said, for example, that he always solved problems by lying down in a darkened room, where he would sometimes stay for many hours, finally emerging with a complete solution. Throughout his life he kept a rough north country accent and rough north country ways. He found the delights of London distinctly alarming and when, on one occasion, he was prevailed upon to visit the theatre to see Garrick as Richard iii, the experience so overwhelmed him that he was unable to work the next day and swore never to go to a theatre again. Brindley, however, in his early days as a millwright had worked in the Potteries, building flint mills. He set up business at Leek in Staffordshire in 1742 and built a windmill for flint grinding for John and Thomas Wedgwood.

The need for a canal was established, the men to build it were available and well-known to the potters, so all that was needed was permission to build and the necessary cash. But that was another "all" that covered a multitude of problems. We had a glimpse of the sort of opposition that was raised against the building of the first Burslem turnpike, but that was nothing compared with the powerful forces that were to be raised against the canal promoters. The plan was not entirely new, for Lord Gower had some time before asked Brindley to survey a line from the Trent to the Mersey. That plan had been put into abeyance but, with the Bridgewater a proven success, the old plans were taken down, dusted and unfolded. Wedgwood, a leading figure in the district and with the experience of the turnpike promotion behind him, was an obvious choice as chief promoter.

> On Friday last I dined with Mr. Brindley, the Duke of Bridgewater's engineer, after which we had a meeting at the Leopard on the subject of a Navigation from Hull, or Wilden Ferry, to Burslem agreeable to a survey plan before taken. Our Gentlemen seem very warm in setting this matter on foot again, and I could scarcely withstand the pressing solicitations I had from all present to undertake a journey or two for that purpose.[1]

Wedgwood needed very little prompting, and few stood to gain as much from the scheme's success as he did. He had two tasks: to rouse the enthusiasm of supporters and to counteract the criticism of opponents. He dragged Bentley into the fray and set him to work organizing support in Liverpool. Bentley, as the acknowledged expert on matters literary, was also given the job of preparing a pamphlet to set out the case for the canal. Wedgwood, as well as co-ordinating the promotion, took it on himself to rouse local opinion and began travelling to secure support. His journeys took him to Lichfield, where he managed to secure the enthusiastic interest of the local doctor of medicine, scientist and poet, Erasmus Darwin.

Darwin is at once a larger than life yet enigmatic figure. In many ways he is similar to that other great contemporary, Samuel Johnson. Both men were physically unattractive. Darwin was, according to Maria Edgeworth, "a large man, fat, and rather clumsy"[2] and suffered under the disadvantage of a stammer. Both men had reputations as wits and men of letters, but whereas Johnson's reputation has risen with the years, Darwin's has sunk. Perhaps Darwin has simply lacked a Boswell. He was certainly unfortunate in his early biographers, since much of the information has come from Anna Seward. This poetess was known in her day as the Swan of Lichfield – history, reversing the conventional process, has now declared her the Ugly Duckling. More importantly, she was jilted by Darwin – a fact that hardly aided her objectivity. However, to return to Johnson, he and Darwin did occasionally meet and showed a hearty, and none too surprising, dislike for each other.

Darwin was a lively and colourful figure, who succeeded in outraging many, including another biographer, Mary Ann Schimmelpennick, the daughter of the eminent scientist, Sir Francis Galton. She found his views on religion even uglier than his appearance, and quoted many examples of the Doctor's attitude, including this little homily he addressed to her: "My dear madam, you have but one complaint: it is one ladies are very subject to, and it is the worst of all complaints; and that is, having a conscience. Do get rid of it with all speed; few people have health or strength enough to keep such a luxury for utility I cannot call it." She made an attempt to convert him to Christianity, but only received this reply. "Before I do that, you Christians must all be agreed. The other morning I received two parcels: one contained a work of Dr. Priestley's, proving there is no spirit, the other a work by Berkeley, Bishop of Cloyne, proving there is no matter. What am I to believe amongst you all."

Idiosyncratic Darwin may have appeared, but he was possessed of a powerful and decidedly lively mind. Few doctors in the land had a higher reputation, and he turned down the offer of a post as official physician to George III. He was, in short, a man of some eminence whose support was well worth canvassing. Wedgwood discussed the proposed canal with him, and described the extensive system of which it was hoped it would form a part. The Trent and Mersey was to be the longest of a group of waterways, known as "the

Cross", which were to link the four major rivers of England –
Trent, Mersey, Thames and Severn. As the most important, the
Trent and Mersey was given the title "the Grand Trunk Canal".

Darwin listened to Wedgwood and reacted at once. He was a
man much given to enthusiasms, and the canal became one of them.
This also marked the beginning of what was to prove a lifelong
friendship between the two men, though there were times, in those
early days, when Wedgwood must have rued Darwin's enthusiasm.
For Wedgwood now had two friends with literary pretensions:
the first was busy writing a pamphlet, and the second was soon
equally busy criticizing it. Some of the criticism was to the point as,
for example, when he told Bentley to make a greater appeal to the
landowners, whose opposition could have proved especially
damaging to the scheme. But much of it was carping or facetious.
In order to make an appeal to the landowners, Bentley inserted a
rhapsody on the delights of having a canal at the bottom of the
garden, even suggesting that the lucky landowner could buy his
own gondola. Unfortunately, he made a minor change in the
wording and incurred this recrimination, passed on to Bentley by
Wedgwood: " 'To have a Lawn terminated by a Canal &c.' Why
change a more elegant & equally simple word for a worse? Why a
Canal is as straight as *Fleet Ditch* – A Canal at the bottom of your
meadows! Foh! it can't be born by the Goddess of modern taste,
but *Water* ay *Water* give me *Water* to terminate or divide my lawn."[3]
The correspondence became increasingly acrimonious. Darwin
noted bleakly: "I cannot see any advantage ye Cause can receive
from the managers appearing bad Writers", to which Bentley
huffily commented that he "doubts not but Dr. Darwin could have
finished it in better manner, if he would have taken the Trouble
upon himself which Mr. B. understood he did not choose to
do". Bentley's resentment was understandable, and eventually
Wedgwood had to step in to sort the affair out and calm ruffled
tempers. There could be too much argument: "The condemnation
or postponing of the whole I can by no means agree to nor persuade
myself that there is any necessity for it. Must the Uniting of Seas
& distant countries depend upon the choice of a phrase or mono-
syllable? Away with such hypercriticism, & let the press go on, a
Pamphlet we must have, or our design will be defeated, so make the

best of the present, & correct, refine, & sublimate, if you please, in the next edition."[4] Sound advice from a good editor.

Wedgwood had good reason to be irritated by petty delays. He had his other concerns to worry about, and the canal business was eating greedily into his time. At the beginning of the year he had written to Bentley: "I have not time to think or write about anything, but *the immediate business* of the day. Public business I mean, for as to my private concerns I have almost forgot them, I scarcely know without a good deal of recollection whether I am a Landed Gentleman, an Engineer or a Potter, for indeed I am all three & many other characters by turns, pray heaven I may settle to something in earnest at last."[5] Now things were ten times worse. The opposition, headed by the two river navigations who saw their trade threatened, the Weaver Navigation and the Mersey and Irwell Navigation, were already active, and were preparing their own pamphlets. They used two approaches. The first was to cry woe over their own "certain and irreperable Ruin"; the second was to cast dark suspicions over the motives of the canal promoters, suggesting that the canal "could only be desired for *private* views, or to make a more *lucrative* Job for Engineers".[6] The argument was joined with very little nicety of feeling on either side.

Wedgwood was trotting all over the countryside, not only answering criticism from opponents, but quelling dissent among friends. The Lancashire subscribers suddenly appeared with a plan to run their end of the canal as a separate venture, a suggestion that earned Bentley a stiff Wedgwoodian rebuke.

> You have strange heterodox notions amongst you at Liverpool about your Port being ruin'd, your not being principals, & I don't know what stuff. Pray who are *principals by the rules of common sense*, in a design of this sort, but those who will receive the *principal* advantages from it. . . . Pray now seriously what will your Lancashire Canal be without the Derbyshire, Stafford-shire, & Cheshire additions – it dwindles so that I can scarce see its *importance* without the assistance of a *mental microscope*.[7]

There was support to be rallied and special interests to be reconciled. Bentley came up with the gloomy news that the Mayor of Liverpool might be less than wholehearted in his support as he had an Aunt

Clayton with shares in the Sankey Navigation. Wedgwood, however, had influential friends of his own. Sir William Meredith began by offering a little mild opposition to the proposals, at which Wedgwood could only exclaim: "Poor Man! how he raves! I hope one Month's Confinement to the Debates in Westminster Hall will perfectly cure him." The cure seems to have worked, and Meredith provided valuable support within Parliament. Wedgwood, in return, offered this guaranteed successful recipe for winning a forthcoming election.

> RECEIPT Bullocks roasted whole – Quantum sufficit.
>   6 small Cannon to be fired at every vote gained from the Enemy.
>   A Fighting Captain to be made use of occasionally with the wavering and timerous.
>   Get Mr. Scraigs (a person well known in Tamworth) to make *querre faces.*
>   A Poet is absolutely necessary & may be heard of at Birmingham.

It is pleasant to find that Wedgwood could keep a good humour through such pressing times, for the business of reconciling interests, out-manoeuvring opponents, flattering here and cajoling there would have tried the wits of a Machiavelli. Only a man of the most tremendous drive and energy could have maintained the pace. Even Wedgwood found it too much at times, as he described in a letter to Bentley: "I have stole a few moments from my wife this morning to converse a little with my friend 'till the world is wide awake for then I must of necessity mix with the bustling crowd. Everything is in the most violent agitation here, by *everything* you know I now mean *Navigation.* . . . My health is now perfectly restored, I could not say so much a few days ago."[8] Illness at times of crisis was to be one of the recurring themes of Wedgwood's life. An absolute stoic in bearing with the often agonizing pains in his legs, his nervous illnesses often quite sank him into melancholy.

In January 1766 the promoters were ready to set out their stall. A grand public meeting was called to launch the petition on its way to Parliament. Lord Gower presided and spoke enthusiastically in favour of the canal, and a number of local MPs joined in with their good wishes. In Burslem bonfires were lit and many a toast drunk. It was a good beginning.

Now there was the long and tedious business of getting the Bill through Parliament, and Wedgwood was forced to spend a good deal of time in London, supervising its passage. There was the final effort to keep supporters up to the mark, the seemingly endless sessions before the Select Committee, until at last, on 14 May 1766, the final stage was reached and the Royal Assent given. The final line of the new canal was to be from a junction with the Bridgewater Canal's extension down to the Mersey, to the Trent, west of Nottingham, a junction at which the new town of Shardlow was to grow. The same year saw the passing of the Act for the Staffordshire and Worcestershire Canal that would join the Grand Trunk to the Severn. Now the funds began to flow in, and at the first meeting of the proprietors of the newly formed company Josiah Wedgwood received due recognition of the leading role he had played in the proceedings. He described the meeting to his brother John with pride but without pomposity: "We had yesterday a very Noble, Numerous & amicable General assembly of the Commissioners & Proprietors of the *Navigation from the Trent to the Mersey* . . . you will see the honour done me, which was quite unexpected & voluntary, without the least previous sollicitation on my part, and without one dissenting voice."[9]
He ended with this list of the Company's officers:

James Brindley Surveyor General   £250 per ann.
Hugh Henshall Clerk of the Works   £150 per ann. for self & clerk
T. Sparrow Clerk to the Proprietors   £100 per ann.
Jos. Wedgwood Treasurer at £000 per ann. out of which he bear his own expenses.

Wedgwood might joke about his new post as treasurer, but it was a great responsibility. In all, £130,000 was to be raised in £200 shares, of which the Wedgwood family between them contributed a handsome £6,000. But the post required more than a simple accountancy for the funds: the treasurer was expected also to act as unofficial banker to the concern. Before he could take up his new office Wedgwood had to provide a surety of £10,000, no mean achievement for a man who, only seven years before, had just enough capital to provide a rent of £10 a year for his new business.

There were great celebrations on 26 July when, at Burslem, Josiah Wedgwood cut the first sod of earth and loaded it into a barrow which was wheeled away by James Brindley. The building of the Grand Trunk was officially begun. Heady days they must have been now that the frantic activity of canal promotion was over and construction work had begun. It was all boundless optimism, but optimism not always well founded. Wedgwood's old teacher had brooded over the difficulties posed by Harecastle Hill, and the canal engineers were to brood again. Eleven long years they were to take pushing their narrow, low-roofed tunnel through Harecastle, eleven years before the whole length of the canal could be opened.

Although he had to wait many years before he could feel the full benefits of the canal he had fought so hard to establish, Wedgwood gained much from the canal promotion. He gained new fame and an enhanced reputation, and he gained new friends, friends who represented the opposite extremes of his own taste and personality. Erasmus Darwin was educated, cultured, a wit, a man of Society: James Brindley was untaught, illiterate, a man who had forced his way to fame by his own efforts and skills. It says a good deal about Wedgwood that he should have highly prized the friendship of each.

[6]

Expansion

WITH the hectic days of canal promotion behind him, Wedgwood could give more attention to other matters. His own business took priority, but there was also more time for family and friends. Having smoothed over the disagreements between Bentley and Darwin, correspondence could be taken up with pleasanter themes. One of these was the constant prodding at Bentley about his single status. Any marriage among acquaintances was an excuse for a fresh attack. "So poor Scarrat is Married! & in the next line allmost you tell me – *his head is turned*, which I suppose are synonymous with you wicked Batchelors & Widowers. Well I could in mere spite wish to see you fairly noosed again, & brought down into the Country, there to be immured in a little Rustick Cott, such as I could fashion for you – you know where, for the Diversion and emolument of the whole Country."[1] Wedgwood's own marriage was prospering, if children can be used as a measure. Sukey in 1765 was followed by John in 1766 and Richard was born the following year – yet another excuse to tease the long-suffering widower, who received the none too subtle suggestion: "You must try your hand at manufacturing something of the kind."[2]

Wedgwood was now consulting Bentley about all manner of things – business matters, new advances in science, family affairs and, with more and more frequency, Thomas Bentley himself and his future. There was an element of hero worship as Wedgwood earnestly pressed his friend to make greater use of the talents which, Wedgwood at least was convinced, could make him one of the

leading figures of the age. He began by urging Bentley towards a
career in politics, encouraging him not to underestimate himself:
"Do not let your modesty prevent your makeing a proper advantage
of your abilitys."[3] But that idea soon faded, and as early as June
1766 there are mentions of Bentley taking an interest in the pottery
business, even if at first that interest was to go no farther than his
receiving commission on pots he sold among his London friends.
Wedgwood also suggested, jokingly, that Bentley might do him a
favour in return: "I expect a small ship Load of Clay at your Port
in 3 weeks at farthest, pray what are the Port dues I am to pay. If
you could get one the honour of being made free of your Corpora-
tion now it might be of some use to me & I would be exceedingly
good & vote just as I was bid, you cannot think how passive I feel
myself to be, & that is surely qualification sufficient for an honorary
Burgess."[4]

The jokes covered a very real problem. Wedgwood needed help.
The hoped-for help from Byerley was clearly not going to be
forthcoming in the near future as that wayward young man continued his career as an eighteenth-century dropout. So increasingly
it was towards Bentley that Wedgwood turned. In the summer of
1766 expansion plans were given a boost with the agreement to
purchase, for £3,000, the 350-acre Ridgehouse Estate. Here
Wedgwood planned to build a new pot works and a new home,
and he at once cast Bentley in the role of a Capability Brown to
aid in the planning.

> My Sally says your *fat sides* require a good deal of shakeing, and
> would recommend a journey on *horseback*, not in the Coach,
> to Burslem, and is half angry with me for coming home without
> you, but your last letter brought her into a little better temper,
> as she expects not only the pleasure of seeing you here in a
> little time, but likewise, a jant to Liverpool in consequence of
> your Visit. Besides she will not fix upon a spot for either house
> or Gardens, no nor even the stables, 'till you have viewed and
> given your opinion of the premises. So now, my dear Sir,
> you are invited to the Ridgehouse Estate in quality of a *Brown*,
> and this may remove my only objection to seeing you here, I
> mean your takeing so long a journey to so little purpose. Ten

Guineas, if I remember right, is the price of a single call, with or without the advantage of his direction, to make a Lawn and piece of Water here – cut down the wood and plant it here – level that rising ground, and raise yonder valley, &c &c. But for ten times the business, fifty miles rideing, and a hundred times the genius, why we must expect to be sure to pay accordingly. One thing farther permit me to mention, that we shall be affronted with a short visit, but very thankful for a long one, so pray settle your business accordingly before you mount your Rosinante, and as a salve, or quietus, to your Conscience for the loss of so much time (which I know to be very squeamish, and am glad it is so, on these occasions) tell the troublesome spirit, that as our connections are to become extensive in the Potting business, it is absolutely necessary you should visit the Manufacture, see what is going forward there, make your bargains accordingly, and lend your assistance towards its farther improvements. Tell him your friend Wedgwood hath some pretty things laid up for you which he cannot send without your first seeing them, and I hope he may be prevailed upon to let you spend a fortnight or so in this neighbourhood.[5]

The letter continues with Wedgwood thanking Bentley for recommending Peter Swift to the job of clerk in Burslem. Swift was to become a highly valued member of the Wedgwood staff – "Cashier, Paymaster General and Accountant General and without him we should all be in confusion at once", as Wedgwood later put it.

This letter has been quoted at such length because it contains a number of important elements. The most obvious point is that it provides much clear evidence of Wedgwood's increasing habit of deferring to Bentley on all matters of taste. And here too we see the idea of a partnership starting to grow between the two friends. Already, we have two characteristics plain before us: in matters of taste, Bentley was to be supreme arbiter: but much of the business sense and ebullient confidence came from Wedgwood. Over the next two years we find these two elements recurring; Wedgwood eagerly accepting advice on the type of house he should build and discussing the various plans put up by Bentley, while at the same time delivering stern moral homilies on the virtues of hard work and hard cash. The language is Georgian, but the sentiments often seem to belong to a later age.

> Endeavour therefore, not after *knowledge*, & *literary wisdom*, of which you have enough, but after the *wisdom* of the *Children of the world*, in plain English – get money – you want some such matters as 4 or £500 per annum in Terra firma (such is the constitution of things in this sub-Lunary Planet) to make the knowledge & abilitys you have acquir'd of the greatest utility to your Countrymen.[6]

By March 1767, when Wedgwood talks of the pottery he is invariably referring to it as "our" business, and a booming business it was too. The newly named Queen's ware was proving a runaway success, selling at home and abroad, and Wedgwood began to consider the implications of its success. Was it intrinsic merit, or was it simply a case of where the Court led the rest would follow? The conclusion seemed obvious: "For instance, if a Royal, or Noble introduction be as necessary to the sale of an Article of Luxury, as real Elegance & beauty, then the Manufacturer, if he consults his own interest, will bestow as much pains, & expence too, if necessary, in gaining the former of these advantages, as he would in bestowing the latter."[7]

The overseas trade was in a thriving way. Even in the Far East, where Europe had traditionally bought its best porcelain, creamware was on sale. As Wedgwood remarked, it looked very much as if the Chinese would soon be sending their potters to Staffordshire to learn new techniques. But the English trade was the keystone of the whole commercial structure, and Wedgwood, in practice, answered his own musings by continuing to cultivate his patrons among the aristocracy. And once having taken that decision, he found the need for Bentley's help all the greater, for he was the man who could mix easily in such circles, the man attuned to the vagaries of fashion.

By November 1767 a partnership between Wedgwood and Bentley was being openly discussed, though with a good deal of wavering on Bentley's side. Wedgwood resorted to the old confidence trick of himself putting up objections for the sole purpose of smartly knocking them down again. He might once have proposed a political career for Bentley, but he proved to be no mean manipulator himself. In a long letter, Wedgwood set about the demolition process, beginning with Bentley's possible worries over his other financial interests. Those possible doubts were soon swept away before the flood of Wedgwood's enthusiastic assessments of the future. Perhaps, Wedgwood suggested, he disliked the thought of giving up home and friends to employ himself among "Mechanicks, dust and smoke". Certainly, Bentley could be expected to have doubts on that score, but Wedgwood was soon offering a new and enticing prospect:

> If this prospect does not fright you, I have some hopes, and if you think you could really fall in love with, and make a Mistress of this new business, as I have done of mine, I should have little or no doubt of our success, for if we consider the great variety of colours in our raw Materials – the infinite ductility of Clay, and that we have universal beauty to copy after, we have certainly the fairest prospect of enlarging this branch of Manufacture to our wishes, and as Genius will not be wanting I am firmly persuaded that our *proffits* will be in proportion to our *application*, and I am confident that it would be beyond comparison more congenial, and delightfull, to every particle of matter, sense, and spirit in your composition, to be the Creator as it were of beauty, rather than merely the vehicle or medium to convey it from one hand to another, if other circumstances can be rendered tolerable. Let us therefore endeavour to take a more distinct view of the outlines of our project, which may furnish us with some amusement at least, and perhaps it may not be the first time we have pleased our selves with future schemes that have eluded our grasp, and vanished away like the morning Cloud or early dew.[8]

In spite of such seductive wooing, it was the following May before Bentley finally agreed to join Wedgwood in the business.

> Your most acceptable letter of the 15th gave me the highest pleasure in setting before me a nearer prospect than I had yet had of a union that I had long coveted, and which I do not doubt will be lasting, delightful, and beneficial to us both. And as

to the time and manner of leaving Liverpool, make it the most agreeable to your self in every respect, and it will be perfectly so to me. At present indeed I am not in possession of the Land you know to build you either a House, or Works, but am now in treaty with the Old Lady's Steward, and you have furnished me with a very strong inducement to comply with allmost any terms they shall propose.[9]

So the actuality of partnership drew nearer, and it came at precisely the right moment in time. The circumstances were just such as to enable their two talents to combine to produce the maximum effect. Indeed, it could very well be argued that, at another time, the pottery of Wedgwood would not have achieved such remarkable pre-eminence. Success came because they met at a time of changing taste. Winckelmann's writings in praise of the antique have already been mentioned, but what was increasingly important in the latter part of the eighteenth century was the work of excavators. To call the majority of them by the title "archaeologist" would be to elevate them to a position too few deserved. They worked with little system and scarcely more sense, destroying at least as much evidence as they unearthed. Nevertheless, the work fascinated fashionable Europe, and the Grand Tour invariably included a visit to the latest diggings. No self-respecting Tourist returned home without his collections of Roman sculpture and Greek vases even if, as was the case with the young Duke of Bridge-water, the collection remained packed away in cases for a lifetime. The point was that it was quite definitely the thing to do.

The great spur to all this frenzied gathering of antiquities was the discovery and excavation of Herculaneum in the Bay of Naples. Here was a rich store of paintings and furniture, vases and statues, made all the more interesting by the reluctance of the Neapolitan authorities to allow visitors to see the new works. Herculaneum was both mysterious and exotic, at first known only from the letters of the few lucky visitors, then later becoming known to a wider public as the first books began to appear. There was a general acceptance of the idea that mankind had discovered in the art of the ancient world a beauty that had been lost for centuries, a perfection of form and grace, an ideal antidote to the excesses of Rococo. The books with their engravings, such as the very influential *Recueil d'antiquités égyptiennes, étrusques et romaines* by Count de Caylus (1752), increased the vogue by including the works of ancient Egypt and, wrongly attributed, Etruscan art. Not that wrong attribution was important, it was enough for most that a work was ancient for it to be certain of a rapturous reception. But for all that it was the sketches from Herculaneum which excited the most interest.

The 1760s were years that saw the spread of the influence of classicism to many different areas, including architecture. Robert Adam had visited Diocletian's Palace at Spalato in 1758, and in 1763 he published his researches in a splendid volume illustrated by engravings. It had an immediate success, but in the long term it was Adam's own interpretations of the classical style – more gentle than the severe originals of the ancient world – that were to have the greatest effect.

Wedgwood was among the many who eagerly acquired the new books as they appeared even if, in many cases, they had to be sent straight off to Bentley for translation. So we find him sending off a whole parcel in February 1767.

> You will as easily imagine what may be of any use to me in the Antiquitys if you find time to dip into them. The colours of the Earthen Vases, the paintings, the substances used by the Ancient Potters, with their method, of working, burning &c. . . . Who knows what you may hit upon, or what we may strike out betwixt us; you may depend on an ample share of the proffits arising from any such discoverys. I have more Volumes of Antiquitys at your service when you can dispence with them.[10]

So we find Wedgwood at once enthusiastic to push forward into this new area where the tastes of Greece and Rome were to dictate the fashions of eighteenth-century Europe, and to help him as intimate friend and colleague a man classically educated, a good linguist and in touch with all the new developments. It is worth stressing just how unusual such a combination was at that time. When one looks at some of the other famous figures who helped to create the Industrial Revolution one finds very different characteristics. Richard Arkwright, the founder of the first successful mill to use water power to spin cotton on machines, was boorish, philistine and tasteless, the very model of the *nouveau riche* industrialist who was later to be a popular fictional image. All that long succession of "where there's muck there's money" clichés have their natural father in Arkwright, whose fortune found expression in the vast mansion he built for himself, Willersley Castle, the house mockingly described as being "in the same castellated style as one sees at Clapham". True, pottery is somewhat different from other industries – there is always something of the art in it – but there were no others at that time who were so sensitive to changes in other, allied arts. Wedgwood and Bentley may have followed a general aesthetic movement, but as far as the pottery industry was concerned they were not followers but leaders. They established new trends which others could only attempt, somewhat haltingly, to follow.

While Bentley laid down the rules of taste, Wedgwood himself was busy looking for improvements in manufacturing processes. His search for better clays, for example, was not limited to Britain and he became interested in "Cherokee Clay", so called because it was found in the Cherokee Indian territory of North Carolina. As was now quite common with Wedgwood, his experiments with this clay were conducted in an atmosphere of much secrecy, all very cloak-and-daggery. In May 1767 he was very preoccupied by the affair and was arranging matters with Thomas Griffiths, the brother of a friend, Ralph Griffiths, who was the publisher of the *Monthly Review* – and, incidentally, one of the few men of intellect and fashion introduced by Wedgwood to Bentley rather than the other way round. Thomas Griffiths agreed to acquire some Cherokee clay for Wedgwood, who at once began sniffing round to see what further information he could acquire on the subject. At the end of the month he wrote to Bentley to describe, with schoolboyish delight, how he had managed to obtain samples from some unsuspecting American visitors who showed them to him, "not knowing who, or what I was, for I kept in Cog". Eventually five tons of the clay reached Staffordshire and proved to be of most excellent quality, but the difficulties of transport were so immense that the cost was prohibitive. The clay was used, but no more was bought.

Wedgwood's early enthusiasm had led him seriously to consider attempting to acquire a monopoly in the Cherokee deposits. Once it was clear, however, that the costs were too high, he simply let the whole matter drop. Wedgwood's enthusiasms were quickly roused but could be equally quickly dispelled if necessary. But the American connections gave him a chance to contemplate American political life, and his comments show that he had rather more prescience than the British Government when it came to considering the affairs of that country. Grenville's administration had begun the calamitous policy of taxing the American colonists without consultation, and was considering the possibility of charging them for the quartering of the British troops in the colonies. Wedgwood was both scathing and accurate:

> Mr. Greenville [sic] & his party seem determin'd to *Conquer England in America* I believe. If the Americans do not comply with their demands respecting the quartering of soldiers, the Alternative, I am told, is to be, The suspension of the Legislative power in America. I tell them the Americans will then make Laws for themselves & if we continue our Policy – for us too in a *very* short time. But I have very little time at present to bestow upon Politicks, if we must all be driven to America, you & I shall do very well among the Cherokees.[11]

A week later, he returned to the subject and noted, with even greater accuracy: "that our policy had a tendency to render the Americans independent a Century sooner than they would be in the common order of events, if treated agreeable to sound policy."[12]

Looking over Wedgwood's life during those two years of 1766 and 1767, one finds so many strands being laid down that were to prove vital in the development in later years. It is as though the last of the warp had been laid on the loom, the pattern was established, and now only the weft needed to be threaded through to complete the piece. Already we have seen the establishment of the canal that was to be vital for the expansion of trade, we have seen the move to a larger works and the steady approach of the partnership with Bentley. These are the main elements in the pattern, but there were other strands that added to its richness. In May 1767, for example, his interest in engine lathe-turning took him to Birmingham, where he negotiated to buy a lathe from Matthew Boulton. "He is I believe the first – or most complete manufacturer in England, in metal. He is very ingenious, Philosophical, and Agreeable. You must be acquainted with him, he has promised to come to Burslem . . ."[13]

Matthew Boulton was to prove in turn associate and rival, but he remained a close friend and was an important influence on Wedgwood's life.

Among his many journeyings, Wedgwood still found time to continue with his experiments. Indeed, no matter how hard affairs might press in on him, he always managed somehow to find the time for such an important activity.

> I am going on with my experiments upon various Earths, Clays &c for different bodys, & shall next go upon Glazes. Many of my experiments turn out to my wishes, & convince me more & more, of the extensive Capability of our Manufacture for further improvements. It is at present (comparatively) in a rude, uncultivated state, & may easily be polished, & brought to much greater perfection. Such a revolution, I believe, is at hand.[14]

In the September, even though his health was none too good, he was still able to plan a visit to the Derbyshire lead mines, where he believed he might find a "Spath fusible" that he needed for a course of experiments.

Not all Wedgwood's scientific curiosity was centred on pot making. He became very excited when the canal navvies digging into Harecastle Hill unearthed fossil remains, which he described to Bentley

> . . . a prodigious rib, with the vertebre of the backbone of a monstrous sized Fish, thought by some connissieurs to belong to the identical Whale that was so long ago swallowed by Jonah! . . . Perhaps by the skill you have lately acquired in Anatomy, you could throw some light upon these matters, but then another difficulty arises – *whether you should be carried to the bones or they to you.* The latter would be very expensive by Land Carriage, & if they come upon the *Weaver* the Boatmen are sure to pilfer them, if only to keep their hands in use.[15]

At the north end of the tunnel, he noted the stratification of coal and sandstone and fossil plants. Although he deprecates his own abilities his conjectures are remarkably sound.

I should be glad to know from some of you Gentlemen learned in Natural History & Philosophy the most probable theory to account for these vegetables (as they once were) forming part of a Stratum, which dips into the Earth to our knowledge 60 or 100 yds. deep & for aught we know, to the Centre! These Strata, the Coals included, seem from various circumstances to have been in a Liquid state, & to have travelled along what was then the surface of the Earth, something like the Lava from Mount Vesuvius. ... I am got beyond my depth. These wonderful works of nature are too vast for my narrow, microscopic comprehension. I must bid adieu to you for the present & attend to what better suits my small capacity, the forming of a Jug or Teapot.

He also took a lively interest in the work of other scientists, though when he came to discuss Priestley's work on electricity, the tone was hardly one of hushed reverence. But then, electricity was still regarded as something of a plaything. Nevertheless, in spite of the general light-hearted tone of the letter, Wedgwood's appreciation of the stature of Priestley the scientist is apparent, and the letter contains an offer of help in the work, an offer that was later to be made good. Indeed, over the years Priestley was to be given ample reason to be grateful for the potter's interest. But that was for the future: for the present, Wedgwood was out to have a little gentle fun at the expense of the scientist–moralist. "But what dareing mortals you are! to rob the Thunderer of his Bolts, – and for what? – no doubt to blast the oppressors of the poor and needy, or to execute some public piece of justice in the most tremendous and conspicuous manner, that shall make the great ones of the Earth tremble!"[16] No pun could have been intended, but that "public execution" sounds like a macabre prediction of the electric chair.

What else was occupying Wedgwood at this time? – not that anyone could describe his life other than full as it was. There was the continuing search for decent showrooms in London, which had to satisfy very particular and apparently contradictory requirements. They were intended as show places to display ware and increase sales, yet at the same time he was concerned that they should not be open to the hoi polloi who might scare away the gentry and nobility of delicate sensibilities. As he put it, "They will not mix with the rest of the World any farther than their amusements or conveniencys make it necessary to do so." He also wanted a place where displays could constantly be changed. "Every new show, Exhibition or rarity soon grows stale in London." He also required an extra room for "my Ladys", who "sometimes come in very large shoals together, & one party are often obliged to wait 'till another have done their business". He looked at a number of possible buildings, but none seemed suitable.

The one area where, at first, everything seemed to be going exactly as planned was in the construction of the canal. There were a few doubters around, but Brindley was on hand to restore confidence. At a committee meeting in March 1767, Brindley stoutly affirmed that everything would be finished in five years and when a querulous voice of scepticism was raised, the engineer at once offered to put a £200 bet on the matter. Heady stuff – but it was the doubter who would have won the bet. Wedgwood firmly believed in Brindley's abilities, but he was beginning to feel real concern that he was taking on too much work. New canal schemes were cropping up all the time, and each seemed to require the services of James Brindley. Even Wedgwood found himself caught up in the activity, and he was called in to advise over the plans for the Coventry Canal, which was to link up with the Trent and Mersey. But the demands on his time were nothing compared with the demands on Brindley. Wedgwood became more and more concerned. He had come to respect the bluff man with his downright manner and hard northern accent, who was described by another friend as "as plain a looking man as one of the boors of the peak, or one of his own carters". But the warning signs were there, and Wedgwood could read them.

> I am afraid he will do too much, & leave us before his vast designs are executed, he is so incessantly harrassed on every side, that he hath no rest, either for his mind, or Body, & will not be prevailed upon to take proper care of his health. . . . I think Mr. Brindley – *The Great, the fortunate money-getting* Brindley an object of Pity! & a real sufferer for the good of the Public. He may get a few thousands, but what does he give in

exchange? His *Health*, & I fear his *Life* too, unless he grows wiser, & takes the advice of his friends before it is too late.[17]

The prognosis proved accurate, for a month later proposed trips to Ireland and Scotland had to be cancelled, and Wedgwood did his best to persuade the engineer to take a long rest. But too soon Brindley was back at work, dressed in his old, shabby clothes and ambling off on his equally old mare. He continued to push himself hard, and under his guidance the skeleton of the canal network was formed, the system that was to provide the major route for bulk transport until the coming of the railways. Wedgwood had no doubt as to the importance of this work, though at this time he was inclined to minimize his own achievements in industry, just as he belittled his own scientific work. Perhaps he had risen from obscurity to the beginnings of fame too suddenly to be quite certain of himself. But the protestations of being just "plain Jos" are not always convincing – at times, one can almost catch the pause as he waits for the denial, but that does not detract from his genuine admiration of Brindley. "Do you think my friend that the *outline* of a Jug, even a Bolingbroke, or the *fine turn* of a Teapot are synonims of *Creating a River*, or *building a City*. No, no, my friend, let us speak softly, or rather be silent on such Fribling performance, your friend shall endeavour to please the Ladys, for the good of his – Family & friends, but he must not be vain of such *trifles*, & mistake them for *great actions*."

Amidst all this activity, Wedgwood's private life had to be slotted into the few remaining hours, but the few mentions we find of "Mrs. Wedgwood and her Wedgwoodikin" suggest a contented family life. But even the family were not kept clear of the expanding business. Sally was very directly involved: "I speak from experience in Female taste, without which I should have made but a poor figure among my Potts, not one of which, of any consequence, is finished without the approbation of my Sally." How she found time to consider every pot between her annual pregnancies remains a mystery. And there were new affairs to be discussed and argued over, the most important of which for the family was the design of their new house. There were long sessions with the architect, Pickford, and Bentley was frequently called on to arbitrate in his role as connoisseur of the arts and architecture.

There still seemed to be some time left over to meet and cor-
respond with old friends. Wedgwood remained addicted to match-
making among his acquaintances and news of a marriage always
delighted him, bringing out in him a streak of whimsy that was
usually expressed in teasing Bentley. But when he heard of the
wedding of another old friend, Ralph Griffiths, he gave him the
benefit of his raillery instead.

> But now Sir pray turn your Eyes another way – you may
> direct them to your dear Betsey if you please whilst I address
> myself to that Good Lady for a moment. . . . Permit me Dear
> Madam to acquaint you that your Naughty Husband has such
> a bewitching way of saying, & doing things, that it is a thousand
> to one he does either good, or mischief by every letter he writes.
> – In this now before me, he has wittingly, & knowingly said
> such things of my Wifes Children, as he well knows must go
> to the heart of any Mother who suckles their own Children
> as my Wife does; & now he invites her to Turnham Green.
> He says it is to see & love you, but I am far from being certain
> that she would not love *somebody else* too. She even now desires
> me to bespeak your first Girl for the Boy she has in her arms, if
> she is not pre-ingaged, this & many other symptoms I have
> observ'd fully convince me that my wife has no small liking to a
> certain family at T.G. And now I have made this discovery do
> you think Madam it will be advisable to bring her with me to
> town. No! I am sure you clearly see the consequences likely to
> attend so imprudent a step, & will leave her behind me 'till I
> am farther satisfyed of her inclinations.[18]

The match-maker seemed to believe in starting young. In fact,
Wedgwood was inordinately fond of his own children, especially
when they were young, and in his anxiety that they should be spared
the pains and miseries of his own childhood, he had them innoculated
against the smallpox. It must have been a desperately worrying time
for him. The treatment was new and relatively untried and the
children were, in effect, given a mild dose of the disease. Sukey and
John both received the innoculation and developed what their father
described as "a pretty smart pox". They were both quite ill, and it

was with immense relief that he could write to tell family and friends when they were well again. Wedgwood needed no reminder of the ravages of that disease, for he was suffering ever more frequent and ever more painful recurrences of his own knee infection. As he watched over the children, seeing the "smart pox" develop, he admitted later that he began regretting the whole experiment. But, at the end, all was well.

All was not well, however, throughout the family. In June 1767 John Wedgwood went to see the fireworks at the Ranelagh Pleasure Gardens in Chelsea and then went to dine at the Swan in Westminster. He had hoped to stay the night, but there was no room and he set off along the riverside walk in search of accommodation. No more was seen of him until his body was discovered the next morning. He had drowned. He might have been attacked by robbers, he might quite simply have slipped on the unlit pathway and tumbled into the water. There was no way of telling. It was a very great shock to his younger brother, for they had been very close. Wedgwood's response was immediate. He wrote to Bentley. His reliance on his friend was never expressed so completely, the depth of his relationship never more clearly seen, than in this moment of grief. At the end of the letter he made this plea, "Let us now be dearer to each other if possible than ever, let me adopt you for my Brother – and fill up the chasm this cruel accident has made in my afflicted heart."

The death of his brother, coupled with the continuing pressures of business, produced one of those periodic bouts of sickness that punctuated Wedgwood's life. He was ready enough with antidotes to everyone else's complaints. "Do not tell me of your shoulders," he wrote to Bentley, "they want shaking, & your whole habits want exercise & fresh Air." Not the sort of advice that puts sufferers into a good humour, and the recipients of those hearty recipes must often have been sorely tempted to mutter: "Physician, heal thyself." For, when one of his nervous attacks struck him, Wedgwood was very far from being an ideal patient. But on this occasion, his health recovered and he was back in the busy world soon enough. This whole hectic period can perhaps best be summed up in his own words: "Why you never knew so busy a Mortal as I am, – Highways – surveying Ridge House Estate – Experiments for Porcelain, or at least – a new Earthenware, fill up every moment allmost of my time & would take a good deal more if I had it – besides all the Hands in the country are not hired but are still coming to me -- '*to know when they must begin*'."[19]

[7]

Artes Etruriae Renascuntur

ETRURIA: that was to be the name of the new works being developed by Wedgwood. Etruria Hall was to be the name of the new house being built for the family. Etruria was to be the inspiration for the new ware that was to make the names of Wedgwood and Bentley famous. What a curious irony that all this extensive building, all this new manufacture, should be based on a misnomer.

The passion for antiquities was at its height, and among those who helped to rouse the passion in Britain the ambassador to Naples, Sir William Hamilton, was pre-eminent. He himself made a great and valuable collection, which should have ensured his name's continuing to posterity if the activities of his wife Emma with Nelson had not ensured an even greater fame for the Hamiltons. In his campaign to popularize a taste for things Greek and Roman he published a book, *Etruscan Antiquities*. The antiquities were not Etruscan at all, but the name came to be used to cover almost any classical find. So it was that Wedgwood, firmly under the spell of the new classicism, came to build his own Etruria.

Between any plans for building and the actuality of construction there seems, inevitably, to be a mighty gulf. Plans whisked between the Wedgwoods, Pickford and Bentley. Wedgwood was now grown sufficiently sure of his own taste to dare even to question Bentley's. "Will not the Gothic Battlements to buildings in every other respect in the modern taste be a little heterogeneous?" he asked rather diffidently.[1] Indeed they would, and battlements duly disappeared from the plans. The house, as finally built, was very much in the modern style – a Georgian mansion, very suitable for a gentleman of property. It was four square and solid, substantial without being ostentatious, set in a fine parkland that gave it an air of spaciousness.

Other worries were less easily disposed of. The new works were planned to stand next to the canal, with the house on the opposite bank. Wedgwood himself was to pay for the section through his property, but when it came to laying down the line he found an unexpected obstacle to his dreams of elegant landscaping. He went to view the site with Hugh Henshall, who was to be responsible for overseeing the work, and found to his dismay that the rules of engineering were to be made to stand above the rules of taste. The "inflexible vandal" would not allow one inch of deviation from the dead straight line decreed by James Brindley, however hard Wedgwood might plead for his "line of grace".

Another problem that arose was rather more serious. Other local potters, who were not to be blessed with a canal at their doorsteps, began to complain. They argued that the passage through Etruria involved an unnecessary and costly detour. The accusation that he was taking advantage of his official position to secure special favours was very bitter to Wedgwood. "This cloud has been gathering for some time, & no pains are spared by the Party who have blown it up, to make it light as heavy upon me as possible."[2] However, he had the support of Brindley and Brindley's reputation as "an honest man". So the plans went ahead again to the accompaniment of the more usual problems of rising costs and interrupted work. The partnership was now sufficiently settled for a second house to have been added, next to Etruria Hall, for Bentley's use.

All then seemed to be going, if not with perfect smoothness, at least reasonably well, and Wedgwood was in fine good humour at the beginning of the year. When in good humour with himself, he was all benevolence to the rest of the world. In February he reported more good fortune, for he had found "an ingenious and indefatigable smith amongst us" who had specialized in engine lathes and promised an absolute secrecy. This fitted in well enough with the usual Wedgwood attitudes, but not with his new magnanimity. He was now above all such petty secrets: "we have renounced these narrow, selfish views & are to let our improvements take a free course for the benefit of our *Bretheren & Country*."[3] Such magnanimity was generally short-lived, and as his mood changed he would swing to obsessive secrecy and an almost paranoid fear of spies. But for a while the optimism remained high.

A further good omen for the future came in March, when Wedgwood at last settled on his new London rooms and warehouse. He rented a house for one hundred guineas a year at the corner of Newport Street and St Martin's Lane. It was a good situation, convenient for his customers and out of the way of the heavy traffic to and from the docks. He was now firmly set, with Bentley's help, in making a thriving trade in ornamental pottery and he saw great things developing around his London base.

> I think of making habitations for a Colony of Artists – Modelers, Carvers &c. I have already agreed with one very usefull Tennant, a Master Enameler, & China piecer. ... I have long had connections with this man, who is sober, & steady, he is just come out of Yorkshire to settle here. He paints flowers, & landskips very prettily, prepares a pretty good powder gold, & has a tolerable notion of Colours. He has an apprentice & another hand. I have set him to work upon Table & desert ware, & shall get his rooms ready in St. Martin's Lane immediately. The having such a man as this under the same roof with the Warehouse, to do Crests, or any other patterns by order – to take sketches &c – is the most convenient thing imaginable, & nobody but ourselves will know what he is doing.[4]

The "tennant" was David Rhodes of Leeds. This was a first step leading, in the following year, to the establishment of an enamelling works at Chelsea under Bentley's direction, where ware was sent from Staffordshire for decoration. The same letter also mentions Sir William Hamilton's brother, Lord Cathcart, the ambassador to Russia. "We are to do great things for each other", was Wedgwood's comment on the meeting, and certainly Lord Cathcart was to do great things for him.

Meanwhile, new artists were being brought into the Wedgwood fold. One of these was a modeller who had worked for Robert Adam, the great architectural champion of Neoclassicism, and he was pronounced to be "a perfect Master in the Antique style". This was a less than happy signing, as the man in question appears to have been John Voyez – one of those awkward, quirky individualists who never fitted into the smoothly efficient organization that was the Wedgwood ideal.

During that spring Wedgwood did a great deal of travelling. He went to Birmingham and had long discussions with Boulton, and he visited Lichfield to view a windmill Erasmus Darwin had designed for him. "This windmill is to grind colours," Wedgwood noted, adding rather rudely: "if it should happen to grind anything." But soon it was Darwin's turn to visit Burslem, not as friend and inventor of windmills, but as physician. It was no neurotic complaint that struck Wedgwood, but an unusually serious recurrence of the old leg trouble. The month of May was an appalling time for Sally Wedgwood. Her husband was clearly getting no better, and at the same time her one-year-old son Richard fell ill. His trouble was gastric, and at first must have seemed a comparatively minor problem in comparison with the condition of Josiah's leg. After much anxious consultation, a drastic treatment was proposed and agreed: the only course open was amputation.

The seriousness of such an operation cannot be overemphasized. Science and technology may have been making immense progress, but medicine lagged far behind. Darwin might scoff at old-fashioned quackery, but too often he could offer only the new quackery in its place. Surgery was performed without anaesthetics and in conditions that at their best were non-sterile and at their worst were downright filthy. There were two grave dangers facing the patient – shock, and an infection leading to gangrene. Wedgwood had two surgeons to attend him, with Mr. Bent performing the operation, which could at least be carried out in the comparatively hygienic surroundings of his own home. Bentley hurried to Burslem to be with his friend. The pain during and after the operation was partially eased by dosing with laudanum, but the patient remained conscious for the whole time. Speed was of the essence. The excruciating pain as the surgeon cut through flesh and sawed at bone soon brought medical shock, stopping blood to the brain. If the amputation took too long, the patient died. The best surgeon was the quickest, and times of under two minutes were not unknown. News of the

James Brindley, the engineer of the Trent and Mersey Canal. The right arm appears to have been borrowed from a friend – the artist is unknown.

Wedgwood's friend and doctor, Erasmus Darwin – looking very Johnsonian.

Basalt ware was another of Wedgwood's important innovations. The hedgehog, which is a particularly charming example, was used as a crocus pot.

An elaborate ewer, in which the figure of Neptune has been splendidly worked into the overall design.

JUNE XIII . M.DCC.LXIX.
One of the first Days Productions
at
Etruria in Staffordshire,
by
Wedgwood and Bentley.

The First Day Vase, thrown by Wedgwood with Bentley turning the wheel to mark the opening of the new works at Etruria in August 1769.

operation was sent to Cox in London by Peter Swift, on 28 May, in these few terse words: "Mr. Wedgwood has this day had his leg taken off, & is as well as can be expected after such an execution." Four days later his progress was still good. Then on 4 June Swift could write even more favourably of Wedgwood, but in the same letter had to report a new tragedy for the household.

> I have now the pleasure to acquaint you that Mr Wedgwood continues in a good way, his Leg was opened on Thursday for the first time & both the surgeons said it could not possibly be better, – & he has every good Symptom so that we have the greatest hopes of a perfect cure.
>
> Poor Master Dicky after being violently seized with a Complaint in his Bowels for some time expired on Thursday morning & was Inter'd Last Evening. Indeed I think Mrs. Wedgwood has had severe tryals of late, but the great hopes of Mr Wedgwood's perfect recovery seem to keep her spirits up in a tollerable degree.

Wedgwood, who could so easily descend into a deep gloom at the onset of one of his psychoneurotic illnesses, showed the most remarkable resilience and fortitude during the whole period of the operation and his convalescence. Within a fortnight he was back taking a lively interest in business affairs and dictating a letter to Cox, which covered a whole variety of topics – the employment of an assistant for the London warehouse, the question of whether there might be objections from the Palace if he was to mention royal patronage in advertisements and that recurring and troublesome theme, accounts. He was frequently short of cash, not because he was not selling but because customers were not paying. At the end of the letter, he was well enough to add a brief note in his own hand.

Bentley was soon satisfied enough about his partner's recovery to be able to move on to Liverpool, where he at once received a letter that contained the now familiar mixture of an almost embarrassing effusion of sentiment, a deep earnestness concerning Wedgwood's relationship with him and a remarkably light-hearted account of the patient's continued improvement.

> I have many, very many, most kind and affectionate letters to be

thankful for to my dear friend, with a thousand other instances
of his esteem – but that is too cool a term to express the feelings
of my heart by; permit me to call it Brotherly love and affection,
as such I do, and ever must regard you, and though I may be
prevented telling you so as often as I should wish to do it, yet
I trust you know my heart too well to think that I could for a
moment cease to love, and be gratefull to you. . . . At present
I am well even beyond my most sanguine expectations, my
leg is allmost healed, the wound is not quite 2 inches by one
& $\frac{1}{2}$, I measured it with the compasses this morning when I
dressed it. Yes, when I *dressed it*, for I have turned my surgeons
adrift and Sally and I are sole managers now, only we give
him leave to peep at it now and then, when he lifts up his hands
and eyes, and will scarcely believe it to be the wound he
dressed before.[5]

There is every indication of good spirits as he passed on various
news items – the wayward Tom Byerley was finally off to America,
building work was held up by the rain – and he would no doubt
have gone on for pages "but Sally says 'give over Joss, and tell our
friend B. that I command it' ".

By 20 June Wedgwood was well enough to visit the works and
take a couple of outings in a chaise, and the pain had eased sufficiently
for him to leave off the laudanum. The wound was healing so well
that he declared that they lived indeed in "an Age of Miracles".
Soon he was fitted with a wooden leg and could stomp off to view
his works again. The only noticeable effect was that he spent less
time on horseback, and more in carriages and chaises. The worst
was over, the amputation was a success, and Wedgwood could
regard the whole affair with such good humour that the following
year he planned to throw a party to celebrate St Amputation
Day.

So it was back to business, and a business increasingly dominated
by the planned expansion of the ornamental ware, and especially
vases. Vase making was not a new activity, but the new Etruria
demanded new Etruscan vases. Quite early in the year, at his meeting
with Matthew Boulton, vases had already featured prominently in
their discussions.

Mr Boulton tells me I should be surprised to know what a trade
has lately been made out of Vases at Paris. The Artists have even
come over to London, picked up all the old whimsical ugly
things they could meet with, carried them to Paris where they
have mounted & ornamented them with metal, & sold them
to the Virtuosi of every Nation, & particularly to Millords
d'Anglise, for the greatest raritys. . . . This alone (the combination of Clay & Metals) is a field, to the farther end of which we
shall never be able to travel.[6]

Throughout that summer he worked, experimenting with different clays and glazes, new designs and models and different colours,
until in August he was sending crates of vases to London and,
triumphantly, two Etruscan bronze vases to Bentley at Liverpool.
The Wedgwood who in January had renounced secrecy now sang
a different tune. To Cox in London he sent a warning that spies
were buying vases to copy, and with Bentley he was even more
insistent: "no Man, Woman, or Child, but your own household,
nor scarcely them, should see these things at present."[7] The wish to
keep the new vases for himself was understandable, for he had
worked hard and long to perfect the bronze colour, which was
burned in. The process was expensive, the result uncertain. As he
explained to Bentley, a prime virtue in a potter was patience:
"Every Vaze in the last Kiln was spoil'd! & that only by such a
degree of variation in the fire as scarcely affected our creamcolour
bisket at all."[7] If the wish for secrecy was understandable, however,
it was scarcely practical: he could not simultaneously publicize
and sell his new vases and keep them secret. There was in any case
little need for such elaborate precautions. Wedgwood's great
strength as a potter derived from his ability to combine an eye for
form with the use of appropriate materials, and the latter came only
as a result of his hundreds of careful experiments. To match his
ware, other potters needed to follow the same process of rigorous
experiment – and even if they succeeded, Wedgwood always
had Bentley ready with new suggestions for changes to meet the
latest demands of taste.

Wedgwood's correspondence through the rest of that year and
on into the next seems to be vases, vases all the way – apart from a

brief interruption when he discovered that some of the items he was including in that category were not vases at all but urns. But vases or urns, it made little difference; always the demand grew, and always he was searching for new improvements, moving closer to his own reinterpretation of the Greek ideal. There were moments of indecision. There was, for example, the awkward problem posed by Matthew Boulton – should he send the ware to Soho for mounting in metal? He recognized the argument that Wedgwood and Bentley were doing very well on their own: "Very true, but he will be doing, so that the question is whether we shall refuse having anything to do with him, and thereby affront him, & set him of doing them himself, or employing his friend Garbett."[8] Wedgwood liked Boulton, but he recognized in him a man with ambitions at least equal to his own. Wedgwood and Bentley complemented each other: Wedgwood and Boulton would inevitably compete unless they could keep a good discreet distance apart in any mutual business. Meanwhile there was enough to keep everyone busy – "Mr Cox is as mad as a March Hare for Etruscan Vases."

In January 1769 Wedgwood visited London to see for himself exactly what was selling and not selling. Etruscan vases were still the rage, but it was not all success – "marbling with gold is hiss'd universally". And the cry was still for more and more vases. There was, he declared, an "epidemical madness" for them which could scarcely be satisfied. While he was away, Sally looked over a good deal of the business of the works, a topic that dominated their correspondence, on her side rather more briefly than on his. There was little of the extravagant about Sarah Wedgwood, but then her husband was quite capable of carrying on sufficient correspondence for two: "I must thank my dear Sally for her last favour, though she did not conclude it so meekly as one might wish, but with a Toss of her head says, I shall not trouble my head &c – Oh Fye Sally Fye, wilt thou never mind? you are a naughty girl, & fill but half a sheet with your letter, whilst I scribble by the Quire."[9]

If 1768 seemed to be the year when vases dominated production, then it soon became clear that 1769 was to be little different. The simple lines and elegance of the vases had touched off an immediate response, and the demand grew rather than slackened. Mrs Byerley,

Tom's mother, visited London and reported on the crowds at Newport Street. "No getting to the door for Coaches, nor into the room for Ladies & Gentlemen & Vases . . . Vases was all the cry." The public knew exactly what it wanted and, as Wedgwood discovered when he tried a new line, it knew what it did not want, in this case confirming Sally's opinion. "Some of the Ladys say the same thing that occur'd to you & me about the sugar dish Vases – that they are like the things on the top of Clock cases, of Bed heads. They certainly are not Antique, and that is fault enough to D_n them for ever with most of our customers."[10]

It became so difficult to meet the demand that Wedgwood had to spend some time on experiments for repairing faulty vases. He was also at work producing what he called "Encaustic vases", which he made in imitation of the black and red vases of ancient Greece. The Greeks made the body of red clay, and coated it completely in black slip. They then produced a design by cutting into the slip to expose the red underneath. Wedgwood, who had already produced his black basalt, used a much simpler technique – he painted the red over the black and fired it on. The effect was very like the original, however dissimilar the method, and in 1769 he took out his one and only patent to protect the process.

By the autumn Wedgwood was characteristically alternating between a wish to keep all his processes secret for fear of imitation and a desire to be seen as the great public benefactor, above such narrow, selfish ideas. So at first we find him writing to Bentley about the difficulties of vase production and the need to monopolize the market.

I want to talk very seriously to my Dear Friend about *Encaustic Vases*, pray sit down, take a pipe, & compose yourself. If our potters once make the black body they will mimick the painting as soon as they see it, this shews the necessity of doing a quantity in as little time as possible. I will ingage to supply you with Vases enough for all the *good* painters in England. You say you can sell a Waggon load a week, if you sell that quantity in the Season, you must have ten Waggon loads of painters to finish them. One Vase per day, with a fine subject, will be as much as one painter will do upon an average. I repeat it again that you shall not want Vases, & it must be your & Mr. Crofts care to collect & make the painters.[11]

Then, only ten days later, he passed on the news that Boulton was considering going into the pottery business. Wedgwood was worried that some of his workmen might be lured to Birmingham, but was curiously excited at the prospect. And why not? If imitation is the sincerest form of flattery, what could have been more flattering than to have one of the country's leading manufacturers following him into the pottery business? "It doubles my courage to have the first Manufacturer in England to encounter with – The Match likes me well, – I like the Man, I like his spirit. He will not be a mere snivelling copyist like the antagonists I have hitherto had."[12] Stirred by this prospect, he promptly proceeded to reverse his earlier attitude and to "generously lay our works open to be imitated by other Artists & Manufacturers for the good of the community at large. . . . With respect to myself, there is nothing relating to business I so much wish for as being released from these degrading slavish chains, these mean selfish fears of other people copying my works." He added, rather spoiling the effect: "This would certainly procure us the good will of our best customers, & place us in a very advantageous light to the Public eye . . . perhaps upon the whole, this skeme might bring us as much *proffit* as *loss*."

Bentley in return very sensibly pointed out that while complete secrecy was impractical, there was little point in making life needlessly easy for their competitors. The final essential was to secure their own market – and not to attempt to introduce too many new lines at one time. Bentley insisted that he was all for securing a place in posterity, but was not too keen at securing it at the cost of profits for the present. Such rather prosaic views were greeted with an enthusiasm they scarcely merited. Yet, in a sense, this correspondence tells us a good deal about the strange balance between the two partners. Wedgwood at this time was swept along by heady dreams, by the vision of an apparently inexhaustible variety of ware flowing from the works. Bentley was more firmly earthbound. He took the great flow of ideas and tested them against his own judgement of their commercial viability. Without Bentley, Wedgwood could easily have dissipated his talents, chasing each and every new idea with equal, uncritical enthusiasm. The enthusiasm is at once both understandable and attractive, but Wedgwood at least had the sense to see that he needed control. Yet when he accepted it, he managed to do even that with enthusiasm.

> Be it so, my dear friend, even so be it, let us begin, proceed, & finish our future schemes, our days & years, in the pursuit of *Fortune, Fame* & the *Public Good.* You will be my Mentor, my Guardian Angel to pluck me back from the confines of extravagance, either in Theory, or practice when you find me verging that way. I will answer to the friendly call; lend a willing ear to your instructions, & most gladly join you in the Paths you have chalk'd out for us. My talents, which your friendship is so apt on all occasions to magnify, are very confined; they lie chiefly in *the Potter*.[13]

There were, in any case, prospects opening up that were even more exciting than competition with English potters or even English metal workers.

> And do you really think that we may make a *complete conquest* of France? Conquer France in Burslem? – My blood moves quicker, I feel my strength increase for the contest. Assist me my friend & the victorie is our own. We will make them (now I must say *Potts*, & how vulgar it sounds) I won't though. I say we will fashion our Porcelain after their own hearts, & captivate them with the Elegance & simplicity of the Ancients. But do they love simplicity? Are you certain the French Nation will be pleased with simplicity in their Vessels? Either I have been greatly deceived, or a wonderfull reformation has taken place amongst them. *French & Frippery* have jingled together so long in my ideas, that I scarcely know how to separate them, & much of their work which I have seen *covered over with ornament*, had confirmed me in the opinion.[14]

It would be possible to fill a book on the subject of vases, so enthusiastic was Wedgwood, so busy the trade. It is a subject in which so many elements of the Wedgwood story come together, and two in particular are powerfully highlighted – the skill of the potter, the business acumen of his partner.

Before leaving the subject, here are two short quotations by way of illustration. Here, first, is the craftsman: "I have been turning two or three faithfull copys from Etruscan Vases & am quite surprised both at the beauty of their forms, & the difficulty of making them."[15] While here is Bentley turning such difficulties to advantage: "If any of your Friends wonder why you have not more & oftener, please to *give them to understand* that it is very difficult to make *fine & perfect* things of *any kind*. How often does our great Mistress Nature fail even in the first order of her Productions! The angelic Sex themselves are not all perfectly straight delicate & beautiful, no more than our Vases & you may contrive to edge in the *Natural Inference,* that *every good Thing deserves a good Price.*"[16]

As Etruscan vases prospered, so Etruria itself gradually neared completion. The planning of the new works was of crucial importance to Wedgwood. This was his opportunity to build to a new design, to regulate the works to fit a new method of production where process could follow process in logical sequence from the arrival of the raw materials to the despatch of the finished ware. The old system, which depended on the idea of a craftsman who could take himself and his skills to all parts of the business, was finally to give way to the new, where the specialist waited for the work to be passed to him. It was to be, in effect, a production line.

Etruria was not at first intended to take all the work: the "useful" ware was to continue to be made at the Bell Works. Etruria was for the Etruscans. It was here that Wedgwood and Bentley ornamental ware was to be produced. By November 1768 the works were covered over, and Wedgwood began to plan for the first workmen to move in to prepare saggars and start building the ovens. This was an area of activity where Wedgwood needed the advice of no man. He kept Bentley informed of each change, but he had no hesitation about what was needed, there was no deferment to other opinions. He considered every detail and made practical trials of his ideas.

I have altered my opinion about the turning room, & unless you think of any objection shall fix the Lathes in the lower corner room under that we before proposed. Here the lights are high enough & a ground floor is much better for Lathes than a

Chamber story, the latter are so apt to shake with the motion of
the Lathe, & as we shall want so very often to be steping into
the Lathe room, for there the *outline* is given, it will be more
convenient, especially for me, to have it without any steps to it.
I have thought of another alteration for the Lathes too. ...
The alteration I propose, is to set the Lathe so that the turner
shall have an *end light* instead of a *front* one, which they now have.
... I have tryed the experiment upon Abrams Lathe & it
answered to my wishes.[17]

By the new year most of the main features, workshops and ovens
were complete, but Wedgwood still had a few changes to make.
He devised a system whereby the different workshops would be
physically separated – first floor rooms having their own external
staircases for access. This was less convenient than an internal
stairway, but it kept the workers apart and so helped to guard the
secrets of production. So, gradually, the form and style of the works
was established. The main range of buildings faced the canal with a
single, wide entrance that gave access to a courtyard beyond. Round
this were ranged, in strict order, the different workshops and ovens,
forming a closed world, within which all the different industrial
processes could follow one another in strict sequence. Raw materials
were brought in, and left to weather. Flints were taken to the newly
installed grinding mill, and when all was ready the ingredients were
mixed in carefully measured proportions. The highly skilled
throwers and modellers had their own separate buildings where they
took the raw clay and formed it between their hands into urn or
teacup, portrait or statuette. From there the process moved on to
the workshops, where mould makers prepared to turn these works
of the individual artists and craftsmen into products for a mass
market. So through the various stages: plate makers pressed out their
plates, "stowkers" spent their days in making handles and spouts,
saggar makers prepared the fireproof containers in which the
unbaked ware was packed for firing. The oven-men plied their
mysterious craft – and it was a mystery, for none but the
experienced eye could gauge just when the great furnaces had
reached the right temperature. Glazers mixed their glazes, enamellers
applied the delicate gilt, and so it went through process after process

until the ware was finished, ready to be packed up for its long journey to the dining tables or mantel-shelves of the customers.

The façade presented to the outside world was interesting, being very similar in many respects to the façade of Boulton's Soho Works. Above the entrance was a Venetian window and a pediment, the whole being topped by a cupola. The influence of Wedgwood on the Potteries became so strong that the style and layout of the buildings was everywhere copied and became the standard for the next hundred years.

On 13 June 1769 Etruria was officially opened in a most fitting ceremony, not without its symbolic significance. Thomas Bentley took over the task of turning the potters' wheel, while Josiah Wedgwood threw six copies of an Etruscan vase. The vases were later painted with three classical figures and inscribed with the date and the simple legends, "One of the first Day's Productions at Etruria in Staffordshire by Wedgwood and Bentley" and "Artes Etruriae Renascunter." The Etruscan arts were reborn.

By November the move to Etruria was completed, very much to Wedgwood's surprise. Business had kept him in London, and he got home after a tedious and thoroughly miserable journey.

> We met with several accidents on the road, such as springs snapping, shafts breaking, &c, which delayed us something in our journeying, but we had no bodily hurt, & the greatest evils we met with were small chaises.
>
> We were three days upon the road though we lost no time & travelled a little by moonlight each evening – but at the last stage – Etruria – I was rewarded for all the risques & pains I had undergone in a tedious long & dirty journey.
>
> I found my Sally & family at Etruria! just come there to take possession of the Etruscan plains, & sleep upon them for the first night – Was not all this very clever now of my own dear Girls contriving. She expected her Joss on the very evening he arrived had got the disagreeable business of removing all over, & I would not have been another night from home for the Indies.[18]

So, there he was at the end of the year, happily set down opposite his new works, with Bentley as next-door neighbour – even if, in general, an absent neighbour. There seemed no end to the expansion of trade. The London showrooms were an outstanding success as the aristocratic patrons packed in like a modern crowd during the sales. Wedgwood had the physical factors of production well under control. But he found the human factors, as always, less tractable.

[8]

Our Humble Friends

THE growth of trade and increasing specialization brought an increase in problems among the work force. Wedgwood was counted a good employer by the standards of his time, but the standards of the eighteenth century were hardly the standards of today. It was not simply a matter of long hours, hard work and poor pay – though in all conscience such matters were serious enough – it was also a matter of attitudes. To understand the relationship between Wedgwood and his employees, one must see it in the context of the times.

To the great majority of thinking men, and to most employers (not necessarily synonymous), the relationship between employer and employee depended on an established order of society. It was the employer's right to give orders, the employee's duty to obey. Right was exclusive to the one side of the equation: it was the employer's right to determine what hours should be worked, what pay should be given. It was a situation where the unscrupulous could play the merciless tyrant. The phrase might sound melodramatic, but such men did exist, though it must be said straight away that Josiah Wedgwood was not one of them. He was not unscrupulous, but he did play the tyrant, albeit the benevolent one. It all centred on this question of attitude.

Wedgwood believed an employer to be inherently superior to the workers beneath him. That was part of the natural order of things. If sometimes he appeared sycophantic in his dealings with aristocracy, he was acknowledging the same order that placed them in a higher rank than himself. If he appeared autocratic to his workers, he was merely being consistent, acting on the same belief in a society of established ranks. So, while he could and did look with a benevolent eye on the men and women who worked for him, he did so from a position of conscious superiority. The attitude is seen crystallized in the few phrases in which he complained about the treatment handed out by the architect–builder Pickford to his workmen. He "does not seem to consider their having any feelings at all. I have seen a great many instances of it, & may perhaps sometime or other find out a mode of conveying a lecture to him upon a proper treatment of our inferiors, & to prove that, *our humble friends* as somebody beautifully calls them, have like passions with ourselves, & are capable of feeling pain or pleasure, nearly in the same manner as their Masters."[1] It is in that "nearly" that the gulf is fixed. Yet such sentiments were almost revolutionary, branding Wedgwood as a radical among his contemporaries. So we find a man, humane and liberal in his outlook in many ways, but conditioned by a climate of thought that attached labels of "superior" and "inferior". He was a "good" employer in the sense that a "good" modern employer in South Africa might look after "his boys".

The attitude led to many problems. New methods had to be imposed on the work force. The methods of generations had to be changed by dictum. There was resentment against this rush of change on the part of the workmen, which was matched by a resentment on Wedgwood's part at their slowness in acquiring the new skills. It was no doubt a great aggravation to him; "Thirty hands employed in making vases, things of which they have no idea when they are doing right, or when they are doing wrong, is alone sufficient employment for three of the best heads in the Kingdom."[2] When things at last came right, when he could see the improvements that he had planned turned into actuality, then he took a major share of the credit. He explained the process while trying to persuade Bentley of the undesirability of going back to make older models.

> In my first essays upon Vases I had many things to learn myself & everything to teach the workmen, who had not the least idea of beauty or proportion in what they did, few, or none of our productions were what we should now deem tolerable, & the

prices were fixed accordingly; but after so long practice from the best models, & drawings, such a long series of instruction as our workmen have gone through, & so very expensive an apparatus, or rather collection of apparatus's as we are now masters of, & all to enable us to get up *good things*, I think we ought not, & I am sure we cannot without great loss return back again to make such things as we first started with.[3]

There was much justice to this claim, for he did indeed lead by example, yet there is also a lack of generosity towards the workmen. The autocracy of his rule is seen at its strongest when one finds the occasional argument over wages. In April 1770, one of the workers employed in London as an enameller had the temerity to ask for higher pay. Wedgwood was angry, but blamed himself for being so foolish as to talk in the men's presence of the great demand for enamelled ware, and the high prices that could be obtained. In other words, the basic mistake was to let the man know the value of the work he was doing. Wedgwood's reaction was not just to threaten the individual with the sack, but to include all the other enamellers in the same threat. As he explained: "It is very probably a settled plan that this man – this *best hand* – shall make the first onset upon his new Masters; if he succeeds, the rest, both those we have at present & shall ingage afterwards are sure to follow the example, & there is no knowing where it will end."

The expansion of Wedgwood's trade brought a more general increase in prosperity to the Staffordshire potters in its wake. That, in turn, meant a general shortage of skilled workers. "What shall I do in this dilemma? not a hand loose in the Country to be hired, this said Creamcolour has made the Trade in general so brisk."[4] One solution to this recurring problem was to take on more apprentices. There was a double advantage – they provided cheap labour, and they could be trained up in the new methods more easily than the older workers who were set in their ways and were such a plague to Wedgwood. "Some will not work in Black. Others say they will never learn this new business, & want to be released to make Terrines & sauce boats again. I do not know what I shall do with them, we have too many *fresh* hands to take in at once, though we have business enough for them, if they knew how, or would have patience to learn to do it, but they do not seem to relish the thought of a second apprenticeship."[5] Or, as he put it later, "I am every day more fully convinced of the justice of our friend Brindley's maxim that where application is expected – 'Half bred things are the best'."[6]

The problem of getting the right kind of workmen became even more acute when it came to the very specialized and highly skilled. Some, such as the modellers and painters, were artists in their own right. They were, perhaps, less inclined to worry about trying something new, but they had other faults which counteracted that particular virtue. Wedgwood thought of employing a painter Willcox and his wife. They had lately been made redundant with a whole group of painters at Worcester, and Wedgwood took them on at a joint wage of £1 5s 0d a week. "I like his appearance much, he seems a sober solid man, & has nothing flighty or Coxcomical in his dress, or behaviour of which most of his Class are apt to contract a small tincture."[7]

Others proved distinctly coxcomical in their behaviour, and none was worse in Wedgwood's eyes than the talented but idiosyncratic and ultimately dishonest modeller, John Voyez. The relationship got off to a bad start when Voyez did not put in an appearance to start work at the time he was expected in June 1768, and it was July before he went on the payroll. He was a good modeller – indeed, at his best he could be a brilliant one – but he was a man who wanted to go his own way and that did not fit into the Wedgwood pattern. On top of that, he was decidedly wayward in his private life. By January 1769 he was out of the works and by April into jail. Wedgwood was faced with a dilemma. Voyez was "vicious", "fickle" and "lazy" but, "to live in this world, as matters, & things are constituted, it is sometimes necessary to make a truce with these sensations, whilst we manage a Rascal, our evil stars have thrown in our way, to prevent repeated injuries which he might otherwise do us".[8] What worried Wedgwood about Voyez was the very quality that had led him to employ the man in the first place, his undoubted skill as a modeller, which was reflected in the unusually high wages he paid him of 6s a day. Wedgwood, in one of his fits of worrying about competition, had argued that the only thing that kept others from copying his successful vases was the want of a good modeller. Once Voyez was free, he could teach others. So, Wedgwood proposed a novel solution – to pay Voyez his full salary, on the condition that he simply did nothing at all. Whether Wedgwood was talked out of this weird scheme or Voyez refused the offer is not known, but in any case, Voyez set up on his own and became one of Wedgwood's special bogey men. In a letter of September 1769, full of plans to "baulk the spies for some time at least who are daily haunting the rooms", he added the heavily emphasized injunction, *"remember Voyez is in town"*. He was to continue to be an irritant for many years, and a dishonest irritant at that.

The modellers worked in Staffordshire, but in September 1769 Bentley established the enamelling works at Chelsea where painters were employed. The painting was under the supervision of Crofts and David Rhodes, and Wedgwood was more than happy to pass over responsibility for one troublesome set of workers. "I wrote to you concerning Warburton a Painter, but have since learnt that he will do us no good he is so poor a hand even at common India patterns. All these matters, I leave to yours & Mr. Crofts better management. I have enough to do to make the Potts, & manage the Pott makers though I would rather, man for man, have to do with a shop of Potters than Painters."[9] Not that, even then, he was entirely free of dealing with painters. They appeared at Etruria, and were then sent on to Chelsea – by foot. He also found the problems from Chelsea returned to him for arbitration. In May 1770 he agreed that the painters should go on piece work, but he showed no greater trust of the artists than he had before: "It will require a good deal of knowledge & attention in fixing the price or the hands will all be ruined, by getting *too much* in a *little time*."[10] And there were frequent problems over individuals. A workman who did not fit could simply be fired, but artists were less easily replaced.

Crofts proved intractable and was soon gone, at which point he began complaining about the treatment he had received, thus confirming all Wedgwood's prejudices concerning the unreliability, greed and egocentricity of painters. "Why if he had been a Nabob himself we could not have behaved with more respect and caution towards him", Wedgwood exclaimed in injured innocence.[11] Not that life was always much simpler with the modellers. Ralph Boot,

An enamelled plaque showing Etruria Hall, the new Wedgwood home, with the Trent and Mersey Canal in the foreground; a splendid example of the delights Bentley claimed for having "a lawn terminated by water".

Etruria, where the Etruscan arts were to be reborn.

Designs for the great dinner service ordered
by Catherine the Great of Russia. The
actual pieces used in the service can be
identified by the frog motif.

Jasper is the ware
most commonly
associated with
Wedgwood. Here
jasper cameos have
been set into cut
steel by Matthew
Boulton for use as
jewellery.

A fine example of the modeller's art: a black
basalt figure of Voltaire, *c.* 1775.

a first class craftsman, showed alarming signs of turning into another Voyez. "I have been obliged to threaten to discharge him for being loose & wild, but he promises to be very good, & will bring up hands to figure making or do anything that we please to our advantage."[12]

This "bringing up of hands" was Wedgwood's favourite remedy for the problems involved in hiring artists as full-time workers. He liked to get them young to raise and tutor them in his own methods and techniques. In a letter of September 1769, after giving a satisfactory report of the erratic Boot's progress, he remarked that he had taken on an "ingenious boy as a modeller, a boy self taught, with no previous experience, but one who did things amazingly!" Wedgwood hired him for five years and looked to him to become, in time, a valuable asset to the business. He was not to be disappointed. The boy was William Hackwood, the greatest success of the training system, who was to rise to become chief modeller.

The same policy of training up skilled workers was applied to the painters at Chelsea – with Wedgwood providing the enthusiasm to rally his more cautious partner. Bentley had been trying, with little success, to find girls who could paint vases in the style he wanted. If they were not there, then to Wedgwood there was only one solution:

> We must make them. There is no other way. We have stepped forward beyond the other Manufactures & we must be content to train up hands to suit our purposes. Where amongst our Potters could I get a complete Vase maker? Nay I could not get a hand through the whole Pottery to make a Table plate without training them up for that purpose, & you must be content to train up such Painters as offer to you & not turn them adrift because they cannot immediately form their hands to our new stile, which if we consider what they have been doing all this while we ought not to expect from them.[13]

He developed the argument further a little later: "I would pick up some likely Boys of about 12 years old & take them apprentice 'till they are twenty or twenty one & set them to drawing .... when you wanted any hands we could draft them out of this school. "The Paintings upon these Vases from W & B school" – so it may be said a 1000 years hence."[14] It was, as Bentley also noted, all part of the process of steady improvement. "We are every day finding out some ingenious man, or curious piece of workmanship; all of which we endeavour to make subservient to the improvement of our taste, or the perfection of our manufacture."[15]

It is very easy, when looking at the great strides being made by Wedgwood and Bentley, to think only in terms of the high artistry of the ware, its immense popularity, the proud message that stood at the head of accounts – "Potter to Her Majesty". This was all very glamorous, and one tends to forget that back in Burslem the useful ware was still being made, under the control of Thomas Wedgwood, and formed the backbone of the whole business. But, as demands grew on both sides, it became increasingly difficult to meet each request. They quite simply did not have the capacity to meet all the demands of Cox and Bentley in London: "You both want Vases, – you want flowerpots, & you both want *Engin'd ware* of various kinds, & we have but two turners & an half for both our works, & for all these things which would employ six or eight."[16] It was very tempting to rob the useful works to pay the ornamental.

> We have got another Lathe up (the third) and I have committed a sad robbery upon my works at Burslem to furnish it. I have taken James Bourn to Etruria! The only tolerable turner of *Good Things* I had at Burslem, and he is far superior to Abram at Vases. I would not have parted with him from my works at Burslem for a good deal on any other account for we have not one Engine Turner left there now. Poor Burslem – Poor Creamcolour. They tell me I sacrifice all to *Etruria* and *Vases*.[17]

Yet this provided no real answer, only exchanging one problem for another, as Cox was soon informing Wedgwood: "I fear we shall lose the Season, the good people here begin to say you neglect the usefull parts of your manufacture for the sake of minding these money getting ornaments."[18] And still the orders came flooding in, and each post seemed to bring only slight variations on the basic message from Cox: "Greatly wanted to Warehouse to supply many Orders that have been long in hand".[19] Wedgwood, with 150 workers under his control, quite simply could not cope, and shuffling them between Burslem and Etruria was no real answer.

"The truth of the case is that all the hands at Etruria are wanted here, & all the hands here wanted at Etruria. Hire more you say. Aye but trade is as good with others as ourselves, allmost everybody wants hands. I have ingaged about half a score Journeymen & as many apprentices, & I think myself very lucky."[20]

There were orders from home and orders from abroad, and each new success also brought a new problem to pile on top of the old. It was splendid, for example, to receive an order from Lord Cathcart in St Petersburg – less splendid to be told, in February 1770, that the ship carrying the ware was stuck in ice in the harbour, inaccessible from the city, but very accessible to looters from across the bay. Transport overseas was always a difficulty: it seemed that if it was not stuck in the Russian ice, it was bogged down in long, overland mule trips in Spain. And then if the goods were lost, broken or stolen in transit, in came a demand for replacements to add to the pile of orders. Expanding trade, continued building at Etruria, work divided between Etruria, Burslem and Chelsea, the ever growing demands for more and more ware were all marks of success, but they were also an extra strain, extra work for Wedgwood himself. It is not surprising to find that at this time there was little opportunity for pleasure and relaxation.

Wedgwood's main pleasure, outside his work, remained the family, to which a young Josiah was added in 1769. At home he could rest, smoke his pipe and be at ease. Some variety was also provided by trips to London, where he could take a more active interest in the political life of the capital, attending debates and catching up on coffee-house chatter. He became fascinated by the campaign to obtain a pardon for Wilkes, who was leading an even more hectic life than Wedgwood, alternating between Parliament and expulsion and jail. He had incurred the wrath of the King and his ministers by his outspoken criticism in his journal *North Britain*, and this led directly to his arrest on a general warrant. The subsequent legal battles did much to improve the freedom of action for the Member of Parliament – and for those who elected him. Wedgwood was decidedly pro Wilkes, but his partisanship did not prevent him seeing the amusement in some of the incidents that can crop up in even the most serious and vigorous of campaigns. "But all are not Wilkes's friends, for a bold Champion the other night when the Populace was shouting around His Majesty's chair as was going to Covent Garden house, A pardon for Wilkes! – A pardon for Wilkes! put his face to the Glass of the Chair & cry'd out D–n Wilkes, & liberty too!"[21]

Politics was only one part of London life that Wedgwood enjoyed. The great attraction was to meet old friends, to talk on into the night about the issues of the day, of the world of arts and sciences or whatever else took their fancy. It was a part of life of which he was too often starved among the pot works of Staffordshire. The house built for Bentley beside Etruria Hall saw little of its owner. In London, he tried to make up the time. Conversation was such a lure that he could even neglect to write his letters home to Sally, so that Cox was left to take over the job for him. "I expected Mr. Wedgwood would have filled up this space but unfortunately for you he is sunk to the Bottom or Center of the earth with three other Deep philosophers and tho' they are helping him with all their powers I am afraid the last post bell will be here before their thorough emergation."[22]

Such times were rare, and savoured all the more for their rarity. As pressures built, circumstances combined at the end of 1769 to make the situation seem scarcely tolerable. For all the improvements that had been made, men were not machines and all Wedgwood's wishing would not make them free from error. It was human error that led to a crisis – and the effect was soon seen on Wedgwood's health. This time it was not his digestion that worried him, but his sight, and again it seems probable that the illness was as much psychosomatic as organic. The crisis concerned money. Collecting money was always difficult, especially for anyone who carried on an extensive trade with the aristocracy. This had never particularly worried Wedgwood, although cash shortages were serious on several occasions. Now he discovered, however, that the trusted Cox had allowed the bookkeeping to get into a thorough muddle. Bills were not being sent where money was owed and, which was much more serious in Wedgwood's eyes, they were being sent where accounts had already been settled. He wrote anxiously to Bentley, begging him to make the circumstances clear to their customers, even if it meant making Cox's mistakes public knowledge. "It is equitable and just, that he should rather lose his Character as a book-keeper which he has deserved to do, than that I should lose mine for honesty, which I have never forfeited." And on top of this, there was Bentley insisting on moving out to Chelsea just when Wedgwood desperately needed someone to overlook the affairs at Newport Street. The final blow came when his father-in-law, Richard Wedgwood, fell ill and Sally rushed away to tend to him.

Wedgwood was left quite alone with his various problems, and the condition of his eyes deteriorated badly. "I am very well in health," he wrote on 29 December 1769, "but cannot help thinking my eyes in a bad way," adding with a totally uncharacteristic lack of confidence, "I do not know what to determine about building any more." The complaint was diagnosed by his doctor as *Mice volanti* and soon the "experts" were called in. Doctor Elliott, "the most famous man in this branch of the healing Art of any man in England", the man who had cured the Duke of Bedford and the Duchess of Norfolk, came to prescribe treatment. On 1 January he received news of his father-in-law's improvement and this, with its promise of an early return by Sally, was enough to put him into a better state of mind, and he began to take a much livelier interest in the state of his eyes and the treatment. The condition fascinated him now, and he described it much as he would one of his own scientific experiments. "The Atoms which appear when I look at the sky, the line or lines which are pellucid, & the little clouds continue still before my eyes when I look at the sky, or any distant object, as usual, & *sometimes* upon the paper when I am reading or writeing, but not allways", and so on in great detail. Others also took an interest. Darwin passed on the unhelpful information that everyone had spots in front of their eyes, "but everybody *did not look at them*." Dr Elliot's remedy, if more tangible, was scarcely more practical: "He has ordered me a Collyrium consisting of Elderflower water, Spirit of Wine Champhorated – Sugar of Lead & something else which I have forgot & with this I am to wash my eyes three times a day, & use them favourably & see him again in March, but in the meantime I must let him know the effect of his prescription, I have made use of it a week & perceive no alteration."

Although the news of Richard Wedgwood continued good, other reports brought only fresh anxieties. "A report has been pretty

current that I was broke, & run away for no less a sum than Ten
Thousand Pounds! This report I believe has been rais'd by Voyez,
& I have sufficient ground for a prosecution, but I believe his in-
significance, & worthlessness will save him. He is not worth any
serious notice & yet I have half a mind to frighten the Rascal a little.
It would be charity to the Country to drive him out of it."[23] He
still found himself unable to concentrate on the building plans, and
he was reduced to ever more miserable forebodings about his
health. "These things altogether, with some other Anxiety I have
lately felt, have at times brought on a temporary suppression of
spirits which I am not accustomed to & which do not naturally
belong to my constitution." For the next few weeks his spirits
were lower than at almost any other time in his life – certainly far
worse than during the menacing time of the amputation. It was not
so much the illness itself, as his own unhappy reaction to it. New
doctors were called in and new and increasingly less likely remedies
applied: "a perpetual blister, or a caustick behind my neck he thinks
is *absolute necessary*." But he clearly had about as much faith in such
remedies as such remedies deserved, for he added gloomily, "I am
often practising to *see* with my *fingers*, & think I should make a
tolerable proficient in that science for one who begins his study so
late in life, but shall make a wretched walker in the dark with a
single leg."[24]

The one bright spot came when, on 22 January, he was able to
fetch Sally and the children home again. But he had been ordered to
rest, and he fretted incessantly about what was happening at the
works during his enforced absence.

> Your advice to make my business an amusement only is very
> good, and would suit me extremely well if I could but put it
> into practice, but 'tis very difficult to see things going wrong
> without feeling *uneasy sensations* & exerting the *necessary* force
> be it *more* or *less*, of the *head* or *hands* to set them right again.
> I do strive to make things pass on with me as easy as possible,
> & hope to be making some progress in that very usefull
> Philosophy, but to keep 150 hands of various professions, &
> more various depositions, in *tolerable* order is no easy task even
> when the mind is otherwise free & in full vigour.[25]

The old human problems still plagued him, and he was now near the nadir, believing that not only his sight, but his life was in danger. He pleaded with Bentley to come to Etruria "to give me an opportunity of communicating many things which I would not have to die with me".[26]

But the effective recipe for recovery had already been applied – not elderflower water and causticks, but the return of Sally and the sorting out of accounts. Bentley had no need to rush to Staffordshire; with the easing of the problems the danger to Wedgwood's eyesight diminished. He stopped his morbid imaginings of a one-legged man groping his way in the dark and quite simply got back to business. He was no nearer his dream of making "such machines of men as cannot err", and the fallibility of the human element in his plans had all but ruined his health. But with recovery, he was soon back in the search for greater efficiency.

[9]

Developing Themes

As Wedgwood recovered and normality returned to the business after the hectic days of the move to Etruria and the financial scandal, for which Cox accepted responsibility and was duly forgiven, there was time to take stock of the situation. Wedgwood set about defining the business arrangements with his two partners, Bentley and his cousin Thomas, and developing the themes already established: improving trade, improving selling techniques and establishing an efficient production system in the works. He was back in health, making his now familiar bustle in the world; and, just as importantly, he was back in good spirit. A sure sign of returning to normality came when he returned to yet another familiar theme, and began teasing Bentley about his relationships with the opposite sex.

> After thanking my Dear Friend for his last good letter with the drawings &c, & assuring him that a moment shall not be lost in executing the fair Ladys commands, in the most *pretty, odd, new, Quere, whimsical, Vase-like* manner possible, I cannot help telling him how much I admire his Gallantry – Ovid himself, after a visit to his most favourite Mistress, could not have infus'd more spirit & vivacity, into so plain a subject, as the ordering a few Potts, than my Good friend has done on the present occasion – The Lovely Countess can elevate him many degrees above the stupid, common, vulgar forms of business: quicken the circulation of his animal spirits & make his pen flow like a feather dipp'd in Oyl, or rather, like his own river Dove, after an April shower.

> After such delicious treats as these, what can we furnish you
> with in the Country that will not be insipid or disgusting.[1]

This proved a light-hearted moment before more serious matters
again dominated, for in August 1770 an argument blew up which
came near to causing a breach between Wedgwood and Bentley.
It began when Bentley proposed that they should start to make
useful ware at Etruria. But Thomas Wedgwood had a share in the
useful works, and although his part of the business was less spectacular
than the ornamental, he had spent much time "upon China bodys
for tea pots in brown, black, grey &c, &c" and would have been
most unwilling to pass the business across to Etruria. When
Wedgwood pointed this out, Bentley reacted by quibbling over the
definition of "useful", arguing that vases had their uses and asking,
rather sarcastically, if a ewer based on a drawing in a book of
antiquities was now to be classified as useful. The tone of the letter
hurt Wedgwood deeply. He was happy enough to discuss the
arrangements and definitions, but was much dismayed at being
treated as a business partner first and a friend second. In a long reply,
written on 3 September, he carefully and patiently put forward
suggestions for resolving the difficulties, but could not disguise the
disappointment and the pain.

> With respect to the difference between the *Useful ware* and
> *Ornaments* I do not find any inclination in my self to be over nice
> in drawing the line. You know I never had any idea that
> Ornamental ware should not be of "some use". You knew this
> from all that we have done hitherto, from the many conversa-
> tions we have had upon the subject, and from the list we wrote
> in your commonplace book of the uses to which ornamental
> vases might be put: I could have wished therefore that you had
> not repeated this idea so often, and asked me if my Partnership
> with T:W would exclude us making Stellas Ewers. Tell me,
> my dear friend, did you ask me this question for information,
> or were you really as angry with me as the question accompanied
> with any other idea would seem to import. I hope you were not,
> for I should be very unhappy to think you would be angry with me
> lightly, or that I had given you any just occasion for the warmth
> some parts of your letter *seem* to express; I say *seem* for I hope I

am mistaken and shall rest in that hope 'till I have the pleasure
of hearing from you again. But as this question has put me upon
thinking a little more upon the subject, and the situation I am,
or may be, in betwixt two Partnerships, it may not be amiss to
enter a little deeper into it, and attempt something like a line in
Theorie, though I hope we shall none of us be too rigid in our
adherence to it in *practice*.

   He then went on to reject the suggestion that "fineness, or richness,
or price, or colour, or enameling, or bronzeing, or gilding can be a
criterion", arguing, very sensibly, that such rules would simply
prevent Thomas trying anything new at Burslem, lest, if it were
successful, it would then be whisked away to Etruria. He then
proceeded to offer his own, simple definition that useful ware
consisted of "such vessels as are made use of at meals". He added to
that that there were other obviously utilitarian objects about which
there could be no argument, objects which today we tend to forget
were once a staple of the Wedgwood works – wash basins, chamber
pots and the like. The letter ends with a direct, personal plea that
might be construed as emotional blackmail, were it not for the
transparent honesty and conviction of the writer. The plea begins
with a note that indicates just how deeply the controversy had
affected Wedgwood, bringing him back to something like the
pessimism of the early part of the year.

   I may not continue long in business, and my life itself is a very
   precarious one, and whom have I then to leave my business to
   capable of conducting it in the manner you know I should wish
   to have it continued but you two; let us therefore, my friend
   and Brother, live and act like Brothers, and friends indeed, and
   not suffer any small matters to put our peace and harmony in
   jeapordie. All I mean by the above distinctions, is, to chalk out
   a path that I may walk in securely, by defineing the limits of
   two interests at present seperate, and of which my situation
   renders me the connecting link, without giving offence to
   either; for if my friend on one side should tell me, in any way,
   that I am too partial to my Burslem works, and my Relation &
   Partner on the other hand be discontent and think I lean too
   much to the ornamental works, and am throwing every

advantageous article into that scale, Think, my friend, you who can feel for me the situation I must be in. Do you think I could bear it. No, and I am sure you would not wish me to lead a miserable life, continually jarring with those I wish most to be at peace with. Next to my *Wife and Family*, my *Partners* are those with whom I must be at peace.

You have for some time past, or at least it has seemed so to me, from very many passages in your letters, been doubtfull of our undertaking being worth the time and attention you have bestowed upon it; and in your last you intimate its certainly coming to nothing upon the present plan. I should be sorry to think so too, but own I have no apprehensions of that sort. – Ornament is a field which, notwithstanding, you have bestowed one years close attention upon it, and I many, yet it appears to me that we are but just stepped or stepping into it, and I am fully perswaded that the farther we proceed in it the richer crop we shall reap, both of *Fame* and *Proffit*. But how, or in what respect, does this first years essay give either you or me any ground for repineing or such gloomy forebodeing? If the first year of a business pays all expences, and furnishes any proffit at all, I should not call it a bad one, but if beyond this it likewise gives a proffit of £500, or £1000 in Cash for goods *really sold*, and an increase in stock in manufactured goods *ready for sale* of one or two thousand pounds more, surely we ought to be more than barely content. I think we have reason to rejoice, and are robbing ourselves of what is more value than money if we do not take satisfaction of a prosperous, and very promising business along with us, as a cordial to support us in every hour of toil and fatigue which our avocations necessarily require at our hands.

At the end of all, the problem was easily solved, and the division established much as Wedgwood had suggested. But for all Wedgwood's confidence, the trade that had been so furious was showing signs of slackening. This was mainly Bentley's concern, but Wedgwood was not slow in bringing forward his own suggestions. There was the familiar refrain of seeking suitable patronage. He proposed that Bentley should call on Lord Mansfield with some examples of Etruscan vases. "He could not be displeas'd with the compliment, you know we were allways received very politely upon the same occasion by other Nobelmen & had their thanks for our trouble, why therefore should we omit doing this where it seems the most necessary."[2] The necessity came from Lord Mansfield's reputation as one of the leading experts on antiquities, a man whose recommendations would make valuable advertisements. Patronage was still seen as the key to success, and the method of collecting dukes and earls is spelled out in this letter in which Wedgwood planned the expansion of Irish business by providing ware to carefully selected shops in Dublin:

> They told me the Duke of Richmond had made a present of a pair of Vases to the Duke of Leinster who is in Raptures with them, & that the Duke is a Gentleman of the first Virtu in Ireland. – That some others had seen our Vases & there seemed to be a violent *Vase madness* breaking out amongst them. . . . We are looking over the English Peerage to find out *lines channels & connections* – will you look over the Irish Peerage with the same view – I need not tell you how much will depend upon a *proper* & *noble* introduction. This, with a fine assortment of Vases & a Trusty & *adequate* Agent will insure us success in the Conquest of our sister Kingdom.[3]

As far as the home market was concerned, the greatest emphasis was still placed on royal patronage and, as is clear from this description by Bentley, both the King and the Queen took a lively and informed interest in their business:

> Last Monday Mr. Wedgwood and I had the honour of a long audience of their majesties at the Queen's palace, to present some *bas reliefs* her majesty had ordered; and to show some new improvements, with which they were well pleased. They expressed, in the most obliging and condescending manner their attention to our manufacture; and entered very freely into conversation on the further improvement of it, and on many other subjects. The King is well acquainted with the business, and with the characters of the principal manufacturers, merchants, and artists; and seems to have the success of all our

manufactures much at heart, and to understand the importance of them. The Queen has more sensibility, true politeness, engaging affability, and sweetness of temper, than any great lady I ever had the honour of speaking to."[4]

A somewhat more generous view of the couple than many commentators took.

Patronage alone was not enough, and Wedgwood was very concerned with the question of middle-class taste. He discussed the matter with Boulton at Birmingham in December 1770. Boulton had begun turning vases in metal which, they agreed, would appeal to "those customers who were fond of show & glitter". There was no element of competition here, since the discerning, they were also agreed, would buy Wedgwood instead. Presumably Boulton did not make his views known to his own customers! But where else could they look for sales? "A third class were therefore called to our aid, composed of such as would of *themselves* choose shewy, rich & gaudy things, but who would be *overruled by their betters* in the choice of their ornaments as well as other matters; who would do as their *Architects*, or whoever they depended on in matters of taste directed them; & with this reinforcement we thought Etruria stood a pretty good chance with any competitor."[5]

Boulton, however, at that time, had more important matters on his mind than gaudy vases. He was busy with arrangements for taking a young Scots engineer, James Watt, into partnership, with the aim of beginning the manufacture of a new design of steam engine. "My idea was to settle a manufactory near to my own by the side of our Canal, where I would erect all the conveniences necessary for the completion of Engines and from which Manufactory We would serve all the World."[6] Serve the world they did, and the partnership of Boulton and Watt was to prove if anything more famous and more important in its long-term effects than that of Wedgwood and Bentley.

There was still a third area for Wedgwood to explore – the overseas trade. The Russian trade, for example, greatly helped by the advocacy of Lord Cathcart, was flourishing, and in 1770 Wedgwood worked on a small service for the Empress Catherine II. It was first taken along to be shown to George III and Queen

Charlotte, who expressed themselves well pleased with it. This was soon followed by more Russian orders, and very welcome they were too, for trade was in a low state in the Potteries. Many potters were either considering or actually cutting their prices, faced, as was Wedgwood, with mounting stocks of unsold ware. In April 1771 the various potters met at Newcastle-under-Lyme to discuss their common problems, as a result of which they formed an association for which Wedgwood was asked to draw up the rules. It provided a forum for the discussion of trade, and saved them from slipping into an uncontrolled price-cutting war.

Wedgwood was, in any case, not intending to cut prices. He was convinced that his ware was of such higher quality that he could both keep prices up and hold sales steady. Here the overseas trade was a great help, and it is interesting to see how far he spread his ware by this date, not just in Russia but throughout Europe. Rummaging through the Wedgwood papers, one is continuously turning up accounts with continental royalty and letters of appreciation together with the all-important promises of recommendation: "Je trouve votre invention fort jolie et je ne manquerai pas de la racommander à toute occasion."[7] It clearly became such a commonplace that such grand gentlemen as the King of Prussia, the Prince of Saxe Coburg, the Prince of Bavaria and numerous others were all lumped together in the ledgers under the unceremonious title "Sundry German Princes". Like Boulton, Wedgwood no doubt kept such undignified cataloguing from the eyes of his customers.

Wedgwood was not prepared just to rest on a growing export trade and leave the rest to aristocratic recommendation, however. He was always on the hunt for "new means of exciting attention to our Vases". He wanted to print cards that could be sent to the houses of "Nobility and Gentry", and he wanted to see advertisements and "puffs" written by friends in the press – he was quite annoyed to find a piece praising Boulton's vases and wanted Bentley to write a similar piece of anonymous self-congratulation. He suggested, and succeeded in organizing, an exhibition of ware made for the King. He also proposed that they should start to sell ware in the increasingly fashionable spa of Bath – an idea Bentley followed up: in April 1772 a shop was opened in the town.

However important sales might be, Wedgwood's preoccupation

with experiments, improvements and innovations never lessened. His last major series of experiments had been on the encaustic painting process, and it is worth mentioning the sheer volume of experiments carried out by Wedgwood; for that set carried the total recorded in the experiment books past the thousand mark. As always, his experiments were secret, and he now had some justification for his obsession with spies and copyists. In spite of the patent, the encaustic process had been introduced by another Staffordshire potter, Palmer of Hanley, and sold by Neale's of London. This particular wrangle dragged on for months, Palmer claiming that he was not copying Wedgwood, but was producing his own pots based on antique designs and a recipe given in a book published abroad. Given Wedgwood's views of such matters, one might have expected an acrimonious and bitter quarrel. What we find is surprisingly quite different. The two men necessarily met quite frequently at Potters' Association meetings, and Wedgwood described such an encounter.

> I meet Mr. Palmer at our Society and other places frequently and we are, or seem to be, very sociable and friendly, nobody would imagine we were over head and ears in Law together, and the People stared abundantly at our walking and talking together so cordially yesterday at the opening of a Bowling Green – a Neighbour joined us and said what a pity it was that two such Men (I am only repeating another's words remember) should be at varience and throw our money away amongst people who did not know anything of the cause they were to decide, and that nobody could do it so well as our selves if we could find in our hearts to talk to one another upon the subject. We looked at each other, I believe, very foolishly for some time, and I was obliged to break silence at last by declareing that our suit at Law had not made any breach in my friendship for Mr. Palmer, and he declared to the same purpose with respect to me.[8]

Eventually it was agreed that Palmer should share in the patent after making a suitable payment, and both sides were saved from the expensive arguments of lawyers.

The new experiments were less dramatic than those for encaustic painting, but no less important in helping the movement towards a steady improvement in the ware. He had long had the idea that many of the problems involved in getting a good, consistent colour in the body started with the introduction of impurities into the flint by the action of the grindstones. As the result of a good deal of patient and careful work, finished in April 1772, Wedgwood proved that this was indeed the case and that, if the old granite stones were replaced by Derbyshire cherts, the problem disappeared. He also found, from the experiments, that the best flints came from chalk pits near Gravesend. All unspectacular, but important, work. A potentially very spectacular line was begun at the same time with experiments on porcelain, but this soon petered out.

Less mundane matters were stirring among other activities. In one single letter of September 1771, a whole string of names and projects is reeled off, each one of which was to lead to an important future development. It begins with a familiar royal refrain.

> Their Majestys are very good indeed! I hope we shall not lose their favour, and may promise ourselves the greatest advantage from such Royal Patronage, and the very peculiar attention they are pleased to bestow upon our productions. It was a good hint you gave them respecting their Portraits. I hope it will work, and have its proper effect, and am fully perswaded a good deal may be done in that way with many of their Majestys subjects, but we should if possible do in this as we have done in other things – begin at the *Head* first, and then proceed to the inferior members. Though we have made some sort of beginning in that way here, for Hackwood has been three times at Crew, by Mrs. Crews particular desire, to model the head of her son and heir. I told her he was quite a novice in Portrait modeling, but she would have him try his hand and I could not refuse her. What he will make of it I do not know. I mentioned bracelets, rings and seals to her with which she seemed much delighted, and to these I think we may add Gemms to be set in snuffbox tops, such as the Cupid and Psyche, &c. or a favourite head, and I finished some of these ready for the oven yesterday – For snuffboxes and Bracelets I mean.

We have company at the works allmost every day. On

Wednesday we had Sir George Strickland and his Lady (a Mr. Freeman of Schute Lodge in Wilts) and her two Brothers. Mr. Freeman has traveled and is a man of Taste, as you will be convinced when I tell you *that he admires our works exceedingly* but says as our materials are so fine, and we execute so well, we should, to be complete, spare no expence in having the finest things abroad modeled for us, and mentioned a Man at Rome who, for a small commission, would get them done for us. He is a great admirer of young Flaxman and has advised his Father to send him to Rome, which he has promised to do. Mr. Freeman says he knows young Flaxman is a Coxcomb, but does not think him a bit the worse for it, or the less likely to be a great Artist. . . .

Yesterday a Mr. Gifford (of Chillington Hall) and his Lady called here and took a thorough view of the works, and expressed great pleasure in what they saw. Mr. Gifford is a Gentleman of a very large fortune and lives near Wolverhampton. He told me he was going to build and should be a good customer for Bass reliefs, both as furniture and to set in stucco. He said a great deal in praise of Mr Adams [Robert Adam] as a Man of Genius and invention, and an excellent Architect, and Mr Freeman assured me that he knew Mr Adam's kept modelers at Rome employed in copying Bass reliefs and other things for them, and he thought a connection with them would be of great use to us.[9]

Here they all are: Hackwood at the beginning of his highly successful career as a portraitist, Flaxman who was to do some of his finest work for Wedgwood, Robert Adam who was to collaborate with Wedgwood to produce the coolly classical interiors so closely associated with their two names, and a new idea for jewellery that was to be developed to splendid effect later. It is really quite astonishing to find so many important themes all leaping into prominence at precisely the same time – more astonishing to us perhaps as we can see the significance of what was, to Wedgwood, just another letter keeping his partner up to date with the latest news. Astonishing, then – but not accidental. Hackwood was available to try portraiture because Wedgwood had taken him and trained him;

the rest came into the Wedgwood orbit because Wedgwood was the most successful potter of his day, with a reputation measured as readily by artistic as commercial standards. "Success breeds success" is a cliché because it has so often proved true as to be worth repeating. It was certainly true of Wedgwood.

Many of the ideas in this letter came out of work already done. The name "Adam" might be new to the correspondence, but the idea of using ceramics in interior design was not. "I am informed," wrote a Lancashire customer in 1771, "that you have invented some composition to resemble Marble for the Tablets Freizes and Corners of Chimneypieces."[10] Some of the ideas probably came through friends – the idea of making jewellery must have been suggested by the association with Matthew Boulton.

Others who appeared in the Wedgwood circle did not always grace it with quite the same distinction. Wedgwood had for some time been using the method of transfer printing devised by Sadler of Liverpool to decorate his ware, though he often complained about the artistic standards of the engravers. In 1771 a new engraver, P. P. Burdett, appeared with a new method. Wedgwood now began to dream of new designs, though one might not always regret his failure to see them realized. "All Country Gentlemen are sportsmen: there is scarcely anything gives them so much pleasure to look upon as Dead Game, a good representation of it is the next thing you know." Burdett's engravings were of very good quality and his artistic standards were high, but there were difficulties in adapting them for use on pottery. Wedgwood found himself tangled up with yet another of those troublesome artists, and it took a long time, much bickering and a deal of acrimony before the two sides disengaged and went their separate ways.

Other changes were more fundamental, for Wedgwood was going through a process of rethinking the very basis of his production methods for ornamental ware. It all came back to the problem of declining trade. At first, when the demand for vases was apparently insatiable, it had seemed sensible to keep up a stream of new designs. Each new type was greeted with enthusiasm, and there seemed no reason why the process should not go on for ever. But this, alas, was not quite the case. Even the wealthiest aristocrat with the stateliest of stately homes places some limit on the numbers of vases and urns he wants to keep around the place. Wedgwood and Bentley were steadily approaching the limit. What was the answer? The overseas market had been tapped by repeating the British operation of establishing a beginning with the aristocracy. But, as all business theories insist, a successful export trade must have foundations in a solid home market, and for Wedgwood the foundation was eroding. The answer was to extend the base, to sell to a wider public. Wedgwood now needed to begin selling to his "third class", the wide middle stratum of society just beneath the gentry.

Now this, however, was where the difficulty appeared. The production methods that suited the old trade were inappropriate for the new. What was needed was a smaller range of ware, produced in greater quantity. Instead of skilled turners producing individual pots, semi-skilled workers could produce large numbers by using casts from moulds. As the overall running costs of the works were the same for either method, the unit cost of the individual pot would thus be reduced. Wedgwood may never have heard the name, but he had just discovered the advantages of mass production. He explained his thinking to Bentley.

> I have had several serious *Talks* with our Men at the Ornamental works lately about the price of our workmanship, and the necessity of lowering it, especially in Flowerpots, Bowpots and Teapots . . . I have promised them they shall make dozens and groces. . . . In consequence of these reasonings and regulations, Robert pays his Boys who wait upon him, which is lowering the price of throwing more than a third. The Turning of flower-pots is lowered full as much, and as I have now got a book for my own use and speculation, with the prices of workmanship of every article, I shall proceed in the same way where I think there is room for it, and the infallible consequence is *lowering the price of workmanship* will be a *proportional increase of quantity* got up; and if you turn to the Columns of calculation and see how large a share *Modeling and Moulds* and the three next columns bear in the expence of Manufacturing our goods, and consider that these expences move on like clockwork, and are much the same whether the quantity of goods made be large or small, you

will see the vast consequence in most manufactures of *making the greatest quantity possible in a given time.* Rent goes on whether we do much or little in the time. Wages to the Boys and Odd Men, Warehouse Men and Book-keeper, who are a kind of Satelites to the Makers (Throwers, Turners &c), is nearly the same whether we make 20 doz of Vases or 10 doz per week, and will therefore be a double expence upon the latter number....

We have now upwards of 100 Good forms of Vases, for all of which we have the moulds, handles, and ornaments, and we could make them almost as currently as usefull ware, and at one half the expence we have hitherto done, provided I durst set the Men to make from about 6 to 12 doz of a sort;. . . .

The Great People have had these Vases in their Palaces long enough for them to be seen and admired by the *Middling Class* of People, which Class we know are vastly, I had almost said, infinitely superior, in number to the Great, and though a *great price* was, I believe, at first necessary to make the Vases esteemed *Ornament* for *Palaces,* that reason no longer exists. Their character is established, and the middling People would probably buy quantitys of them at a reduced price. . . .[11]

The arguments are sound enough, but one notices that none of this increased productivity is to benefit the producers – quite the contrary, in fact, since Wedgwood made it quite clear that he would be reducing piece work rates to ensure that men would produce more simply to keep up to their former income. The common argument among manufacturers of the day was simplicity itself – keep costs as low as possible. That included the rule – keep wages as low as possible. The justification for this was seldom spelled out, since it was axiomatic that it was an employer's prerogative to set wages at any level he saw fit, though any attempt to raise wages might be condemned by other manufacturers as attempted employee-poaching. But when justification was given it went something like this: it is the wisdom of the employer that increases the business, and it is the capital of the employer that makes the increase possible, therefore it is to the employer that any rewards should go. In this case, however, it is ironical to note that the suggestion that constant change was too expensive came, in the first instance, from the men themselves. They must have regretted their suggestion when they saw rates start to fall. The point cannot be stressed too strongly that Wedgwood was, by the standards of the time, a good employer: it was simply that, by those same standards, there was no thought that the ordinary workman should participate to any great extent in the growing prosperity of a concern.

The men did not share Wedgwood's philosophy, but their attempts to combine at the useful works were soon scotched by their employer, astonished by their demands for "most exorbitant" rates. The way in which the matter was handled was not untypical.

> The ring leader, who was to try the experiment with us yesterday, after several consultations amongst themselves, insisted on having *his own price* or *his discharge*. I had before argued the matter cooly with him, and told him we would pay him 4/6, his demand was 6/-, and set another person to make the articles, and if we ever gave more than 4/6 we would pay him the 18*d* or in proportion as we gave him more than 4/6. This proposal was so reasonable that it silenced him, and he went awəy, as I thought, satisfyed, but it seems nothing less than a complete conquest would content them, and after another consultation, and when I had left the works, the man returned with the above formal demand, and our T:W as we had agreed gave him his discharge, at which the man was visibly chagrined. . . . I expect more will follow him.[12]

That year, 1772, was a bad one for relations between master and men, partly as a result of the imposition of the lower piece rates, but also from other causes. There was a continuing trouble with London accounting, but this time not as the result of some incompetent bookkeeping, but through dishonesty. In short, the warehouseman, Mather, proved a rogue. It seemed Wedgwood was doomed to have money troubles in London. Then he even found the trouble spreading to his own home where he discovered, to his great horror, that the servants were making free with the Wedgwood larder and were carrying on a roaring old trade in food and drink with the estate tenants. Wedgwood reacted promptly and sternly. "This will render it necessary to sweep the House of every servant we have in it, Male and Female, some from the field Men, and others from the works. My head Farmer is in this list, whom I have turned adrift, and given several of my Tennants notice to quit their houses."[13] All in all, then, a bad year for staff relations. But by early 1773 that was all behind him, and Wedgwood was ready for another dramatic coup that would rival the establishment of Queen's ware. Before looking at that event, however, we shall pause to see something of Wedgwood's life away from the factory and its problems.

[10]

Domestic Interlude

WEDGWOOD'S own letters are so full of talk and business, so packed with new ideas and projects, that we catch only occasional glimpses of his private life; and those few glimpses tend to give a distorting picture, since it is usually only serious illness or some other dramatic event that can lay claim to valuable letter space. But it is possible to piece together a picture of his interests and amusements, his concern for family life – wife, children and friends.

The life of the family rarely gets mentioned, seemingly taking its place as an accepted background to other events, but we do at least know the value that Wedgwood placed upon it. The absence of his Sally was always unwelcome. Even when they were at their busiest, visiting London, for example, with its hectic round of business meetings and dinners, the time they could spend together was important to Wedgwood: "We are under the necessity of in-croaching upon regular bed time, to have an hour's rest, or enjoy-ment of ourselves in peace, & tranquility."[1] Peace and tranquillity were clearly important to his wellbeing, though home life could have its livelier aspects. In the middle of the negotiations with Burdett over the engravings, Wedgwood asked Bentley to invoke his aid in selecting a barrel organ. "He is an excellent judge of musick, of the *Tone* and other qualitys of an instrument, and if you will be good to tell him what is expected from the Machine – that it is to put, or keep us in *good humour*, and to make us laugh, sing, and dance – and tell him too, that Joss sends him a nod, Jack a scrape, and Sue a Curtsey, he will perhaps be so good to take the commission off your hands, or at least assist you in it."[2]

For many years, Sally's regular appearances in the correspondence coincided with the equally regular appearances of her pregnancies. They were important events in the family, made doubly so by the always attendant risk to mother and child in that age. So we find Wedgwood writing early in 1771: "In April Mrs Wedgwood is to present me with another Boy, and there is no being from home at such a time on my account."[3] The dates were a little awry, but the forecast of a boy proved accurate, and Wedgwood was delighted with the whole thing. He had just begun a letter to Bentley, explaining that the midwife had come and gone and "My Wife as pert as a maggot and talks of holding out another month!", when he had to come back and add a postscript:

> This is chiefly to tell stories of my Wife – Would you think, my dear friend, she could have served me so slippery a trick. After my waiting here so long to receive a certain present, that she should bring it forth in my absence, when I had only turned my back of home for a few moments without thinking anything of the matter. I left her at near 8 last night, to go for an hour to our Club, quite well as usual. Came home before ten and just as I came into the house, little Tom (for so they call him), came into the world, and a very fine lad they tell me he is. A month old at least, and all are *well as can be expected*.[4]

The following year Sally's health began to deteriorate, with a painful attack of rheumatism, which left her so stiff in her limbs that she was unable to dress herself. Wedgwood was inundated with business problems, for he was in the middle of moving the useful works to a new site at Etruria, but at the end of May he and his wife set off from Staffordshire to try the healthy waters of Bath. He may have left the works behind, but could not quite leave work. They had already established a shop to sell Wedgwood pottery to the crowds that thronged the fashionable resort, and Wedgwood himself was soon visiting the premises. What with taking the waters, selling vases and nosing around the other vase-sellers, time must have passed quickly and agreeably enough. Then came news from town to add extra spice and interest to life. After years of teasing by his friend, Bentley at last announced that he was to remarry. His intended wife was Mary Stamford, a governess and daughter of an engineer in Derby. Wedgwood was left with one last whimsical letter to be dispatched before events removed the subject from him.

> You are tired of living by your self, and wish to know when we think of returning – Poor Man! he counts the minutes for hours, and thinks Old Time drawls along like a Broad wheeled Waggon. How many years now do you think it is since some good Ladys departed into Derbyshire; or can you count over the months since we left you alone at Chelsea. Be comforted my Good Friend, the time will come, however tardy he may seem; but every body tells us Mrs W must stay about three weeks longer. In the mean time we drink your health every night, wish you could be conveyed here some how or other to spend your evenings with us at Bath, but, as that cannot be, we pity your solitary condition, and hope you will take care of your self in the best manner you can 'till we arrive at Chelsea to set you at liberty for a week that you may be made a Happy Man for life.[5]

After years of being urged into matrimony, it must have been more than slightly galling to Bentley to find his partner showing so little sense of urgency. In the event, he did not wait but set off for Derbyshire, leaving the Wedgwoods to follow on to London some three weeks later, Bath not having done its work for Sally: "Mrs Wedgwood has left off bathing, it did not agree with her; she is now trying the pump, but thinks of leaving the Pump, and Bath, and Water, and the City too behind her."

By the time the Wedgwoods were back at Etruria in July, it was apparent that Sally was pregnant again – "sick, but I hope not *unto death*, but *rather unto life*." This time, however, things went far from well and there was much anxiety. She was suffering from recurring sickness, and Darwin was called over from Lichfield to help out the regular doctor. The former diagnosed a liver complaint, the latter a "Breeding case", and neither could do much to alleviate Wedgwood's worries about "my Dear Girl". He had cause to worry, for early in September 1772 Sally had a miscarriage – or so it seemed, for there is some doubt as to whether it was an actual or a phantom pregnancy. But the result was a marked deterioration in her health. The doctors could respond only with the familiar prescription of bleeding. Perhaps it was as well for her that the doctors left her welfare in the hands of her husband, whose own remedies, if somewhat startlingly robust, were at least unlikely to further weaken an already weak woman.

> My Dear Sally continues to recover, and has been up to day and bore it very well. But well as we think her compared with her situation a few days since, you never saw such a changling, nothing but skin and bone, pale as her cap, and does not seem to have a drop of blood in her body. Her lips to day begin to incline towards a blush of red, and as she relishes what she eats I hope to give you a better account of her soon.
>
> Doctor Darwin has left me to act as Physician in his absence but I believe I shall not gain much credit in my office amongst the female Nurses here, as I have prescribed what they durst not think of for my Patient.
>
> When nothing would stay upon her stomach I gave her fruit, ripe plumbs &c as often as she would eat them, and she has never vomited since. For the wind, I have given her Cyder that blows the cork up to the Ceiling. She relishes it vastly and it does her good.[6]

Wedgwood was a great believer in his own remedies of fresh air and exercise, as he explained to Bentley, whose wife was also ill. "She rides out every day let the weather be what it will, and I hope Mrs Bentley will do so too, for I think the gentle exercise and shaking of a Carriage, the diversion of the thoughts it creates, and the *open Air*, are preferable to being confined in a Parlour in almost any weather."[7]

But for all the fresh air, Sally's condition again worsened and became so serious that she was taken to stay at Lichfield, so that Darwin could have her under constant supervision. The strain told on Wedgwood, but he applied his own dictum, going out to work in the field for an hour or two every day. For a time Sally seemed better, but at Christmas she suffered a severe relapse.

A sudden sickness and giddiness seized her betwixt nine and ten o'Clock, which was immediately followed by faintings, attended with cold sweats, and her legs and arms and face as cold as clay. In this terrible situation she continued for many hours when we thought every moment would be her last. When she could be sensible of anything she complained of most severe cold which baffled all our endeavours with hot flannels, hot bricks, chafeing &c to remove 'till about 3 in the afternoon, when her natural heat began to return and her sickness began to abate a little, and from that time she has had no return of it, and we are very willing to flatter ourselves with the pleasing hopes of her recovery, though that must be a work of time; she is again reduced to such an extreme weak state, and will be confined mostly to her bed for some time.[8]

Darwin, who had been called in immediately, came and confirmed that the worst was indeed past. The spring saw a gradual recovery, though Wedgwood did not dare leave home for a full two months.

During Sally's illness, Wedgwood showed something of the depth of his feeling for her. There can be no doubt that it was a close and affectionate family circle, and that affection spread to the children. He seems to have had a very easy relationship with the children – at least while they were children. In 1772 Sukey was seven and John (Jackey) was six. Both were ready for school – an item in their lives to which their father attached the very greatest importance. And in spite of his preoccupation with Sally's illness, he still found the time to ferry them to and from their respective schools. Sukey went to Manchester with her cousins Jenny and Kitty Willett, Jackey to Bolton with John Willett.

Wedgwood took more than a passive interest in their education. He was especially concerned that science should be included in Jackey's curriculum, and as this was not a normal part of eighteenth-century schooling he was prepared to make good the deficiencies by his own efforts. Examples of Wedgwood the parent–teacher can be found in correspondence of 1774, a series of letters sent to Jackey. The letters are delightful, vivid and open, and the more remarkable in showing none of the condescension common in letters from father to son, especially when the son was only eight years old!

My Dear Boy

Having a parcel to send to your good master, I take that opportunity of inclosing a few lines to you, well knowing you will be glad to hear that your mamma, your brothers, & all your friends, are well and continue their good will & affections to you – Your brothers often talk of you, & seldom omit drinking your health at dinner. Joss wants much to go to school with his brother Jackey, that he may learn to read, & so learn many things out of books which he is very earnest to know, but finds there is no other way of gaining the knowledge he wants, but by becoming a scholar, and reading and studying for himself; for if he prevails upon his cousin Jackey or any body else who is at leisure, to read a little for him, they are no sooner got into the midst of an entertaining story, or something he wishes to learn, but they are called away to other business, and leave him unsatisfied & distressed. "Oh I wish I could take up the book, & read the story out myself, papa"! – but finding he is not able to do this at present, & being convinced that a little application will enable him to read for himself, he is determined to be more attentive to his learning, to say double lessons and if it were possible, to overtake even his brother Jackey in scholarship. I do not know how this may end, but am persuaded he will find it no easy matter to overtake one who is so active & ready at learning as I am told you are.

I suppose you have received two samples of Lead ore, with some flower pots, &c – I sent you the ores, & now send you some account of them, because I find you are attentive to what I told you of them & of some other natural bodies, & because I wish you to know a great deal of some things, & not be quite ignorant of any thing you may meet with in your journey thro' life. You must therefore begin to learn early, but more of this in some future letter – Believe me, my dear boy, your truly affectionate father – Jos. Wedgwood.[9]

The rest of the letters contain no similar pictures of the family at home, but they do show the same directness and the same most commendable ability to take his son seriously. Later he wrote from Matlock:

". . . a most delightful & romantic little village, where company meet in the summer to bathe & drink the waters, which are said to be good for many complaints & disorders of various kinds; but as I do not go there on account of my health, I spent a great deal of time upon the hills & mountains, & amongst the lead mines with which this country abounds, in search of different specimens of ores, spars & fossils; and in this search I had your amusement and instruction in view as well as my own, and I am the better pleased with my labours since I find by your last letters that they are not likely to be thrown away upon you.

Wedgwood then continued his course of lessons on lead, which apparently were being passed on to the rest of the school. The essay is not without its moral note. He mentioned that lead was sometimes used to remove acidity from wine, but with poisonous results: "Wine when unadulterated is a proper cordial for old, infirm and sick people. You, my dear boy, are young & healthy, and want no cordials; & therefore when wine is offered you, thank your friends for the civility, but I would wish you to *think of the lead* and if you are thirsty, ask for a little water or small beer."[10] He ends with a compliment which shows the pride of the father as much as a wish to please the son. "I have paid you a compliment in the pieces of granite, supposing you already too much of a philosopher to be offended with their nature roughness." Finally, when he went to collect Jackey, he promised to spend "a day or two with my Pupils, They having made me Professor of Metallurgy to the College there".

The main pleasures for the Wedgwoods, when Sally was fit, lay in travelling and visiting friends, though Josiah for his part could seldom travel anywhere without finding something that reminded him of business. Typical in many ways was a journey they made in December 1770, when they returned from a trip to London via Oxford and Woodstock. At the former they went to see the drawings and paintings at Christ Church, which they enjoyed, though Wedgwood could not help adding a disgruntled remark that there were not many vases and he had seen them all before anyway. At Woodstock they visited Blenheim, where they were very courteously received by the Duke of Marlborough's steward, which at once suggested to Wedgwood the whiff of possible patronage. As he remarked to Bentley: "You have so often drawn upon these phenomena."[11] From Oxford their route went through Birmingham, which of course meant a stop at Soho where talk of business again dominated over pleasure. The visit is worthy of note on another account, as an indication of the comparatively small world in which these people moved. There on that day with Boulton and Wedgwood, two of the leading manufacturers of the time, was one of the leaders of taste, the architect and painter, James "Athenian" Stuart, and conversation centred round the work of the other leading architects, the Adam brothers, whose new buildings, the Adelphi, were just available for renting. For a time Wedgwood and Boulton considered taking rooms there, but the plan came to nothing. The rest of the conversation was more mundane, and what the ladies discussed was not considered to be worth the mention.

Such excursions were limited in the early seventies, gloomy years too often marred by illness in the family and among friends. The Brindleys had become regular visitors to the Wedgwood home, and valued visitors at that. Wedgwood often declared that he learned as much from conversation with the unlettered Brindley as he did from any man. But Brindley was desperately overworked, and unexpected difficulties had added to his burden. At Harecastle the tunnellers had found every kind of obstacle in their path – quicksands, water, hard rock – and for every obstacle a new technique had to be invented to overcome it. Brindley's boast that all would be finished in five years seemed sadly wide of the mark. What the proprietors of that and the other canal schemes did not know as they harried their chief engineer – what, indeed, he himself did not know – was that Brindley had diabetes. Only when the engineer was taken ill and Darwin was called to attend him was the disease diagnosed. For nearly two weeks, in September 1772, Wedgwood was a daily visitor to the sick man's bedside. He died on 27 September and Wedgwood wrote to Bentley a letter that is as fitting a memorial to one of the great men of the age as any he received.

> I told you in my last letter that Mr. Brindley was extremely ill, and I have the grief to tell you that he is no more. He died the

27th inst. about 12 at Noon, and died in a sound sleep, for about 3 o'clock in the morning, after giving him something to wet his mouth he said *'tis enough – I shall need no more*, and shut his Eyes, never more to open: he continued to the time of his death (about 9 hours) seemingly in a fine sleep, and yielded up his breath at last without a single groan.

He has left two young Children behind him, and poor Mrs Brindley inconsolable for the loss a of sensible friend and affectionate Husband. What the public has lost can only be conceived by those who best know his Character and Talents, Talents to which this Age and Country are indebted for works that will be the most lasting Monuments to his Fame, and shew to future Ages how much good may be done by one single Genius, when happily employed upon works beneficial to Mankind.

Mr Brindley had an excellent constitution, but his mind, too ardently intent upon the execution of the works it had planned, wore down a body at the age of 55 which originally promised to have lasted a century, and might give him the pleasing expectation of living to see those great works completed for which Millions yet unborn will revere and bless his memory.

Do I need to tell you that he bore his last illness with that fortitude and strength of mind which characterised all his actions.

If you have so much leisure perhaps you will send an account of this event to some of the papers, with such accompaniments as your esteem and friendship for the deceased shall dictate, and if a premium is required from the printers I will gladly pay it. The Duke of Bridgewater might, and indeed ought, to have a handsome compliment paid him on this occasion, to encourage others to *bring Genius to light* and support its first efforts as he has Nobly done.[12]

Another death among the circle of friends was that of Darwin's wife in 1770. They had had five children, of whom three died in infancy. Darwin, however, was left something less than prostrate with grief. Instead of going into deep mourning, he went more than slightly wild. He began a mild flirtation with Anna Seward encouraging her limited poetic talents with extravagant praise. The young lady was quite overwhelmed by his attentions, and seems to have been deeply chagrined to discover that his interest in her ended with his interest in her brain and he was actively seeking other gratifications elsewhere. He had a very open affair which resulted in the birth of two illegitimate children. The "Misses Parker" were always acknowledged by Darwin, accepted as members of the family and eventually set up with their own school and a pamphlet on the precepts of female education by the Doctor. When Darwin eventually remarried, the children of that marriage were sent to school at the Misses Parkers.

None of this unconventional behaviour appears to have affected his friends – though it might explain why he was spared the usual Wedgwood witticisms on the subject of sex and marriage. But then the ties that held Wedgwood to Darwin were hardly social in that sense – they were held by their common interests, especially their interest in science. In 1766 Darwin had got together with a few friends, including Boulton and William Small, who was Boulton's partner in the Soho works before Watt arrived and engine-building began. They agreed to meet regularly in each other's houses to have dinner and discuss science and the arts, though the former soon came to dominate the talks. As the streets were unlit and meetings ended late, they agreed to meet on the Monday nearest the full moon, and this arrangement gave them a name – the Lunar Society. There were some remarkably eminent men to be found in the ranks of the Lunatics, as Darwin called them: the printer Baskerville, James Watt after his move to Birmingham, the engineers William Murdock and John Smeaton, the president of the Royal Society Sir Joseph Banks, and Joseph Priestley.

Mary Ann Schimmelpennick, who was invariably scathing about the atheistic Darwin, was more interesting and perceptive on the subject of the other luminaries. Boulton "was tall and of a noble appearance: his temperament was sanguine, with that slight mixture of phlegmatic which gives calmness and dignity; his manners were eminently open and cordial; he took the lead in conversations, and with a social heart had a *grandiose* manner like that arising from position, wealth, and habitual command. He went among his people like a monarch bestowing largess." From the description it is easy to see why Wedgwood should have regarded this imperious man as a potentially dangerous rival and uncomfortable partner. As it was, they were fortunate in generally meeting as equals, each pursuing an independent line. Boulton's new partner Watt was, by contrast, "one of the most complete specimens of the melancholic temperament". He was introverted, retiring, speaking seldom and when he did in a very strong Scots accent. Parallels are often drawn between the partnerships of Boulton and Watt and that of Wedgwood and Bentley, but whatever similarities, and even in business terms these are frequently overstated, they stopped far short of similarities in personalities. Of all the Lunatics, the one who earned the most lavish praise was, not surprisingly, the minister of religion Joseph Priestley. "I can never forget the impression produced on me by the serene expression of his countenance. He indeed, seemed present with God by recollection and with man by cheerfulness."

· Darwin was not the least eminent among this company, but as Boulton had appropriated the role of monarch, he appears to have cast himself as court jester. A letter to Boulton, apologizing for missing a meeting, gives the Darwin tone, but also conveys something of the excitement of the meetings:

> I am sorry the infernal divinities who visit mankind with diseases, and are therefore at perpetual war with doctors, should have prevented my seeing all your great men at Soho today. Lord! what inventions, what wit, what rhetoric, metaphysical, mechanical, and pyrotechnical will be on the wing, bandied like a shuttlecock from one to another of your troup of philosophers! while poor I, I by myself I, imprison'd in a post-chaise, am joggl'd, and jostl'd, and bump'd, and bruised along the King's highroad to make war upon a stomach-ache or a fever.[13]

As another distinguished member, Richard Lovell Edgeworth put it, the Society contained men of different characters "but all devoted to literature and science. The mutual intimacy has never been broken but by death."

Wedgwood himself was not a member of the Lunar Society, but he was a regular guest at their meetings, knew all the members well and corresponded with them on scientific subjects. And this was the true importance of the Lunar Society: it provided a forum. Here the different members could put their ideas forward and have them knocked around and criticized by friends whose criticism was worth regarding: here they could bring their problems and have those problems intelligently discussed. There was such a wide range of interests and expertise among the members – from civil engineering to astronomy – that if one could not provide the missing piece to a puzzle, there was a fair chance that another would. And much of the help was of a thoroughly practical nature: suggestions for improving experiments, advice on new materials, and one member, James Keir, even undertook the chore of translating a new treatise on chemistry, which earned from Wedgwood the comment: "I would not be without it at my elbow on any account. It is a Chemical Library." In his turn, Wedgwood was welcomed for his own contribution to the group – "Wedgwood, with his increasing industry, experimental variety, and calm investigation", as Edgeworth described him.

The Society did not confine itself to scientific discussion. Politics, though theoretically no part of the group's business, invariably cropped up from time to time, and in the turbulent years at the end of the century came as near as anything to causing breaches and schisms. America was one of the first subjects for dissension. Benjamin Franklin was a personal friend and correspondent of many in the Society, and men such as Wedgwood were among the early supporters of the colonists in their struggle for representation and just treatment. As the War of Independence drew nearer, there was inevitable disagreement between the conservative group, led by Watt, and the more radical majority.

The Lunar Society gave to Wedgwood an opportunity to extend his own scientific work. It must be remembered that he was largely self-taught in science, and here he had the possibility of getting his own rough techniques polished by experts. The stimulus they gave to his ideas was as important as the practical help over specific details. It helped too to confirm Wedgwood in his belief in the value of scientific work in industry, so that in 1775 he had the confidence to suggest that the Staffordshire potters band together to support scientific research – one of the first proposals ever made for the establishment of a scientific research establishment in an industry. The Society also stimulated Wedgwood's continuing work of self education, helping him to turn into a confirmed bookworm. He began to build what was to prove an extensive library. His taste was catholic. Just one account with one bookseller includes the following polyglot selection: Bryant's *Antiquities*, Ferguson's *Astronomy*, Thucydides, Xenophon, Pennant's *Tours*, *A History of England in Letters*, and *British Biography*.[14]

Wedgwood's spare time, such as it was, could hardly be said to be idled away, what with reading such a variety of subjects, planning, discussing and executing his experiments, talking politics and providing educational programmes for the children. All this was based on the solid platform provided by a loved and loving family. So his life continued through the years, with his interests continuing to develop much as his business continued to grow.

[11]

Russia and Jasper

In the spring of 1773 Wedgwood received an order that rivalled that from Queen Charlotte in importance and far exceeded it in scale. It came through Alexander Baxter, the Russian consul in London, and was for a dinner and dessert service to be used by the Empress Catherine at the Chesman Palace near St Petersburg. It was to consist of 952 pieces of creamware, each of which was to carry the distinguishing emblem of a frog – the original name of the palace in Finnish meant Frog Marsh, and it was also known as La Grenouillere. This in itself constituted a gigantic order, but what made it difficult, expensive and time-consuming to produce was a further condition: each piece was to be decorated with views of an English house or garden, and each view was to be different. Small wonder that Wedgwood's elation was tempered with nervousness, not least at the expense and the chances of recovering the money. European royalty were notoriously more generous at giving out orders than at paying for them when completed.

> I have no idea of this service being got up in less than two or three years if the Landskips and buildings are to be tolerably done so as to do any credit to us, and to be copied from pictures of real buildings and situations – nor of its being afforded for less than £1000 or £1500 – Why all the gardens in England will scarcely furnish subjects sufficient for this sett, every piece having a different subject. I think Mr. Baxter should be spoke to very particularly to know what expence he thinks it would be prudent

to lay upon the service, for he cannot but know that any sum almost may be expended upon this commission.

Suppose the Empress should die when the service is nearly completed: as it will be a very expensive business it may not be amiss to mention something of the kind to the Consul.[1]

Price, invariably, became a source of some disagreement: Baxter proposed keeping the total cost to around £500, while Wedgwood argued that such a cost would be impossible to meet without reducing the standard and the decoration far below anything that the Empress had in mind. Wedgwood's judgement proved the sounder.

> The Empress has again prov'd her self to be what we had before all the reason in the world to believe she was – A Woman of sense, fine taste, and spirit. I will have some real views taken and send them to you from Trentham, Keel, Lawton, Booth, Swinnerton, Shugboro', Ingestry, Etruria, and many other places. Pray have you Wilson's Views from different places in Wales? If you have not Mr. Sneyd will lend them us; he was a subscriber and says they were sold only to subscribers, he believes.
>
> The Consul should not talk of *doing them as much lower as we can*. If his Mistress heard him she would rap his knuckles. We could do them as much lower as he pleased, but to do them in the manner the Empress wishes to see them, and as we (I mean the Consul and all of us) may receive due honor from the execution of the noblest plan yet laid down, or undertaken by any Manufacture in Great Britain, the price agreed upon is cheap beyond comparison with anything I know, and you will make no doubt of it convince the Consul of it *in due time*.[2]

In the event, even Wedgwood's estimate of a maximum cost of £1,500 proved to be pitched too low. The ware itself was not the major problem, but the decoration, the 1,224 separate views. Early trials were in colour, but this was reduced to monochrome, otherwise the cost would have been prohibitive. The service was of such importance that Wedgwood took a personal interest in even the most minute detail, as this note in a letter from John Wood of the

London warehouse to Etruria indicates. "The new round cream bowls sent for the Russian set, Mr. W begs leave to observe are a full inch too large, the handles thrown too far from the body of the vessel, & the holes for the handles too large, likewise thinks the crinkling too deep."[3] There speaks the authentic voice of the perfectionist – and the practical potter.

When the service was at last ready in the summer of 1744, it had occupied a good deal of the time and talents of the two partners. It is rather difficult to disentangle the profit and loss accounts for the work, but it appears that the production cost came out some-where in the region of £2,500 and the Empress paid approximately £3,000 – and, in spite of Wedgwood's worries, she paid promptly. But the cash value of the manufacturing profit is virtually insignifi-cant in comparison with the value of the service in other ways. Before it was sent to Russia the whole set was put on display in London in June 1774. Altogether four rooms were needed, so that the service could be set out on tables. Once ready, the exhibition was widely advertised and proved immensely popular. It was just what was needed to revive the slightly flagging interest in Wedgwood ware. It was as if the intoxicating days when the world was vase-mad had returned all over again. Aristocracy and nobility crowded to the rooms, and the peak of achievement of this exercise in public relations was reached when the Queen herself came to view the service. She had a special interest in it, for many of the illustrations were of royal palaces and gardens. Wedgwood and Bentley were firmly re-established in their roles as potters to royalty, more importantly for the sales figures, as potters to every-one with pretensions to being dubbed fashionable.

The emphasis on selling as an activity deserving as much care and thought as manufacture set Wedgwood and Bentley apart from their contemporaries among the potters. This was where Bentley's main contribution lay. He was the arbiter of taste, who made the sugges-tions of what would sell – suggestions that determined much of the production of the ornamental works – and once the appropriate ware was available it was his concern to improve the selling techniques. The success of the partnership lay in a perfect symmetry: Bentley could sell what Wedgwood could produce, and Wedgwood could produce what Bentley wanted to sell. By this time the variety of the ware was immense, and it was becoming increasingly obvious that this profusion of shapes, patterns and glazes needed bringing into some sort of order. So in 1773 Wedgwood and Bentley set about producing their first catalogue.

There is no better way of assessing the diversity of Wedgwood's ware than to look through the pages of this and subsequent catalogues. There are vases of different shapes and sizes, engine-turned vases, basalt vases, encaustic vases; there are busts and statues of all manners of people from ancient Romans to contemporary politicians; there are candelabras and chimney-piece tablets, cameos and urns. No collection of Wedgwood could hope to show all this variety, and the years added to the numbers of types and the numbers of designs within each type.

From a business point of view, the catalogue must have made life considerably easier for everyone: now customers could order what they wanted, even if they could not get to London or Etruria. This was particularly useful for overseas customers, so that one finds, for example, among the early orders for catalogues one from the Chevalier Pinto requesting a copy for the King of Portugal.[4] For later generations it remains a marvel, a treasure house of information on the production of Etruria. Of even greater value to later collectors, however, was the practice introduced at much the same time of putting a mark on all the ware that was produced. By the end of the year a Queen's ware catalogue was in preparation, and it joined the ornamental catalogue the following spring.

The year 1773 was a busy one for Wedgwood – few years were not. It was also one which involved him in a good deal of travelling. One line that preoccupied him was the making of seals, a difficult job requiring much skill if the detail was not to be lost, and in his travels he usually found time and opportunity to promote their sale. A good deal of this travelling stemmed from concern over the health of various members of the family. In July Sukey returned from school "Full of pouks and boils and humours" and was trundled off to the seaside near Liverpool, where she could benefit from fresh air and salt water. The latter was considered so good for the unfortunate child that, as well as being allowed the pleasure of bathing in it, she was also encouraged in the less enjoyable activity of drinking it. From Liverpool they went to Buxton, where Sally was to take the waters in the hope of curing her rheumatism. But the Derbyshire spa proved no more efficacious than its more famous rival, Bath, had done. Still, on all these travels Wedgwood noted the great demand for his seals, and his mind began to turn more and more towards ways in which these small delicate objects and equally delicate cameos could be improved to both meet and expand the demand.

The journeyings included other useful visits – to Birmingham, where Boulton was setting ceramic pieces in metal, to Manchester, where Wedgwood made a valuable connection with an enterprising merchant, Radcliffe – but more and more his thoughts turned to Etruria, the works and new experiments. In particular he began to apply himself to planning for improvements in the small ware that was proving so popular. He put his thoughts down on paper in the spring of 1774.

> The main thing we want at present, to complete our Cameo's and Bass reliefs and to add a little variety to our Vases, Candlesticks, &c, I believe will be managed, and as to the Blanching of our ware in general, when that step is absolutely necessary I hope it may be done. I have for some time past been reviewing my experiments, and I find such *Roots*, such *Seeds*, as would open and branch out wonderfully if I could nail myself down to the cultivation of them for a year or two. And the Fox-hunter does not enjoy more pleasure from the chace, than I do from the prosecution of my experiments when I am fairly enter'd into the field, and the farther I go, the wider this field extends before me. The Agate, the Green, and other colour'd Glazes, have had their day, and done pretty well, and are certain of a resurrection soon, for there are, and ever will be, a numerous Class of People to purchase *shewy* and *cheap* things. The Cream-color is of a superior Class, and I trust not yet run its race by many degrees. The Black is sterling, and will last for ever. These are a few of the Roots which have been selected and put into a state of cultivation, and I never look over my Books but I find many more which I should very gladly bring into action: but the too common fate of schemers is ever before my Eyes, and you

George Stubbs spent some time at Etruria, experimenting with ceramics, and one result was this delightful set of horse studies in jasper.

The modelling room at Etruria. Wedgwood himself casts an expert eye over a new vase.

below and opposite A rare set of photographs from the early years of this century, showing that the work rooms at Etruria had scarcely changed.
below The throwing room, where the assistant weighs the clay, while the thrower fashions the ware. Notice the grand "going home" hats on the wall.

top The grinding mills, where the flints were reduced to powder.

below, left and right Workshops, and part of a bottle kiln. The outside staircase kept the different departments isolated, preserving secrecy; and saggars containing ware to be fired stacked inside an oven.

The Wedgwood family painted in 1780 by Stubbs. Josiah and Sarah sit beneath the tree. On horseback, from right to left, are John, Josiah II, Sukey and Tom. Catherine holds the cart handle, Mary Ann is in the cart and Sarah stands beside her.

Jasper fitted in well with the new ideas in interior decoration: a marble chimney piece inset with green jasper plaques, made for the Master of the Dublin Mint. The centrepiece is Flaxman's "Apotheosis of Homer".

have given me many excellent lectures upon the bad policy of hurrying things too fast upon one another.

I have been looking over our Cameos, Heads, &c, and we shall send you an account of some new ones soon. . . .

I have not been on Horseback for a week! This morning some business calls me from my Books and Vases and trumpery, and I am very thankful for it, for I have scarcely power, *of my own mere notion*, to quit my present pursuits for a few hours.[5]

Delays to the experiment programme were inevitable, for there were always matters of a more mundane, but nevertheless important, nature to be attended to at the works or in London. It is easy to lose sight of such matters, crowded out of the centre of the picture by the dramatic highlights of royal visits and the like. Yet the problems that exercised Wedgwood and his employees were still there to be dealt with, and many of them are as familiar today as they were then. To take just one example, there was the business of getting goods from factory to the customer. The ware might be brilliant in design and wonderful in construction, but if it failed to reach the customer it was useless. So we find John Wood writing from London: "Desire Mr. Thompson to cause our Goods to be regularly forwarded, for of date the Waggoners have kept a whole weeks goods behind which delay is a great hindrance & disappointment to our business."[6] There follow complaints about packing, with invoices and goods not matching, and, worst of all, delays in crates intended for export. So that, a week later, he had to write: "Oh! those waggoners, they have left Captain Jackson's goods behind, & I fear he will be sailed without them." Some of these problems were exacerbated by the inconvenience of the London warehouse and showrooms, so that Wedgwood was forced to break off his work at Etruria to come to London to arrange for new premises. He was successful, and in the summer of 1774 he was on hand to supervise the move to Greek Street in Soho. In July he was back at Etruria and back at his experiments.

The problem that was exercising Wedgwood was that of producing a suitable body for cameos, seals and other gems. The requirements were that it should be a pure white, yet hard enough to be polished on a lapidary's wheel. For this he needed to start with a clay free from impurities, and that part of the problem was not too difficult to solve. He had already tried the Cherokee clay and, rather more conveniently, the West Country clays, both of which answered the requirement. The clays however needed to be hardened by fusing in a powdered rock or stone, and finding the right type of rock proved more of a problem. A great deal of work had to be done, endlessly experimenting with different minerals to find a suitable type that not only did the job but could be relied on to do it consistently.

> Moor stone and Spaith fusible are the two articles I want, and the several samples I have of the latter are so different in their properties that no dependence can be had upon them. They have plagued me sadly of late. At one time the body is white and fine as it should be, the next we make, perhaps having used a different lump of the Spaith, is a Cinamon color. One time it is melted to a Glass, another time as dry as a Tob:Pipe – And this way it has led me a dance ever since I came home, without my knowing why 'till I tried each separate lump by itself. I am afraid this said S. Fusible is too Proteus-like ever to make a fixed solid base for a Manufacture, and I have now begun a series of experiments upon Materials which are easy to be had in sufficient quantities, and of qualities *allways the same*.[7]

He received much help in his search from friends in the Lunar Society. John Whitehurst, a scientific instrument worker at Derby, sent him samples of "terra ponderosa" or "cawk", a barium sulphate ore, which proved to answer very well indeed, and was used for many years until a better substitute was found in Cumberland witterite, a barium carbonate ore. Though helpful suggestions and samples came from friends, the long work of making careful trials of the different samples under different conditions fell to Wedgwood – and that it was a long process the experiment books amply testify. Wedgwood went on working to improve the body for many, many years.

The first hint of success in the experiment showing itself in the factory production comes in a rather unlikely place. The French translation of the ornamental catalogue contains a mention of a very white, very strong body suitable for cameos, portraits and bas reliefs. By November 1774 Wedgwood had given the new body a name – jasper. By early 1775 he was producing coloured jasper, including the famous blues and greens. What distinguished this new ware was the fineness of the pottery, almost equal to that of porcelain, and the combination of this with a hardness which matched that of the strongest stoneware. It needed no glazing, and so there were no problems with polishing. First experiments were with a colour wash, but then the colour was burned into the body itself, and finally Wedgwood developed a jasper slip into which the white jasper was dipped.

Jasper made it possible for the potter to combine a delicacy of detail with great durability. The contrast between the blues and greens and the pure white of the applied figures exactly hit the mood of cool elegance that characterized the taste of the age. And Wedgwood was very quickly on to the possibilities offered by the new materials, making plans for new vases, medallions and modelled figures. By one of those seemingly fortunate coincidences that so often, on closer inspection, have their roots in earlier plans and policies, Wedgwood had on hand an artist whose talents exactly matched the needs of the day – John Flaxman. He had been a brilliant child artist, entering the newly established Royal Academy school in 1769 at the age of fourteen and carrying off their silver medal in his first year. Wedgwood's first reactions to such a precocious talent were, not surprisingly, unfavourable, and he was promptly classed with all those other eccentric, odd, individualistic artists who had plagued the potter: "It is but a few years since he was a supreme Coxcomb, but a little more experience may have cured him of that foible."[8] Indeed it had, and Flaxman was to become the leading figure among the group of artists who did regular work for Wedgwood, and he had sufficiently shed his coxcombery to become a close personal friend.

The development of jasper brought Wedgwood face to face with an old and very familiar dilemma – how much should he make known, how much keep secret? He wanted to put the new materials to use at once, but how was he to gather in the materials in sufficient quantity without attracting attention and giving away the secret of the process? He could apply for a patent, but, as he had already discovered with encaustic painting, the eighteenth-century patent was more likely to give rise to large lawyers' fees than any real protection. His friend Boulton was to have success with the steam engine patent he took out with Watt in 1775, but he was very much an exception. In any case, Wedgwood decided against the patent, and instead preferred to rely on his own precautions to keep the process concealed; and, if the worst happened, then he always had his inventiveness to keep him a step ahead of imitators. It was to prove a sensible and successful policy.

The experiments on jasper took up an immense amount of time, though at first no one seems to have been aware just what a success they had on their hands. Wedgwood was pleased with the results, but in general life went on much as before. His letters still manage to combine business details with jottings on his private life, with little more than a hiccup between the two. So, for example, we find him, in November 1774, a proud father one minute and a distrustful employer the next.

> I know my Dear Friend kindly interests himself in every event by which I am materially affected, and will rejoice with me in Mrs Wedgwood's safe delivery, and the welcome addition to our Family of a fine, healthy and perfect Child.
>
> My Dear Girl gave me, as usual, a very short notice of the approaching critical moment. At past four this morning she gave me a gentle notice to leave her bed and call the Midwife; and a quarter before five news was brought me that I had another Daughter, and all was well.
>
> Mrs. W. continues in a good way, and I hope to see her below again in a few days: for it is becoming fashionable for the Ladies in the straw to become well and leave it as soon as they are able; and even a Lady of Fashion may be seen in her Carriage again, without shame, in ten days, or a fortnight after delivery. – Mr. Wood to send me £1000 in Cash, in different boxes, and at different times as received or rather faster – it should all be here in a Month. You'l perhaps have some Busts, or other matters to send by the Waggon along with it. The boxes should not be too small to give suspicion, and if JW could pack the cash without our other People knowing, it would be much better, and advise me particularly of every sending upon some

convenient place in the sheet of accounts for me to cut it off before I send it to the Counting house.[9]

For a time Sally and the baby were not too well, in spite of the optimism after the birth, but they soon recovered and young Catherine (Kitty) took her place in the family to reinforce the heavily outnumbered distaff side.

Politics again came to provide interest and variety to the scene. Wedgwood was interested in political affairs, but was not active in party politics: a businessman with many influential customers with conflicting political views is not always well advised to broadcast his own opinions too widely. In fact, as John Wood explained to Wedgwood, there was more than one sense in which it was safer to keep quiet during elections.

> I suppose Mr. Bentley will have left Etruria before this comes to hand, but hope he will spend some time with his friends in Derbyshire upon his return whilst the Electioneering is a little abated: or perhaps if he is absent the whole Poling for the City of Westminster, it may not be altogether imprudent, for I fear his presence would occasion some offence: A few days since Mountmorris & Mahon called with several of our good Customers to solicit your Votes, & today Her Grace the Duchess of Northumberland called in purpose for the same purpose in favour of her son, & if we mistake not she suspected the Truth of both you Gentlemen being in Staffordshire for this evening Lady Percy visited us merely to ask questions. Lord Besborough interests himself very much in Mountmorris & Mahon's favour – We are very well provided at present with an Apology for either party.
>
> On Saturday night the whole town was obliged by a Mob to illuminate for Mountmorris & Mahon, or submit to have their Windows broke. Indeed many Windows were broke before the inhabitants could possibly put up lights however we escaped by setting a few candles in the front room.[10]

Wedgwood, very wisely, remained aloof from such proceedings. He considered that reforms to the system were necessary before a sensible man could take an interest in politics – and, in any case, elections were bad for business, as John Wood sadly recorded: "You will perceive by Our Sales that we have very little Company comes, & I fear we shall not have more 'till the Parliament meets."[11]

In foreign affairs Wedgwood played no very active part, but he had decidedly firm views, particularly over the subject of America. He had long been prophesying that British policy could have only one conclusion, the end of British rule and American independence. In 1774 the Boston Tea Party was followed by the punitive closure of the Port of Boston, and in Philadelphia the colonists met to form what was, in effect, an independent government. The prophecies were rapidly reaching fulfilment. Wedgwood's sympathies were all with the Americans, but public clamour insisted on dubbing them traitors and rebels. "All the world are with the minister and against the poor Americans." So, he played the part of prudence, and limited his comments on affairs to Bentley and fellow sympathizers in the Lunar Society, many of whom kept up a correspondence with their old friend Franklin. In February 1775, on a visit to Lancashire, he saw something of the activities of the anti-Americans, for Roebuck, a violent propagandist, was hard at work. Petitions and counter-petitions wafted everywhere.

> Doctor Roe had been at Manchester about a week before – exceeding hot and violent against the Americans. Dr. Percival told me he quite frothed at the mouth like a —— and was so excessively rapid in his declamations and exclamations, that nobody could put in a word 'till his story was told, and then away he flew to another House repeating the same Rigmirow over again. . . . The good Doctor was thought by the moderate at Manchester to be an Agent, under immediate employment, for that particular purpose, and no doubt he likewise *will have his reward*.[12]

When war finally came, Wedgwood continued his support of the American cause – but continued to keep that support "within the family". Later, when the conflict was at its height, he even decided it was necessary to caution the usually cautious Bentley to "Write anything to me but treason", as he was convinced his mail was being opened. Not that he always remembered his own advice and a fresh example of British stupidity could be relied upon to bring out, if not a tirade, then some notably wry comments.

> How could you frighten me so in your last letter? It was naughty of you. I thought of nothing less than some shelves, or perhaps a whole floor, of vases and crockeries had given way, and that you had been carried down with them! But on reading a little further I found that it was only the nation that was likely to flounder into a French war; and, having been fully persuaded of this event for a long time past, I recovered from my shock and blessed my stars and Lord North that *America was free.* . . . We must have more war, and perhaps continue to be beaten – to what degree is in the womb of time. If our drubbing keeps pace with our deserts, the Lord have mercy on us.[13]

But in 1775 the war was just beginning, the full ramifications of the skirmish at Lexington were still to be felt, and Wedgwood continued to put his role of man of business a long way in front of any possible political ambitions or ideas. He had too little respect for the prevailing parliamentary system to wish to be part of it, and too much respect for his own business to jeopardize it by expounding unpopular political views, however strongly held. The only area of political life where he was prepared to make a public noise was in that area that directly affected the pottery trade. There he was very willing to play an active role, and in 1775 he was to lead a parliamentary lobby.

[12]

Cornwall

WEDGWOOD, by this time, had established firm connections with the West of England clay trade, and enjoyed very cordial relations with the men who ran it. The Trent and Mersey Canal was open to the Trent end, which meant that clay could be shipped all the way to Gainsborough where it could be loaded into narrow boats for the rest of the journey. Costs were thus much reduced, which made it worth Wedgwood's while to go on scouting expeditions in Dorset to look for even better varieties of clay. Thomas Hyde of Poole was his main contact, and Hyde was ever anxious to help in the matter of improvements. "It was my opinion," he wrote, "when you saw the White Clay at the first Work we visited in our way to Corf Castle that it would answer and I think that I sent you specimens of it – in point of colour, if that is the object, I should think would excell any other." He added that he could not get to see Wedgwood, who was then in London, but "When friends get together is generally the Time for forming Excursions. Why cant You all conclude to visit Dorsetshire? I give you my Word that when I get next to London, I threaten to see Staffordshire."[1] It was a prosperous and thriving trade, clearly conducted to the mutual advantage and satisfaction of both parties. Yet there was a limit set on the clays that could be taken from the West Country, a limit that Wedgwood resented and that set him on the road to Westminster in 1775.

The story dates back to the discovery by William Cookworthy of Plymouth of a method of making porcelain from native English materials – a true, hard porcelain, that is, not the porcelain made of soft paste, hardened by use of a flint. Cookworthy got a patent and the patent gave him exclusive use of Cornish china clay and china stone. In 1774 a Bristol merchant, Richard Champion, bought up the patent and laid plans for a new works where he intended to make porcelain. The earthenware manufacturers of Staffordshire showed little interest, until Champion applied to Parliament to have the terms of the patent extended. He argued that he needed time to develop his manufacture before he could recover the costs of the patent and later experiments. The Staffordshire potters now took exception to the extension of a patent that not only prohibited them from making porcelain, but also kept them from using the raw materials in other ways.

Champion got his patent bill through the Commons without opposition, but the Staffordshire potters were able to baulk its progress in the Lords, largely through the influence of Lord Gower. The complex process of eighteenth-century lobbying then began: petitions were sent to Parliament and a pamphlet published, to the accompaniment of identical manœuvres from the other side. Wedgwood produced his own pamphlet, in which he argued that, as raw materials were freely available, they could not be described as "an invention", in the sense that Watt's engine was an invention. Champion replied that Wedgwood, as a manufacturer of earthenware not porcelain, ought – though Champion used more convoluted language – to keep his nose out of other people's business. Wedgwood, in turn, adopted a high moral tone:

> When Mr. *Wedgwood* discovered the Art of making Queen's Ware, which employs ten times more People than all the China Works in the Kingdom, he did not ask for a Patent for this important Discovery. A Patent would greatly have limited its public Utility. Instead of *one hundred Manufactories* of Queen's Ware, there would have been *one*; and instead of an Exportation to all Quarters of the World, a few pretty Things would have been made, for the Amusement of the People of Fashion in *England*.

Considering that, in developing creamware, Wedgwood had invented nothing, and that it was hardly through Wedgwood's open-handed generosity that anyone had got access to his well-guarded secrets, the statement has more than a whiff of hypocrisy about it. But then, campaigning pamphlets were not generally expected to be models of accuracy, and it was probably no worse than a hundred others. Pamphleteering and lobbying had their effect, and through Lord Gower's advocacy the Lords introduced substantial amendments to the Bill. The main point the Staffordshire interest gained was the requirement that Champion should publish full details of his porcelain mixture. This would then be covered by the patent, but the same ingredients could then be used in other proportions for other ware.

So at the end of the day Champion was left with his porcelain, and the Staffordshire potters were free to invade Cornwall. In May Wedgwood, together with another successful potter, John Turner of Lane End, and Thomas Griffiths, who had bought Cherokee clay for Wedgwood in America, set off on a Cornish clay hunt. The trip is interesting in showing Wedgwood at work, exploring new possibilities, but it has more significance than that. Normally, when travelling he sent home a flurry of business letters into which he slipped the occasional anecdote or description, but on the Cornish trip he kept a detailed diary of his travels.[2] Here we find him writing about the scenery, the people he met along the way, the places he visited. We see his interest in the world about him, but we also see how business continued to obsess him, intruding into the least likely situations. It is a fascinating document and no apologies are offered for quoting from it at length.

At the very start of the journey, Wedgwood himself produces the main theme, bemoaning the pressures of business.

> We have now a Serpentine road before us – The great Brown himself could not trace a finer line of beauty – through an extensive grove of oaks, interspersed with neat farm houses, which are seen thro' the trees in the most picturesque stile imaginable.
>
> It is impossible to pass through these finely varied scenes, and comfortable haunts of man, without wishing to spend more time amongst them than these hurrying chaises will allow; and I often form hasty resolutions, that the next time I visit

such places, I will take more time to stop, to indulge myself
with a ramble amongst them; but the next time is like the
preceding – every journey has its main object, & all others are
sacrificed to that – We must reach such a place at such an hour;
– and this leaves room for none of the pleasing episodes we
have before promised ourselves, – and thus we continue to be
cheated with vain & delusive promises as long as we live.

By the time they reached Devon, he was beginning to comment
on the differences and peculiarities not just of the countryside but of
the people and their way of life. At Exeter he was surprised to find
no signs of carts and waggons, only pack-horses: "A droll appearance
the horses make, scarcely any part of the horse being seen, so that it
looks like an animated stalking bundle of green vegetables." West
of Exeter, they climbed to the top of a hill where they were "amply
repaid for the trouble, by one of the most extensive & finely varied
views imaginable". But matters closer to hand, or rather to foot,
soon distracted his attention away from the panorama. "The soil
is full of loose flints, most of them white throughout, as if they were
calcined, without any ferruginous crust on the outside from long
exposure to the air – which is the only instance I know where that
has not happened to flints long exposed to the atmosphere out of
their native beds – They fetch their flints from this place to a
pottery at Bovey Tracy, not far from hence." Bovey Tracy,
however, did not pass the great potter's inspection – "a poor
trifling concern, & conducted in a wretched slovenly manner" –
and with that and a terse note that he could not understand a word
the natives said, he was on his way again.

If Devon seemed strange, Cornwall was positively foreign. Here,
for example, is the description of an encounter in Truro, "much the
handsomest town I have seen in Cornwall", which aroused
Wedgwood's curiosity if not his gallantry.

> We met a very numerous procession of females, all dizened out
> in their best habitments. We were much struck with such a
> troop of young women, marching in regular order, and enquir-
> ing into the occasion of it were told that it was the annual
> meeting of two female clubs, who had associated for the same
> purpose that the men in this & other parts of this island do, –

A bill of 1775 for a substantial order from one of Wedgwood's grander customers – His Serene Highness Prince of Anault Dessau

to lay by a little money whilst they are in health & can spare it, & receive it again in time of sickness. I am sorry I cannot say much in favour of the beauty of this groupe of the fair sex, indeed there were scarcely three faces in the two clubs that were tolerable.

They moved on to Gwennap, or Guenep as Wedgwood called it, in the heart of the tin and copper mining district. "It abounds greatly with mines. There are no less than 11 fire engines in it [Newcomen steam engines] (or inians as they call them here) and in some parts the grass is totally destroyed, so that it has a very singular, & indeed a very dreary aspect. We found the Growan clay here in great abundance, and of a very fine white colour." They reached Redruth, decided not to stop and set off on what was to prove an alarming journey to Penzance.

Being strangers, we did not know that we had an arm of the sea to pass through with the chaises, and some time after it was quite dark, the open sea, as it appeared to us, presented itself right before us. When we came to the water edge, the boys who drove us said there was no other way but to go through it, that they did not know the tide would be in, nor did they know its depth now it was in; besides, they said, there were plunge holes made by the tide, which would take the chaise almost overhead, in places when it was good sand before the tide. In this dilemma, we ordered our two chaises abreast, to call a council, and whilst we were debating this matter over, whether we should turn back to Redreuth, or what we should do, a man came up on horseback, who said he was going to St. Ives, & must cross the water, that he would go before the chaises as far as his way & ours lay together, & give us directions for the remainder of this water road, and wisely observed that if we saw him plunge into very deep water, we did not need to follow him. Upon this fortunate circumstance of meeting with a guide, we determined to venture through, and followed the tract he led us, but more from the sound of his horse's plunging in the water, than from any sight we had of him. At last however he stopt, & told us we must then part unless we would go with him to St. Ives, which was many miles out of our way, indeed the whole breadth of this part of the Peninsula for St. Ives lies on St Georges channel, & Penzance to the English channel. Our guide then left us, with directions to go straight on till we came to the opposite shore. We had not gone far before we discovered a vessel, I suppose a barge, right ahead of us. I did not like this appearance, as I thought it impossible for the barge and the chaise to live in the same water. I believe we all now wished heartily to be on either shore, though no one thought proper to express any fears, – but suffered the boys to drive straight on as they had been directed, by which means we passed the barge, and to our great joy got safe to the opposite shore.

The excitements over, they continued on to the very tip of the county, noting many interesting specimens both mineral and animal. "As we approach near the Lands End, the people came out of their little huts to see us, and droll figures, from their dress & singing way of speaking, they appeared to us, and no doubt we were an equal novelty and entertainment to them. I believe most of them make their own clothes, & the little furniture they make use of, themselves." On the return journey he paused briefly to view St Michael's Mount, declared himself unimpressed, and got back to the serious business of the journey. He decided to try and acquire the mineral rights in some land near St Austell. The process of haggling with the farmer was lengthened by the farmer's wife joining in with the not unreasonable argument that land was land but money, as far as her husband was concerned, was just so many pots of ale. The wife lost and Wedgwood secured the rights for a year.

The business completed, they turned for home and Wedgwood had one last chance to raise his head from an inspection of the clay and rocks when, at Glastonbury, they were greeted with a majestic sunset.

But the most truly magnificent scene was still preserved for our nearer approach to the town, which truly beggars all description. It was literally speaking a heavenly one; for the clouds rose out of the sea like immense towers, battlements, rocks, and a thousand fantastic forms, to meet & hail the sun before he dipt into the Western ocean. ... when the last finishing was given to this truly august scene, when the fine lucid gilding was given to these airy forms, by the sun passing behind & shooting his rays through them, it was beautiful and sublime beyond conception.

Poor Wedgwood, there was little enough time in his life to stand and admire. But then, his was not a temperament that allowed for such luxuries. He was not a watcher he was a doer, and however much he might complain about the pressures that kept him moving on, the notes on his Cornish trips show very clearly that the strongest pressures of all came from within himself. On the hills of Dartmoor, the fine view and magnificent scenery could not keep him for long from the much more interesting phenomenon of the flints at his feet. The more romantic side of his nature might appear at times, but it had to take its place and grab such time as it could.

Soon he was back in Staffordshire to receive the congratulations of his fellow potters at the successful opposition to Champion's Bill and their interested inquiries into the results of the Cornish expedition. Wedgwood proposed setting up "an experimental work" in the form of a joint-stock company, to which all the principal potters who had helped with the parliamentary lobby could subscribe, to test the Cornish clays. It was a splendid idea in itself, and one that could have led to wider researches that would have benefited the whole industry. But it was a concept far ahead of its time, and after months of negotiations the whole scheme was abandoned. At least that left Wedgwood free to conduct his own experiments and benefit from the results of importing the growan clay from Cornwall – the clay that is still used in earthenware manufacture.

Apart from his work on the Cornish clays, the year was very much "a business as usual" kind of year, a period of consolidation, of the steady improvement of such promising lines as jasper. Things were well enough in train for the Bentleys to visit Etruria and for the combined families to go off visiting in Derbyshire. Mrs Bentley – "my governess", he called her – remains strangely in the background. For all Wedgwood's encouragement of matrimony before the event, he seems to have taken very little interest after it. "The governess" does not seem to have found very ready acceptance into the circle.

Sukey was the only one of the children to join the party, but Jack got a very full account of it all from his father. As usual with a

Wedgwood excursion, business managed to get mixed up with the pleasure.

> We are surveying a course for a branch from our Canal at Etruria to the West End of Calden Low [the Caldon Canal] by which, if we succeed, our Country will be supplied with Lime at little more than half the price we now pay for it, which will enable us to improve our Land, and the face of our Country very much, and is therefore a great object to us. The course of this intended Canal runs parallel with the road from Leek to Ashbourne for some miles; to view this ground was my principal motive for prefering the Leek to the Cheadle Road.[3]

Wedgwood assumes, as a matter of course, that these matters of business and land improvement will be of interest to a nine-year-old boy. At least he was paying him the compliment of not talking down to him, and he never wrote about matters unless he himself was interested – which, in a way, was a second compliment.

The account continued with a description of the scenic splendours of Matlock, suddenly made popular by the ecstatic writings of the new admirers of the picturesque. They all climbed the rock over-looking the river, where they would stand "and rival the birds in their view of the enchanting scene". Wedgwood took the opportunity for a brief digression to issue a homily on Mr Adam, who had first cut the steps to the top of the rock: "let me here stop a moment to tell you, My dear Boy, that this poor Man – This Adam of Matlock – by a well timed exertion of his ingenuity and industry, has acquired more real fame than many noble Lords, and his name will be remembered with gratitude and respect when theirs are totally forgotten."

What a mixture the boy got in his letters: accounts of lead mines, ore collecting, dances and parties all jumbled up together. Their one disappointment to be recorded was a visit to Cromford to see the new cotton mill built by Richard Arkwright. Here Wedgwood found a manufacturer even more jealous of his secrets than he was himself, and they were flatly refused a glimpse of the new spinning machines. Finally they returned home, leaving Sukey to travel on to London to stay with the Bentleys. "Your poor Sister was a good deal affected when the time came that we must take our final leave of each other. The last farewell was hard to be borne, but she behaved very properly and very affectionately, as I hope my Children will always do." There was a present for Jackey from his sister, and one suspects father's part in the choice – "a beautiful specimen of polished Spar". It might, perhaps, have seemed small compensation to a small boy stuck in boarding school while his sister was off scrambling up crags.

There was a pleasing openness between the children and their father during their younger days – an openness to be found on both sides. Here is Sukey, in London, writing to Wedgwood:

> I hope to here by your next letter that you are all quite got rid of your colds. Mamma told me yours was a navigation cold. At first I was sorry you had begun another navigation then it was hinted that it would keep you know who in London a good while & then as you may suppose I was only sorry that you had got a cold by it. . . .
>
> Do you think a journey to London to Brother Jacky would be disagreeable at Christmas with you. I dont think it would. I will try to make it as little as possible when he comes I shall be very glad to see him if it could be made convenient however I will not set heart on it too much for fear.
>
> I think this is a very long letter & that it is quite time to give over.[4]

If problems did arise in later years, then it was not from want of affection on either side, but from a familiar difficulty – the wish of the father to see his children fit into the moulds he designed for them. One cannot help seeing in the letters to Jackey a correspondence course in matters suitable for a potter-to-be. Sukey was perhaps luckier in that respect – there was no expectation that the girls would ever follow any career.

The following year began badly for Wedgwood with his falling ill and being laid up for a whole month. But typically he put the time to good use by bringing his experiment books into order and indexing them. This still left time to spare for conjecturing about the future, especially considering the possibility of making porcelain. But this line was never followed, and we are left to conjecture in our turn what might have been achieved.

Early in the year an old and most unwelcome face from the past put in an appearance – Voyez. He was found to be selling seals similar in style to the products of Etruria, which of course he was perfectly entitled to do. What, however, was somewhat less defensible was his practice of stamping them "Wedgwood and Bentley", and then selling them at a price much below that of the genuine article. He was, according to Wedgwood, nothing if not a bold forger.

> When he is asked by any Gentleman whilst he is selling his seals why he puts Wedgwood & Bentley upon them, "I borrow and lend with them, he says, when I am out of any particular sorts or they want any that I have, we borrow and lend with each other." So you see, we are on very friendly terms, and it might be a pity to interrupt this mutual exchange of good offices by an Action for Trespass. What do you think of it? I do not know how far this kind of forgery is punishable by Law, but it is not very pleasing, and should in one way or another be contradicted.[5]

After an "impudent" apology, Voyez faded back again into the background and disappears from the Wedgwood story.

In many ways, 1776 was a more eventful year for Bentley than for Wedgwood, and provided a pleasant opportunity for some role-reversing, with Bentley playing the eager innovator and Wedgwood the attentive listener. When he went up to London in April, Wedgwood found his partner deep in plans for a new chapel in Margaret Street, where morality was to be taught rather than any specific creed. This was an idea that had grown and developed since the days of the Octagon Chapel, and it appealed greatly to Bentley. He envisaged a universal liturgy which could be used for all men to worship together. "Are we not all the children of one benevolent parent? Do not Jews and Gentiles, Christians and Mahometans, own his power, his wisdom, and his goodness?" Wedgwood helped with the chapel, but he did not share Bentley's revolutionary zeal and was content, the following year, to deal with his own more modest plan to get a new minister for the Unitarian Chapel at Newcastle to take over from old Mr Willett. Unfortunately, the congregation could not raise enough money to tempt their first choice, Mr Yates, to leave the Warrington Academy. Wedgwood was disappointed.

> Mr. Yates is every thing I could wish, and far more than I ever durst hope for in a Minister at Newcastle; and as we have amongst us upwards of sixty young folks, sons and daughters of subscribers, it is of considerable consequence who we bring amongst them, as a teacher and companion, and I cannot avoid interesting myself very much in the choice.[6]

There is a hint of the underlying reasons behind Bentley's early reluctance to enter into the partnership: he had other dreams of his own. Unlike Wedgwood, he could not see the building of a commercial empire as being sufficient of an objective in itself.

Nevertheless, Bentley did continue to devote the greater part of his energies to business, travelling to Europe to help drum up more trade. "To conquer France in Burslem!" – only a short while ago, this had seemed the impossible dream, the highest of ambitions, and now Bentley was visiting Paris and calmly pronouncing on its imperfections.

> It is a very large city, perhaps about three fourths of the size of London. The houses are all of soft stone, which is white when fresh, and very soon extremely black and dirty. The streets are narrow, dirty, and badly paved. . . .
>
> Many of the buildings are *grand*, but few of them *beautiful*. The famous Louvre is an incomprehensible jumble of magnificence and meanness – of grandeur and bad taste – and ruins. The Seine, at Paris, is but a poor dirty river. Their bridges are not worth speaking of. Their gardens are in the old Dutch taste, Kensington gardens are infinitely superior to the Tuilleries or Versailles. The palace of Versailles merits the same character as the Louvre. Some parts of it, both within and without, are very magnificent, while others are only fit to excite disgust. The insides of their houses and palaces are almost all in the same style: as much glass and gilding as they can either afford or contrive to put into them: – and nothing can be uglier and more tasteless than their chimney pieces, which are all alike, from Calais to Versailles.[7]

So much for France. In general, overseas trade was expanding, but Wedgwood and Bentley were plagued by the unreliability of the agents who conducted their business. Du Burk of Amsterdam was the worst offender, and it was only when he was finally sent to prison that Wedgwood was able to retrieve the stock he had sent to Holland. There were similar staff problems nearer home, where Mather continued to give trouble, drinking heavily and neglecting the enamel works. Wedgwood considered sacking him but eventually, after being given a severe drubbing by Bentley, he was allowed to stay. One cannot help wondering whether Wedgwood was simply unfortunate, whether the world was full of rogues, or whether Wedgwood's judgement of human character was rather badly at fault. Du Burk, Voyez and Mather were but three among many in whom Wedgwood put his trust, only to find that trust abused. It seems most likely that there was a general lack of probity in most eighteenth-century business dealings. The many cases of blatant patent infringement, industrial spying, denigration of competitors and dictatorial attitudes towards employees hardly combined to create an atmosphere of trust. We even find, for example, in the correspondence between Etruria and W. Brock, the agent in Dublin, that Wedgwood himself regularly evaded duty on his goods by concealing the more expensive ornamental items in crates of useful ware, or by putting small items inside ewers and jugs. Given such a general climate, the frequent individual lapses seem less surprising.

The years 1776 and 1777 might not seem especially eventful, but the latter did see two events of some significance. At last, after eleven years of work, the Trent and Mersey Canal was opened throughout its length and Etruria at last had its waterway connection with both the east and west coasts. It was an event that provided immense satisfaction to the canal's chief promoter, though even he found some of the eulogies on the new canal somewhat startling. The most curious was a poem sent by a local enthusiast, the Rev. Sneyd, which was as notable for its length as its clumsiness. The ecclesiastical poet describes how, when walking along the towpath, he was surprised – as who would not be – by the goddess of the waterway rising from its depth.

Up rose the guardian – genius of the wave
I knew the goddess by her sweeping vest
And dewy locks that hung in ringlets loose.

Then followed the mandatory plaudits to Commerce and Britannia. But Wedgwood's literary education had come a long way from his early uncritical enthusiasm for works such as Thomson's, and though he tried to avoid giving offence, disguising his criticism by explaining that he is only saying what other critics might say, he clearly enjoyed penning the "critic's criticism":

> What a change. What a country you have painted. No object can withstand the magic of your pencil. . . . Even our dirty tiny canal no sooner becomes the subject of your creative muse, than its stagnant ochery surface, which before reminded us of one of the plagues of Egypt, becomes a gentle current – glossy stream – with *flowering banks*. Our long, naked boats, groaning under their sooty burthens, which yesterday looked like so many half-burnt masts scraped from a wreck, are now bedecked with rustling canvas. . . . Nothing but gentle Zephyrs – Dryads & Naiads! – Blest abodes! Woodlands & Spacious lawns surround us – Ha-Ha-ha.[8]

Wedgwood needed no Naiads to praise his canal; he knew its worth.

And finally, to complete the happenings of the year, Tom Byerley came home, his various dreams of a more glamorous life finally faded, to take his old place in the pottery business. Here, at last, was one man who was amply to justify Wedgwood's patience and trust.

[13]

The Children

As the children grew older, Wedgwood took an active interest in two particular aspects of their lives: their education and their health. As the former depended so much on the latter, that had necessarily to be his first concern. Sally Wedgwood bore the last of her eight children, Mary Anne, in 1778: one child had already died in infancy and the health of the rest was a constant preoccupation of the parents.

Sukey was old enough now to take regular long holidays away from her parents, usually staying with the Bentleys, who had settled in Chiswick. At the end of 1777 she went, for a change, to stay with Richard Lovell Edgeworth and his wife. He sent back reports likely to swell any proud parental bosom. Wedgwood's was suitably swelled: "We have received a very friendly letter from Mr. Edgeworth wherein he assures us that we may depend upon his sincerity in telling us that our daughter possesses an extremely good solid understanding, and is capable of learning any thing we may please to teach her, and, so far as he can judge, has the strongest desire to improve herself and acquire proper habits, and that her obliging behaviour and good disposition give much pleasure to himself and Mrs Edgeworth."[1] In March of the following year, however, she was back with the Bentleys and the disquieting news came from Chiswick that Sukey was unwell. Wedgwood made the appropriate comments on the Bentley ability to look after his daughter, but for all that he wanted her back home, and in April she made the long, tiring journey back to Etruria. She arrived in apparent good health, but a few months later she was seriously ill again. The trouble, described as a "bilious fever", began in the September, and a week later Wedgwood was still anxious about her condition.

> My poor girl recovers a little upon the whole, but it is so slowly, and she is so extremely weak and emaciated that I am afraid for her, and sent for Dr Darwin to her this morning. She lies in bed almost constantly, and in that situation is cheerfull, and often merry, but when she is got up for a quarter of an hour, which is generally twice a day, her spirits and strength, what little she has, forsake her, and she seems quite miserable 'till she is put into bed again. I wish I may be able to give you a better account of her than my fears suggest after seeing the Doctor.[2]

Sukey recovered, but the following year it was young Joss's turn to be taken ill and his parents rushed up to his school at Bolton to collect him.

> On my return from Bishton I found a letter from Mr Holland acquainting us that one of our boys (Joss) had been poorly for some days, which they supposed proceeded from some little indigestion, but as the complaint had not yielded to a few days' rest, gruel, and kitchen physic, they thought it better to acquaint us. Upon this intelligence my wife and self set off for this place the next morning and found our little fellow very poorly. I called in Doctor Taylor, who tells me he does not apprehend any danger but thinks the country air, with gentle exercise and a recess from his buseness will be very necessary for him. A puke and some opening physic has had a good effect, but there is still a considerable fever upon him. We shall take him with us back to Etruria as soon as he is able to travel, but am afraid that will not be of some days yet.[3]

The journey to Lancashire and back proved more exciting and eventful than the Wedgwoods could have imagined when they set out. Their arrival coincided with the start of one of the most serious outbreaks of rioting that the North of England had seen. Richard Arkwright had only recently established his cotton mill at Cromford in Derbyshire, which being well away from the traditional textile areas met with little hostility. But the new machinery that took cotton spinning out of the home and put it into the factory had come to Lancashire when Arkwright opened a mill at Chorley, and it soon found many imitators. Britain was at war, foreign trade had slumped and the new factories seemed the final blow to the already depressed domestic workers. In October 1779 they rose against the new mills and the new machinery, and Josiah Wedgwood was there to see and record the events.

I wrote to my dear friend last from Bolton, and mentioned the mob which had assembled in that neighbourhood, but they had not then done much mischief; they only destroyed a small engine or two near Chowbent. We met them on Saturday morning, but I apprehend what we saw were not the main body, for on the same day in the afternoon a capital engine, or mill, in the manner of Arcrites, and in which he is a partner, near Chorley was attacked, but from its peculiar situation, they could approach to it by one passage only, and this circumstances enabled the owner, with the assistance of a few neighbours to repulse the enemy, and preserve the mill for that time. Two of the mob were shot dead upon the spot, one drowned, and several wounded. The mob had no fire arms and did not expect so warm a reception. They were greatly exasperated and vowed revenge: accordingly they spent all Sunday, and Monday morning, in collecting fire arms and ammunition and melting their pewter dishes into bullets. They were now joined by the D. of Bridgewater's colliers and others, to the number, we were told, of eight thousand, and marched by beat of drum, and with colors flying to the mill where they met with a repulse on Saturday. They found Sir Richard Clayton guarding the place with 50 Invalids armed, but this handfull were by no means a match for enraged thousands: they (the invalids) therefore contented themselves with looking on, whilst the mob completely destroyed a set of mills valued at £10,000.

This was Monday's employment. On Tuesday morning we heard their drum at about two miles distance from Bolton a little before we left the place, and their professed design was to take Bolton, Manchester, and Stockport in their way to Cromford, and to destroy all the engines, not only in these places, but throughout all England. How far they will be able to put their threats into execution time alone can discover.[4]

He narrowly missed seeing the rioters in Bolton but Jackey, left behind, took up the story and Wedgwood passed on his account to Bentley:

By a letter from Bolton I learn that the mob entered that place on Tuesday the 5th when we had left it not more than an hour. They contented themselves with breaking the windows, and destroying the machinery of the first mill they attacked, but the next, the machinery being taken away, they pulled down the building and broke the mill wheel to pieces. They next proceeded to Mr Keys of the Folds, and destroyed his machine and water wheel and then went to work with the lesser machines, all above so many spindles: I think 24. When they had completed their business at Bolton, I apprehend they went to their homes. Jack only says things are quiet now, and that 100 of the Yorkshire militia are come to defend them. I hope the delusion is ended and that the country may be in peace again.[5]

In fact, the rioting died down and the march to Cromford never occurred. Sir George Saville arrived with three companies of militia and Arkwright, who had turned his Derbyshire mill into a miniature arsenal, was left in peace.

Wedgwood's attitude to the riots was much what one would expect from a manufacturer of that time. There was a strange kind of quasi-religious belief that changes in economic conditions were divinely inspired and that to fight against such forces was a form of impiety. At his most generous Wedgwood could only refer to this wish to reverse processes of change as "a delusion". Looking back with the advantage of hindsight, it is easier for us to see that the changes were indeed inevitable, in the sense that once begun the changes were pushed through by forces far more powerful than any that the opposition could muster. Yet we can at least understand the feelings of a family faced with starvation, seeing work taken from their homes and their families and given to strangers in the new mills. But for Wedgwood – and he was by no means alone in his attitude – such matters did not enter into his consideration. He could not see them as men and women driven by poverty to take desperate measures: they were simply "the mob", or even as he once referred to them "the enemy". Mistaken the rioters may have been, but they deserved more than the blank incomprehension and implacable hostility of Josiah Wedgwood and the other great manufacturers.

Among all this excitement, there was still young Josiah to be got home, and his brother Tom was added to the party when it was discovered that he too was far from well. The cause of all these ailments was diagnosed to be the same as in the case of Sukey – school. The food was bad, the rooms stuffy, and, in general, whatever benefits the minds of the younger Wedgwoods might be receiving, their bodies were being made to suffer. Diagnosing the cause of the illness was not quite the same thing as prescribing a cure, however, and in any case the eventual solution of the problem had to be put to one side for there were even more pressing problems to be dealt with. Mary Ann was now ill. The letter in which Wedgwood described her condition is as revealing of the sad state of medical practice as it is of the father's concern. Darwin congratulated Wedgwood that he had the best of modern medicine at his command and had no need to rely on old wives' remedies. But, really, reading of the unlikely diagnosis and incredible treatment, one cannot help feeling that though the old wives might not have done much good they could well have done less harm.

> Our little girl, Mary Ann, breeds her teeth very hardly, and unfortunately several of them are pushing forward at the same time. This brought on convulsions which lasted thirteen hours without intermission the first attack, which was on Friday morning, and when this left her we found she had lost the use of her arm and leg on one side. She had a slight return for about half an hour the last night, but is better again today.
>
> Doctor Darwin was here on Friday with my father and ordered our little girl to be electrified two or three times a day[6] on the side affected, and to be continued for some weeks. We are willing to flatter ourselves that she has received some benefit from electricity already, as she begins to move her arm and leg

a little, and this will encourage us to proceed in the same course. The Doctor gives us great hopes of our poor little girl's limbs being restored, even without the assistance of electric shocks, but apprehends they will hasten the cure and thereby prevent the diseased limbs being shorter than the others which must be the case if they continue long in their present inactive state. We have lanced her gums and keep them open, as the teeth do not yet appear, by means of the sharp end of an ivory modelling tool. I am the electrician upon this occasion which must confine me at home for some time, and my father continues so very poorly that I cannot entertain the least thought of leaving home at present.[7]

Whether because of or in spite of treatment, the poor girl recovered, but she was never in good health. Wedgwood now had time to ponder over the advisability of moving his children away from school and setting up a schoolroom for them at Etruria. It was not an easy problem to resolve. Wedgwood's own education had been hard won, a long process and one that was still continuing. He had become an avid buyer and reader of books, though the latter activity could scarcely keep pace with the former. This resulted in a familiar complaint from the bibliophile's wife – why did he buy new books when he had not read the old books, and where were they all supposed to go? The result of this orgy of learning was that Wedgwood had become a great enthusiast for education and he was torn between the conviction that education was better supplied in the school than in the home, and the very evident fact that the conditions in the school were undermining the health of the children. In the end there was no real question over which direction he had to take, as he had no wish to be the father to a brood of well lettered invalids. Now there only remained the other difficult question of what form education in the Etrurian schoolroom should take.

Wedgwood, like many a father, had decided views on what the future should hold for his children – the male children, that is, since there was no question in those days, long before female emancipation, of a career for the women in the family. Jack, he decided, was to be a gentleman farmer and Joss and Tom were to take over the family business. The children did not, with the exception of Joss, follow the lines laid down by father, but those were his intentions and it was with those intentions in view that their education was planned. The advice of friends was sought and both Bentley and Darwin were consulted. But such thorny questions as the need to learn Latin were discussed at length: Wedgwood was at first unconvinced of the need for a classical education among businessmen, but Bentley finally convinced him to change his mind. Teachers were employed, including a French prisoner of war, M. Potet, who Darwin declared was "very well qualified to teach his own language". The curriculum being decided, the school plan was laid down by the head of the household.

Masters for our school.

French and drawing master: A French prisoner from Lichfield who has got his exchange but chuses to remain in England with an agreeable situation.

Latin master: Mr Byerley, and in his absence Mr Lomas.

Writing and accounts: Mr Swift.

Scholars, who are to be attended at their own houses.

Susan, John, Josiah, Thomas and Kitty Wedgwood.

With three boys and a girl at our Mr T. Wedgwood's.

Two of our young clerks, one of whom may perhaps be kept here as a reserve to be sent to Greek Street if wanted, and therefore must learn to speak the language.

These to attend the master at his own rooms, morning and evening.

One day's schooling for our own five scholars:

Rise at 7 in winter, when I shall ring the school bell, and at 6 in summer.

Dress and wash half an hour.

The boys write with Mr. Swift one hour along with Mr T. Wedgwood's (if I approve of company) in some room fitted up for the purpose at the works.

The little girls an english lesson with their nurse *in the school*, which happens to be a room near the nursery. I would instil an early habit of *going to school at stated times* in the youngest of our scholars, as it will make it so much easier to them by as much as it seems a necessary and connected part of the routine or business of the day. My young men are quite orderly in this respect since I let them know that it was indispensible, and they are very good in keeping my eleventh commandment – *Thou shalt not be idle.*

Breakfast – as school boys.

From 9–10 French.

From 10–11 Drawing.

From 11 to 1 Riding or other exercise which will include gardening, Fossiling, experimenting etc. etc.

Susan fills up these intervals with music besides her exercise.

From 1 to dinner at half past 1 washing etc. in order to be decent at table.

Half past 2 Latin one hour.

Then french one hour, and conversation in the same, in the fields, garden or elsewhere as it may happen half an hour, to 5 o'clock.

From 5 to 7, exercise, bagging, etc.

At 7 Accounts, one hour – Supper, and to bed at 9. The little lasses I had forgot they must have two more english lessons in the school, and Kitty as much french as she can bear.[8]

It all sounds slightly heavy going, especially for the younger children, but Wedgwood brought a lot of humanity and affection to his role of educator. We saw in earlier letters how he encouraged Jack in his "fossilising", and he showed the same interest in his daughters. He tried to make education appealing to the children, to rouse their enthusiasm. In March 1780 he went on a visit to London and sent back to Kitty a long description of his journey.[9] But it was more than a mere description – it was a lesson in geography, English, morality and any other subject that could be fitted in. Some of the sermonizing may seem leaden, but there is so much honest feeling in it, such sympathy of father for daughter, not least in his understanding of the disappointment a little girl would feel at not going on an exciting journey. It is worth remembering when reading these extracts from what is, after all, a very long and quite complicated letter that Kitty was still only five years old. There were clearly no illiterates at the Etrurian school:

A short History of A Long Journey to London
From a pappa in Town – to his good child at home.

27th March 1780

My dear Kitty,

   Should you like to have come to London with me? I dare answer for you that you would like to take a journey with your pappa, to see new places, and learn many things which you do not know at present, especially when the weather is so fine as it has been since I left home. You would like, I know, to see the hedges and trees beginning to put on their new spring clothes of leaves, buds, & flowers, of various colours, green, yellow, red, white, blue, purple, and shades of different hues for which there are no names. You would like to hear the pretty birds singing, and see the little lambs frisking and playing in the fields as you passed along – But all this you may see at home, and your sister Sukey can tell you what a long, long way it is to London, and how sadly she used to be tired in coming hither when she was a bigger girl than you. But as you could not travel with me all this long journey, you will perhaps like, the next to that, to hear how I travelled, & what I met with upon the road.

   Come along then, my dear little companion, and you may invite your sister Sally to travel with us in this way. I will not take you too far at a time. You may rest a while when you are weary, and we will call every resting place a *Stage*, or a *chapter;* and the first shall end here, to give you time to put on your riding-dresses and mount your horses.

Chapter the Second

Are you both ready? – very well – we will only go to Stone this stage, but we must first call at Newcastle, & bid your aunt Byerley farewell. – Your mamma & sister Sukey, you know, went with me to Stone, but your cousin Byerleys asked if they were going with me all the way; so your sister, who you know is a funny girl, took the hint, and bid them farewell as if she was going in earnest. Your mamma joined in the joke, & away we drove towards Trentham.

   Trentham is a village & not a market town – you know the difference between a village & a market town. At Trentham there is a large fine house belonging to Lord Gower, with a garden, – and a park with bucks, does, and deer in it, – a large pool of water, with fish in it, – pike, trout, perch, – & swans swimming on it. I will tell you a story of a swan and a pike in this pool.

A swan was trying to catch some fish, for they eat fish when they can catch them, – and putting its long neck and head under water for that purpose, a pike, who was as hungry as the swan, saw the head and neck poking in the water, & thought it would make him a fine dinner; he came nearer & nearer, and at last swallowed up the head and got it into his throat, but he could neither swallow the whole body of the swan, nor part with its head again, so the pike was choaked, & the swan smothered, and they were both taken out dead together.

After this somewhat chilling anecdote he described reaching "a barren common".

I will tell you some of its uses. Do you love mutton? This common is covered with sheep, and mutton you know comes from sheep. Do you love lamb? These sheep bring lambs every year. Wool of which our clothes are made, and the blankets which cover our beds & keep us warm in winter, all come from the sheep & lambs; and the sheep of these barren commons make the finest wool & the sweetest mutton. – Do you love rabbit? They live & make their houses here, and these commons feed them ready for our table – Do you love clean & dry gravel walks? This common is full of the best gravel, which makes the hardest and nicest roads – so you see we must not be too hasty in saying a thing is good for nothing because it happens not to be pretty, or to please us in all things.

Later he described a visit to the Sparrow family at Bishton.

Mrs. Sparrow says she lives in the garden, & looks after the trees, & is quite delighted with seeing them in the spring, & watching them every day to grow, bud, & blossom, & put out their leaves, – the currants & gooseberries, the rasberries, the vines, apricots, peaches, nectarines, cherries, & plums, one after another, and her face looks as healthy & red as a cherry, by being

One of Flaxman's illustrations of Homer demonstrating the splendid clarity of his design work which made him so invaluable to Wedgwood

so much amongst them – Mrs Sparrow is so fond of the garden, that she has made her house into one, and has various bulbous-rooted flowers in full blow, in the windows and other places. Your sister Sukey will tell you what these are, & how they are to be managed, and if you little folks wish to have such a garden in the house another year, for it is now too late for this, I will give you flower pots and roots for the purpose.

Bishton is a very pretty place. The river Trent, and the canal, are both within view from the door, and both full of fish. We had some of them to dinner, and as you love to learn things, I will now tell you a good way of cooking small fish, which I have learnt upon this journey.

First grate a quantity of white bread, then beat some eggs in a cup with a wooden spoon; scale the fish, and gut & wash them ready for frying; then dip them in the beaten egg, roll them well in the crumbs or grated bread, and lay them a while upon a clean cloth before they are put into the frying pan. Fry them afterwards, but not in too much butter, and they will be brown, & crisp, & very nice.

At Ridgeley, he found the best shop shuttered and this gave an excuse to set out that fundamental of the manufacturer's creed – the virtue of hard work. The unfortunate shopkeeper who had once been so successful could have made his fortune, "but instead of this, all his goods are sold to pay his debts, and he is obliged to leave his house, his home, and friends, and dares not be seen for fear of being sent to jail.

"What a sad change! It is worth while to stop a little, to enquire how it happened – It was because he *played too much*, – and *worked too little*."

So the story of the trip to London continued, each event providing an opportunity for another lesson. It is interesting, however, to notice that Wedgwood did not just dish out homilies, he made suggestions for practical work – starting a garden, cooking a meal – and it was always the sort of practical work that would have been fun for a small girl.

Another example of Wedgwood the educator can be found in a play[10] written for Sukey and Kitty, where the same idea of using incidents to draw morals is used. It takes the form of a dialogue during a walk to Newcastle. Kitty, after being told which towns are in which directions, asks how she can find the different compass points. Sukey replies:

> *Sukey:* Look at Mrs Barbauld's pretty book when you come home – and that will tell you. Have you not read that part of her book where she teaches Charles to find them out?
>
> *Kitty:* Yes, I think so, but I have forgot how it was.
>
> *Sukey:* I wonder you have. You should not forget what you read. Learn it once more very well, and you will never forget it. . . .
>
> [The short play ends with this unlikely dialogue:]
>
> *Sukey:* Shall I hear you a french lesson as we go.
>
> *Kitty:* If you please sister, I should like to say a lesson out of doors very well.

Wedgwood seldom missed an opportunity to provide a little extra education for his children. Even in his ordinary chatty letters to them he underlined certain words which they were then expected to translate into French. Considering the hectic life that he was still leading, and the ever present pressures of business, there is something very pleasing in finding that he not only took an interest but such a very active interest in their education. His rather heavy-handed moralizing may be out of favour with modern educators, but his technique of using stories and plays to suggest new projects and new directions for work are very much in line with present-day theories. As in his manufacture, so in his school, Wedgwood was ahead of his time.

[14]

End of a Partnership

THE late seventies were dominated for all manufacturers by the war in America, which was steadily involving the rest of Europe and having a bad, if not disastrous, effect on trade. Throughout the campaign the British Government showed exactly the same muddled incompetence that it had shown in the years leading up to the war. All the most dire prophecies of the pro-Americans were coming true. They, and Wedgwood was among their number, continued to show considerably more common sense than either the King or his ministers. Lord North proposed, years too late, to grant the tax concessions that had been at the root of the conflict. But the Americans had received recognition for their nationhood from the French. What would have been a major concession three years before was meaningless in 1778. Wedgwood expressed the scorn that many felt over North's pathetic attempts at reconciliation.

> I thank my dear friend for his good letter of the 25th ultimo and agree with him entirely and heartily, that somebody should be made to say distinctly what has been the object of the present most wicked and preposterous war with our brethren and best friends. You will see by my last that I had the same ideas upon this subject, and I have not yet seen a paper in the public prints, nor a speech in the house, that has handled this recantation at all to my satisfaction, nor made that use of it to expose the absurdity, folly, and wickedness of our whole proceedings with America which the minister's confessions and concessions have given

ample room for. You will perhaps say that the minister has done all this so fully and effectually himself that he has left no room for his friends in the minority to assist him. Something of this kind may be the case, but some of the most violent tories here abuse him most heartily, and kindly offer me their assistance in that line to any extent.[1]

So North's offer was rejected and the war went on, to the dismay of Wedgwood and his friends. It had brought Wedgwood one benefit, however, for it had driven Tom Byerley back from America. He returned a more serious and sober young man than the one who had left to teach or to act or to trade or to do whatever else held the fancy of the moment. He rejoined his uncle in the pottery business and was to prove one of its most valuable members. This might appear a small glimmer in such surroundings of general gloom but, in fact, the general economic condition did not show itself in the production of Etruria. This proved on the contrary to be a period of the very highest artistic achievement for Wedgwood and Bentley. The modellers Hackwood and Flaxman were at the peak of their powers, and jasper was being constantly improved so that now large plaques could be made for use in interiors as chimneypiece centres. Jasper was seen as an admirable complement to the architectural work of Adam and the furniture of Sheraton. It continued in use for the more familiar vases, urns and medallions. It was at this time that Flaxman produced the most famous of all his designs, the "Dancing Hours" figures, and he had already produced another design which perhaps more than any other caught the mood of classicism at its most perfect – the "Apotheosis of Homer". The vase incorporating the design was made in 1784, but the design itself is of an earlier date and it received the ultimate accolade of praise by Sir William Hamilton.

I have had the Pleasure of receiving safe your delightful Bas relief of the Apotheose of Homer, or some celebrated Poet indeed it is far superior to my most sanguine expectation, I was sure that your industry would produce in time something excellent in the way of Basreliefs from the specimens I saw before I left England but I realy am surprised & delighted in the highest degree with this proof of the hasty strides you have made towards perfection in your art. ... Your Basrelief astonishes all the artists here, it is more pure & in a truer Antique Taste than any of their performances tho' they have so many fine models before them.[2]

This was triumph indeed for Flaxman, for Jasper and for Wedgwood – a triumph too for Bentley, who had set Wedgwood in this particular path. If one looks at the jasper vase it seems indeed to represent a "truer antique taste" – the crisp white modelling stands out against the blue, the delicate curves of drapery and the poet's lyre echo the curves of the vase itself and the winged Pegasus seems to add to the feeling of lightness as though it would actually lift the whole piece bodily from the earth. The elements combine so perfectly together that it could well be termed the Apotheosis of Wedgwood.

The chance of a new type of collaboration between artist and potter came in the late 1770s.[3] George Stubbs, famous as a painter of animals, especially horses, had become interested in the idea of painting in enamel but was unimpressed by the results obtained by painting on the conventional copper plates. Bentley suggested that he approach Wedgwood to discuss the possibility of using enamels on earthenware plaques. Wedgwood agreed with some enthusiasm, though that enthusiasm must soon have begun to falter, if only slightly, as the difficulties of firing the large tablets that Stubbs wanted became apparent. It is not clear exactly when the collaboration began, but at the end of 1777 we find Wedgwood writing, rather tetchily: "My compliments to Mr. Stubbs. He shall be gratified, but large tablets are not the work of a day."[4]

Indeed they were not, but early in 1778 there was the first success and a plaque was successfully fired. In spite of that hopeful sign, however, there were more troubles ahead.

When you see Mr. Stubbs pray tell him how hard I have been labouring to furnish him with the means of adding immortality to his excellent pencil. I mean only to arrogate to myself the honor of being his *canvas maker* But alass this honor is at present denied to my endeavors, though you may assure him that I will succeed if I live a while longer undisturbed by the french.[5]

So the experiments went on into 1779, when again there were only small successes, but they were successes enough to make it worth while for Stubbs to visit Etruria. While there, he was engaged to paint a family portrait. This may have been partly a wish to have a portrait by Stubbs, but as the experiments on Stubbs's plaques had taken so long and proved so costly, Wedgwood might well have been looking for a way to get some payment, if not in coin of the realm then in paint on canvas. The potter and the painter turned out to have rather different views on how the Wedgwood family should be portrayed, and it seems that the painter won. It looks as though Wedgwood might have had his own way over the very right-hand side of the painting, where he and Sally are shown sitting by a tree with a basalt vase at their side and a kiln can be seen smoking in the distance. For the rest, it is a competition for attention between the horses and the Wedgwood children, with the horses emerging as clear winners. The figures of Sukey and Joss have some vitality, Tom and Jack rather less and the young girls show all the vivacity of rag dolls. Wedgwood was never happy with the painting and one sympathizes with his views. But, for all its faults, it does give us a picture of the whole Wedgwood family in the summer of 1780 as they appeared to one of the leading artists of the age. It adds faces to familiar names. It also shows us Wedgwood not as a businessman but as a prosperous country gentleman in his estate.

After the long initial period of trial and experiment, Wedgwood at last succeeded in making the large tablets and Stubbs produced some exceptionally fine works, including individual portraits and other, more ambitious subjects. The collaboration continued right up to Wedgwood's death. It is a story of painstaking research on the part of one man matched by a growing confidence in the use of a new medium by the other. It was, as the organizers of the Tate Gallery's 1974 exhibition of the work called it, a "unique alliance".

Stubbs was not the only artist Wedgwood was considering as a possible portraitist for the family. He was also in touch with Joseph Wright of Derby, a painter who in many ways was better suited than was Stubbs to the task of picturing a manufacturer. Wright already had a considerable reputation, based largely on his original treatment of lighting in the paintings. He often chose scientific and industrial subjects, showing them lit by a single source of artificial light. It was, inevitably, Bentley who first suggested Wright in 1778, when the painter had six works on show at the Royal Academy.

Wedgwood however was somewhat anxious at the prospect of having two eminent artists at Etruria at the same time. He was spared the problem. Wright wrote to Wedgwood in July 1779 to report that he had been away on "a ramble for my health" but had caught a cold and was unable to leave home. The connection however was made, Wright and Wedgwood remained in touch, and later Wright was to paint a number of canvases for Wedgwood.

There was one more important development in this period: the introduction of a new ware. To the deep disgust of Wedgwood, who remarked tartly that some people would get tired of the company of the archangel Gabriel if they saw too much of him, patrons began to complain about the lack of novelty in Queen's ware. The creamy white was no longer as acceptable as it had once been, and Wedgwood set out to provide an alternative. One obvious answer was to make use of the Cornish clays, but here he had the problem of using them in a way that he did not infringe Champion's patent – that is, by not making a transluscent ware. Wedgwood was successful, and introduced a trace of cobalt blue into the glaze. He realized long before modern detergent-makers reached the same conclusion, that for some reason a touch of blue can convince people that they are looking at something "whiter than white". Wedgwood wrote to Bentley asking for suggestions for a name for the new ware and then sent more details, explained the difficulty of avoiding the appearance of producing china in the Champion manner.

> You wish to see the babe before you baptize it, and kindly warn me to beware of making china. I find to my grief that I cannot make any great improvement in my present body but it will be china, though I have endeavoured all in my power to prevent it. However to give the brat a name you may set a cream-color plate and one of the best blue and white ones before you, and suppose the one you are to name another degree whiter and finer still, but not transparent, and consequently *not china*, for transparency will be the general test of china.[6]

Eventually a name was found and the baby was duly baptized "pearl white". It was popular enough but never matched the spectacular success of Queen's ware.

Tom Byerly, Wedgwood's nephew and later partner, modelled in sober middle age – very little hint here that he was once a wild and wayward young man.

Wedgwood produced hundreds of these cameos for the Society for the Suppression of the Slave Trade – they could be thought of as early examples of campaign buttons.

A centre for the fashionable to gather – Wedgwood's London showrooms.

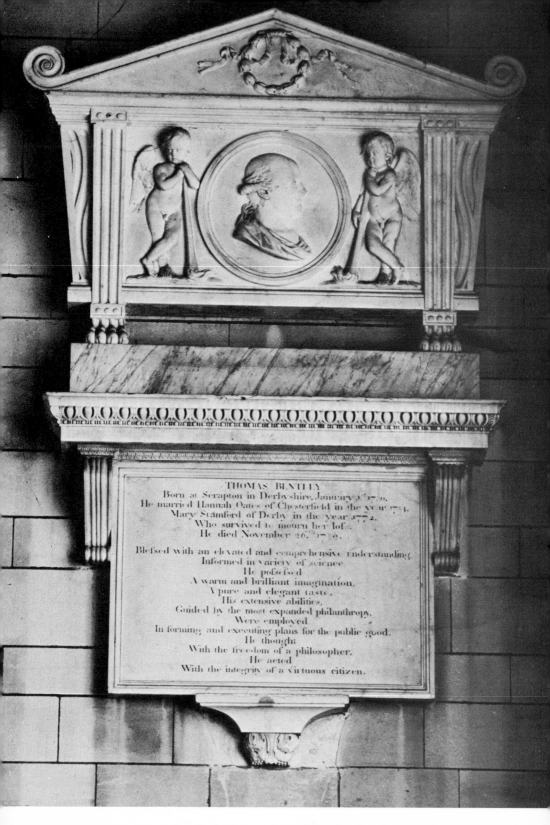

THOMAS BENTLEY
Born at Scrapton in Derby shire, January 1 1730.
He married Hannah Oates of Chesterfield in the year 1754.
Mary Stamford of Derby in the year 1772.
Who survived to mourn her loss.
He died November 26, 1780.

Blessed with an elevated and comprehensive understanding.
Informed in variety of science
He possessed
A warm and brilliant imagination.
A pure and elegant taste.
His extensive abilities,
Guided by the most expanded philanthropy,
Were employed
In forming and executing plans for the public good.
He thought
With the freedom of a philosopher.
He acted
With the integrity of a virtuous citizen.

Bentley's memorial in Chiswick Church.

There were other changes at Etruria, but they concerned people rather than pots. Swift, a steady and reliable figure among so many unsteady and unreliable employees with whom Wedgwood was cursed, had hit on the idea of going into business on his own account. He bought a pub in Burslem and went into a partnership in a pot works – he soon grew tired of the former and lost money at the latter. Wedgwood, pausing only to remind everyone that that was exactly what he had said would happen in the first place, welcomed the prodigal back. "I was afraid this poor man's mind was debauched by his situation and connections, but hope he may be still pretty sound, and I will endeavour to give him stronger motives for continuing in virtuous habits than he may meet with for falling off from them."

Tom Byerley, that other returned prodigal, was set to work as the concern's first commercial traveller. He set off early in 1779 with the somewhat unromantic brief of selling inkpots in the north of England. This early representative found the familiar problems that were to plague his later counterparts – the frustrations of travel and the sales resistance of customers. Of a journey to Wigan he wrote: "I have got this far upon my journey which hitherto has been attended with some unfortunate incidents, such as the shattering to peices nearly of my vehicle. . . . of all bad Towns this is surely the worst. Four Shopkeepers declare to one that there is not a man in it of spirit enough to give 18*d* for an inkpot."[7] At the end of the trip he had notched up sales of £125 16*s* 7*d* and an expenses bill of £7 9*s* 9*d*, which he acknowledged was a little high. Nevertheless the venture was deemed sufficiently successful for him to set off again, this time towards Worcester to sell inkpots and, to a select few, vases. Byerley had been fully accepted back.

Wedgwood in Etruria was more fortunate with his staff than was Bentley in London. Mather again went astray.

I am much grieved to find by my dear friend's last letter that he is still tormented with that plague to our enamel works, and foe to all order, Ben Mather. We have both of us suffered sufficiently, and much more than sufficiently, for such an abandoned worthless wretch, who has nothing of the man left but his form, and who is self devoted to destruction whither he would have brought us too, if we had depended only upon that branch of business with the conduct of which he has been entrusted.[8]

Mather was at last sent on his way.

Wedgwood remained in remarkably good spirits as the seventies passed and the eighties began, even though the new decade showed no signs of a lifting of the general political and economic gloom. He had sufficient confidence to begin planning further expansions at Etruria and at the same time he began taking a more active interest in politics. In April 1780 the Society for Constitutional Information was founded, the first of many societies aimed at promoting parliamentary reform, and the forerunner of the London Corresponding Society. Wedgwood very soon expressed his approval. "I wish every success to the Society for Constitutional Information and if I was upon the spot should gladly not confine myself to wishes only. If at this distance I can in any way promote their truly patriotic designs, either by my purse or my services, they are both open to you to command as you please."[9] He favoured annual Parliaments and an increased suffrage and though he was too far from London to play a very useful part in the Society, his friend Bentley became a member.

Wedgwood did however have a chance to play a more active role when Lord North went to the country in September 1780. Not that there was much doubt about the issue locally, where the parliamentary seats were handed out by Lord Gower; but elsewhere there were stern battles to be fought. In Stafford the election appears to have been unusually corrupt even by eighteenth-century standards. "Matters are not conducted quite so smugly in our county town. They have four candidates and the highest bidder must carry it, for no cornish borough is more venal. Sheridan the manager is one but the inhabitants say to him, Master player you must bring Mr Punch or you have no share here."[10] The Sheridan referred to was the famous playwright, and Mr Punch was a gentleman required not to play but to pay for votes – a performance that met with enough success for Sheridan to be elected. Wedgwood's support was canvassed for Liverpool and he did his best to rally the opposition against the government candidates. It was one occasion when he was sufficiently involved in the political questions of the day to make a thorough effort and to let it be known he was making an effort, whatever offence he might give to potential customers. But for all the outcry against North, the Tories were returned to power or, as Wedgwood himself put it, "a corrupt majority" was back "to compleat the blessed work of the last session".

If the political news was bad other things seemed to be going on much as before. On 12 November 1780 there was a typical letter to Bentley, discussing improvements in ware, passing on a tasty piece of gossip about Edgeworth, who had eloped with a local Stafford-shire girl, Elizabeth Sneyd, and describing a rather surprising meeting with Champion.

> He is come amongst us to dispose of his secret – His patent etc. and, who could have believed it? has chosen me for his friend and confidante. I shall not deceive him for I really feel much for his situation. A wife and eight children (to say nothing of himself) to provide for, and out of what I fear will not be thought of much value here – The secret of China making. He tells me he has sunk fifteen thousand pounds in this gulf, and his idea is now to sell the whole art, mystery, and patent for six, and he is now trying a list of names I have given him of the most substantial and enterprising potters amongst us, and will acquaint me with the event.[11]

That was to be the last letter that Wedgwood ever wrote to his partner and friend. Within a few days, messages came from London that Bentley was ill. "I went to Turnham Green this morning and found Mr Bentley very poorly indeed, he is confined to his Bed since Friday; Sir Richard Jebb was there last night, and Miss Stamford thinks (for I did not see either Mr or Mrs Bentley) seemed a little alarmed. Sir Richard ordered Dr James's Powder to be given, which had its proper effect." Reports continued bad, and Ralph Griffiths sent off a hurried note to Wedgwood: "Our poor friend yet breathes; but alas! it is such a breathing as promises but a short continuance. Almost every hope seems to have forsaken us! I dread the thought of what will be the contents of my next! adieu! R.G."

That was on 25 November, and Wedgwood left at once for London. The following day, Thomas Bentley was dead.

[15]

Wedgwood without Bentley

THE sudden death of Bentley came as an appalling shock to Wedgwood. He was ill for a time but, though he soon recovered his health, he could not again recover the friendship he had known with his old partner.

The influence of Bentley on Wedgwood has often been stressed: his effect on the potter's taste in art, the introductions to notables of the day, the brilliant entrepreneurship that was such an important factor in the growth of the business. Yet that was only part of the story and, in a sense, by the time of Bentley's death it was no longer the most important part. Bentley had set Wedgwood in certain paths and those paths could still be followed, but now there were to be no more exciting new paths opening up. This does not mean that Bentley was responsible for all the innovations of the past few years – far from it. But Wedgwood responded to stimulus. Given a problem, he could worry at it until it was solved and in doing so would often turn up new problems and find new solutions. Bentley, with his drive to keep always in the forefront of taste, set these problems. Wedgwood, of course, had ideas of his own but those ideas often came in a chaotic rush. With Bentley he could put that chaos down on paper, letting the ideas flow straight from brain to hand, and he could do so confident that Bentley would not be deterred by the fine flow of words. He was there to give the responses whenever Wedgwood called. There were other friends, but none with whom there was such complete rapport, such total understanding, none with whom there was so much freedom.

In business matters Wedgwood turned more and more towards the help of Tom Byerley, but Byerley could never be an equal in the way that Bentley had been. In personal matters he moved closer to Darwin. But Darwin was no businessman, no cosmopolitan: he was a doctor who dabbled, albeit successfully, in literature and science, and he was a confirmed provincial. There was much in common between Darwin and Wedgwood – similar interests, common friends – but there was also much that was in direct contrast. Wedgwood had been in the habit of teasing Bentley and other unmarried friends, but what he had wanted for them was a solid, married respectability such as he himself had with Sally and Bentley found with his "governess". He certainly did not encourage Darwin in his behaviour towards women, behaviour that in modern times would probably have seen him struck off the medical register. For Darwin had been called in to attend the children of Colonel Chandos Pole and had promptly fallen in love with Mrs Pole. He wrote verses to her and about her, including this intended farewell to the Pole household:

> Farewell! A long farewell! – your shades among
> No more these eyes shall drink Eliza's charms;
> No more these ears the music of her tongue! –
> O! doomed for ever to another's arms!

Not as it transpired doomed for ever, since in 1780 the Colonel conveniently died, leaving a beautiful and wealthy widow surrounded by a horde of very eligible young men. To everyone's surprise and to the extreme annoyance of the ever hopeful Anna Seward she chose Erasmus Darwin. This continued to annoy Miss Seward so that the bitterness shows even when she was writing some five years after the event:

> Almost five years are elapsed since Dr Darwin left Lichfield. A handsome young widow relict of Colonel Pool, by whom she had three children, drew from us, in the hymenal chain, our celebrated physician, our poetic and witty friend.
>
> The Doctor was in love like a very Celadon, and a numerous young family are springing up in consequence of a union, which was certainly a little unaccountable; not that there was

any wonder that a fine, graceful, and affluent young woman, should fascinate a grave philosopher; but that a sage of no external elegance, should by so gay a lady, be preferred to younger, richer, and handsomer suitors, was the marvel; especially since, though lively, benevolent, and by no means deficient in native wit, she was never suspected of a taste for science, or works of imagination. Yet so it was; and she makes her ponderous spouse a very attached, and indeed devoted wife! The poetic philosopher, in return, transfers the amusement of his leisure hours, from the study of botany and mechanics, and the composition of odes, and heroic verses, to fabricating riddles and charads! Thus employed, his mind is somewhat in the same predicament with Hercules's body, when he set amongst the women, and handled the distaff.[1]

This was all very fascinating for Darwin's friends, but was not the kind of behaviour likely to endear him to the somewhat puritanical Wedgwood. So, although there was much toing and froing between the Wedgwoods and the Darwins, the relationship could never match the closeness of that with Bentley. Even if it had done so, it could never have completely filled the gap left by Bentley's death, for the importance of the Wedgwood–Bentley relationship lay in the fact that they were as much in accord as partners as friends. Something now seemed to have gone from Wedgwood's own personality. One misses the note of easy familiarity; from being an open, eager man he began the descent into an irritable middle age and a curmudgeonly old age. There were no longer brave new ventures to be announced in long enthusiastic letters studded with Wedgwoodian exclamation marks and underlinings. The death of Thomas Bentley diminished the life of Josiah Wedgwood.

Over the next few years, Wedgwood devoted more time to his scientific work and his scientific friends. Priestley was the most important of these, and it was Priestley who was among the first to write to Wedgwood on Bentley's death:

Few of my friends interested themselves so much as he did in the success of my philosophical pursuits, and I shall now feel myself less interested in them myself. For the pleasure of communicating our discoveries is one great means of engaging us to enter upon and pursue such laborious investigations. Indeed every friend we lose (and none of us have *many* so justly entitled to that appellation as Mr Bentley was with respect to me) makes life itself of less value, and prepares us for leaving it with less regret.[2]

Wedgwood corresponded regularly with Priestley and was one of those who, when his patron, Lord Sheldon, suddenly withdrew his support, helped to finance his work by providing 25 guineas a year. Just as importantly, he kept him supplied with ceramic equipment such as retorts and crucibles.

An important step in Wedgwood's own scientific career was taken in 1781 when he employed Alexander Chisholm, who had been assistant to the chemist Dr William Lewis, to teach science to the children. The idea of employing a science teacher grew from a very successful series of lectures given by John Waltire, a well-known popularizer of science, in 1779 which had greatly interested the boys and got Jack "very deep in chemical affinities". In the event, it was Tom who was to prove the scientist among the children, but in the short term it was Wedgwood himself who was the principal gainer from the appointment.

Chisholm was a careful, methodical scientist who was able to bring order into the myriad experiments of Wedgwood. He was able to take Wedgwood's own descriptions of the work and rephrase them in a properly scientific language. He also brought with him a vast accumulation of material in the form of notes, translations of foreign scientific papers, articles and jottings. A glance through Chisholm's commonplace books reveals the astonishing catholicity of interests of the eighteenth-century scientists. One turns from learned treatises on latent heat or Lavoisier's latest work to solemn pronouncements on the benefits of substituting felt for whalebone in ladies' stays.

Wedgwood's main scientific work at this time was concerned with designing a thermometer to measure high temperature. As with all his experiments, the interest grew from a practical problem in the making of pots. As he put it:

Most of these productions of art, which owe their existence to the action of fire, have their beauty and value effectively influenced by the minute deficiencies or excesses of heat; and the artist is frequently precluded from availing himself of the advantages that might result even from his own experiments, where the heat has passed under his eye, by not being able to ascertain the degree of such heat; much more so from those of others, who have no means of communicating to *him* even the imperfect ideas which they have *themselves* of the heat made use of in their operations.[3]

The principle on which the thermometer was constructed was the contraction of clay when heated. Blocks of carefully prepared clay were placed between two converging rods, so that as the blocks shrank they slipped further down into the V. It was highly successful in the special circumstances of the pot works, but was not so easily applied in general use. In the first place, its success depended on an individual judgment in making the clay blocks: "for the formation and adjustment of the pieces require those particular niceties and precautions in the manual operation, which theory will not suggest, and which practice in the working of clay can alone teach". The next problem arose because the thermometer could not be calibrated against any recognized temperature scale, though in practice this did not prove too important. Wedgwood, for example, could make his own scale for the oven temperatures he needed, and the instrument could be used by anyone working with high temperatures who could calibrate it to meet his own requirements.

Whatever its shortcomings, the work on the thermometer impressed the Royal Society. A paper was read to the members in May 1782 and thoroughly discussed as Wedgwood reported to James Watt: "My Thermometer paper was read in the R.S. last Thursday. It underwent the examination of many chemists & philosophers here before that time & they gave it their approbation very fully."[4] Two weeks later Wedgwood was proposed for fellowship of the Society and at the next ballot, in January 1783, he was duly elected. It was a much prized honour.

Wedgwood's concern in national politics declined after the Tory victory in the general election, but in 1783 events brought him back to Westminster as lobbyist for the Staffordshire potters. That was the year which saw the long-awaited end to the war in America, leading to a whole new series of trade treaties and a good deal of scrambling after favourable terms by all the interested parties. The potters were greatly hampered by a variety of regulations, some imposing high duties, others acting as outright bans on imports into certain countries. Lord Gower was a sturdy advocate for the potters and was able to acquire some powerful allies including Pitt, who promised to use his influence in attempting to reduce French duties, stressing "my disposition to promote their interest as far as may be in my power".[5]

The end of the long and ludicrous war was warmly greeted by all manufacturers. The years of declining trade and high provision costs had affected them all and had also affected the working people. By the end of the war there was unrest throughout the country. In the small, well organized trades this could take the form of effective strike action – industrial disputes that fitted the modern pattern. Such action had its effect on other industries, as Wedgwood discovered when the price of gold went up in 1782 for reasons spelt out by his regular suppliers:

> I have sent you a Small Box of Gold and think myself Happy in Having it in my powers to send it the Reason is the Journeyman Gold Beaters have all Quitted Business for near three Weeks and Returned to Business only on Monday Last. Before they left Work they presented a Petition to the masters Stating that their Wages is the Same now as it was fixed at 36 years Ago and that every Necessary of Life is so Considerably encreased in price since that time that they could not support themselves on the present Wages the Masters Refused to Comply with the Request of their Petition and for near three weeks we had no work done. The Journeymen in the Whole trade are but 51 in Number, in Consequence of which at last we were Obliged to Advance their Wages And at a General Meeting of the Whole Trade of the Master Gold Beaters it was Unanimously Resolved to Advance the Price of Leaf Gold.[6]

For most of the poor, however, there was no organization, no planning, only a growing despair as unemployment and low wages were matched by high prices and severe scarcities. Inevitably there were rumours of profiteering, and the 1780s saw a series of riots in which grain was taken from farmers and merchants and then sold off cheaply by the poor themselves. In March 1783 just such a riot broke out in the Potteries, and the troubles reached Etruria itself. Wedgwood was away from home but had a full account of events from the boys.

The trouble began when a crowd started following a boat loaded with grain which had been sent by canal from Manchester. Joss began the story:

> I think they had notice of it from our works, there were several hundreds of them men, women and children who followed it to Long Port & there a man jumping into the boat the boatman cut the rope & with the knife struck at the man, immediately half the mob cried *put him into the canal* which they would certainly have done if some gentleman had not interfered & got into another boat. Then they brought the boat in triumph to this place & lodged the contents in the crate shop: this was between 3 & 5 o'clock this evening. About half past seven four men came up to the house & asked for something to eat & drink as they were to sit up to guard the corn flour &c. John went to them & told them a great deal my mother followed and said some more & then they went off.[7]

The story was taken up by Tom. He described how the master potters, John among them, met to harangue the mob and to raise a subscription to keep up the price of grain. The meeting ended with a reading of the Riot Act.

> An hour gone and they did not disperse. Dr Falkener had got the word "fire" in his mouth when two men dropt down by accident, which stopt him, and he considered about it more. The women were much worse than the men, as for example, Parson Sneyd had got about 30 men to follow him, he huzzaing, but a woman cried: "Nay, nay, that wunna do, that wunna do", and so they turned back again, and it was agreed that the corn taken in the boat should be sold at a fair price.[8]

The ringleaders were taken by the authorities and one, Barlow, was sentenced to death. The riot was over. Wedgwood returned from London to lecture the poor on their behaviour. He printed an address directed not at the rioters themselves but at their children, asking them to repudiate their parents' action. It is not an endearing document. It is yet another example of the inability of Wedgwood, as of most leading manufacturers of the day, to understand the conditions and feelings of the poor. If he had ever stopped to imagine his own reaction on seeing a document published asking his sons to turn against him, he would surely never have produced the pamphlet. His concern at finding violent events virtually on his own doorstep was natural enough, but there is an assumption of superiority in the address that is decidedly unattractive.

He began by rehearsing the arguments of the rioters – provisions were too dear, retailers cheated them and the rich took no notice unless the poor rose in a body to demand action. His answer to the first complaint was the classic response of the eighteenth-century, the gospel of Divine Economic Law.

> It is admitted that provisions are dear: but before any censure and abuse is on this account offered to people who may be as innocent as ourselves we ought first to enquire if the hand of providence is not visible, to all who will see it, in this dispensation; and surely that consideration may be sufficient to stop the most daring man, and induce him to bear with becoming patience his share of the public calamity, and submit quietly to the will of Heaven.[9]

On the second point, he suggested that dishonest retailers should be reported to the authorities and punished by them – one of those statements that sound eminently reasonable until one looks at the results when the poor did attempt to get justice from the magistrates. On the last point, he pointed out that the poor had not attempted to approach him peaceably to ask for relief. Again this sounds reasonable enough until one remembers the fate of Wedgwood's own workers who were foolhardy enough to ask for a rise in wages. But of course Wedgwood had not been thinking of wage rises but of charity. He ended his discourse with a reminder of the old days: "the inhabitants bore all the marks of porverty to a much greater degree than they do now. Their houses were miserable huts; the lands poorly cultivated, and yielded little of value for the food of man or beast, and these disadvantages, with roads almost impassable, might be said to have cut off our part of the country from the rest of the world." He pointed out that wages had risen, housing was better and there were now decent roads. "Industry has been the parent of this happy change." All this is incontrovertible but did not alter the basic fact that the workers in the Potteries were going hungry and that a general growth of prosperity would always be accompanied by a general raising of expectations.

The same year he produced another pamphlet – *An Address of the Workmen in the Pottery on the Subject of Entering into the Service of Foreign Manufacturers*. Wedgwood, the advocate of an open trade in pottery, was the opponent of a similar trade in potters; the writer who preached the inevitability of the prevailing conditions now opposed those who wanted to look for better conditions elsewhere. But Wedgwood did have some powerful arguments on his side. Foreign potters were often heavily subsidized and Wedgwood's ability to compete depended mainly on the superiority of his workmanship. There was a strong suspicion that what was being bought was not a skilled workman but a trade secret.

This pamphlet, then, leaves none of the unpleasant after-taste of the address to the young potters, but it does provide an entertaining glimpse of the extravagant arguments used by eighteenth-century pamphleteers. There were two main recruiting drives to be opposed. The first was from America, and Wedgwood painted an alarming picture of storm-tossed crossings and disease-ridden arrivals with the result that "recruits could not be raised from England sufficient to supply the places of the dead men". An equally alarming future was said to await those looking for happier prospects in France. There they would find that they were used to train up the local who would then take over the works and throw them out to exist on "frogs, hedge-hogs, and the wild herbs of the field". And there would be no escape, for the French would never let them out to tell their ghastly story to the world. "In this foreign land, then, suspected, watched, despised, and insulted, you must continue to the end of your wretched days." The workers, he concluded, would be well advised to stay in England, "a land truly flowing with milk and honey".

Science, politics – and then art. Wedgwood continued to interest himself in painting and painters and he became particularly concerned with Joseph Wright of Derby, who began work on a canvas for him, the Corinthian Maid. The correspondence between the two men is fascinating for the contrast between the robust – not to say downright bawdy – Wright and the rather prudish Wedgwood. In 1782 they began a discussion of the Corinthian Maid. It pleased Wedgwood very much, but some aspects of the painting caused him concern.

> I could not speak to you when I was with the ladies at your house about the particular sort of the drapery of the Corinthian Maid which I liked the least; but finding afterwards that some of the ladies had seen that part of the drapery in the same light with myself, and not being able to wait upon you again, I begged Dr Darwin to mention it to you.
>
> The objections were the division of the posteriors appearing too plain through the drapery and its sticking so close, the truly Grecian, as you justly observe, gave that part a heavy hanging-like (if I may use a new term) appearance, as if it wanted a little shove up, which I only mention in illustration of the term hanging as used above. I do not say that I am *satisfied* with the lover, but that I think it excellent. I had almost said inimitable, and I should quake for every future touch of your pencil there. It is unfortunate in my opinion that the maid shows so much of her back, but I give it as my *opinion* only, with great diffidence, and entire submission to your better judgement. In one word you have been so happy in your figure of the lover that almost any other must appear to disadvantage in so near a comparison. Make her to please yourself and I shall be perfectly satisfied.[10]

Wright replied: "I this morning received your very friendly & polite letter & be assured I shall do everything in my power to make the pictures agreeable to you in every respect. I will cast a further drapery upon the Corinthian Maid which will conceal the Nudity." This was Wright on his best behaviour, for he was not a man who was in the habit of turning a bashful eye on nudity or much else, as this reply to comments on a sketch for a painting of Penelope demonstrates with refreshing vulgarity:

> I am glad you like the disposition of the Groups & composition

of light & shadow. As it was customary among the Antients to make their Statues naked I had designed Ulysses to be so, but being seen nearly in profile, the private parts became too conspicuous for the bed chamber of the chaste Penelope. I therefore made him rest on his bow & put the Quiver in the other hand so as to cross the body & conceal that part which might give offence to our delicate Ladies. I consulted my friend Hayley upon it, he seems to object to it "I am afraid says he, the Quiver crossing the bottom of the Hero's Belly, may to some saucy imaginations produce a ludicrous effect, & make some prophane Wag exclaim, 'Happy is the man that hath his Quiverfull.' "[11]

At a less exalted artistic level – if a somewhat higher social one – there was another new designer who came to collaborate with Wedgwood, Lady Templetown. She was a lady possessed of a good deal of both spare time and talent, and, unlike most aristocratic ladies, she was willing to put the two to good use. Wedgwood, who could be informal and chatty enough when dealing with a Stubbs or a Wright, was reduced to obsequy when dealing with the aristocracy.

Mr. W presents his most respectful compliments to Lady Templetown and is very happy to learn by his nephew Mr Byerley that his attempt to copy in Bas relief the charming groups of little figures her Ladyship was so obliging as to lend him has met with that approbation which he durst not flatter himself with, and is sensible he owes much to Lady Templetown's politeness on this occasion.

Mr Wedgwood is afraid to trespass farther upon the goodness he has already experienced, and is sensible that nothing but experience could justify his expressing a wish to be indulged in copying a few more such groups, but however earnest his wishes may be, he begs to be understood [to express them] with the most perfect submission to Lady Templetown's pleasure.[12]

The designs, such as "Domestic Employment", are delicate but sentimental, very reminiscent of some of the popular eighteenth-century silhouette pictures. They have none of the strength shown in the work of Flaxman on Hachwood, but they do have a certain charm and were immensely popular, and jasper was an ideal medium for them.

The business side of Wedgwood's life during these same years had nothing dramatic to show although there was one event, sad in itself, that demonstrated the continuing attraction of Wedgwood earthenware. With Bentley's death the partnership was necessarily ended, and "his governess" was left with the problem of a shortage of funds but a large stake in a business in which she had no interest and to which she could make no contribution. The somewhat drastic decision was taken to bring the whole thing to an end by selling off all the joint Wedgwood and Bentley stock of ware. The sale took place at Christie's in December 1781 and was widely advertised in advance. "Mr Wedgwood, having had the Misfortune to lose his much-lamented *Friend* and *Partner*, Mr BENTLEY, has found it necessary, in Concurrence with the Wishes of Mrs *Bentley*, the Widow, to dispose of their joint Stock by PUBLIC AUCTION. The Nature and Quality of the Ornaments made by *Wedgwood and Bentley* are generally known throughout *Europe*, as well as in these Kingdoms. ..." The whole affair lasted for eleven days and £169 was taken on the first day alone, which was almost the equivalent of what Wedgwood had calculated as the *annual* turnover for a pot factory at the beginning of the century. One cannot even imagine such a sale today, let alone guess what prices would be reached, for here was every type of ornamental ware produced during the partnership. The crowds thronged in every day so that at the end Wedgwood was able to place another advertisement thanking "the Nobility, Gentry and Publick" for their support. The comfort of Bentley's widow was assured and the continuing demand for Wedgwood ware confirmed.

Other matters were more mundane. There was a nasty little incident at the Trent and Mersey Committee in 1782 when Wedgwood, who was repeatedly elected as chairman, was the subject of a slanderous rumour begun by a Mr Boyers. He accused Wedgwood of corruptly profiting from a bankrupt's estate, but hurriedly retreated as soon as Wedgwood turned on him. The accusations were withdrawn and buried. Other aspects of canal business also took up a good deal of time, and Wedgwood was pushed into another bout of pamphlet writing in 1784. He wrote a long argument about the advisability of the company continuing to run their own boats even though they produced "nine-tenths of the anxious care" of the concern. But this was all time well spent, for the canal continued to prosper and proved to be well worth the many years of battling and struggling for its completion.

Wedgwood himself at this time was beginning to attract the sort of anecdotes that inevitably surround the famous, and many were concerned with his irritable perfectionism. The best known, told by Samuel Smiles, has Wedgwood stomping around the works smashing any pot that fell beneath his standards to the accompaniment of the growl "not good enough for Josiah Wedgwood". His irritability may have been partly caused by ill health, though it could just as likely have arisen from the prescriptions handed out by way of treatment. A typical concoction, recommended by Darwin in 1781, involved boiled bark and tincture of bark, "four or five large spoonfuls twice a day, rhubarb mixed with oil of cinnamon and twenty drops of elixir of vitriol in small beer at mealtimes".

Certainly one cannot blame the state of trade for his bad temper. Tom Byerley, who had taken over the London end of the business, was continually sending letters complaining of lack of sufficient ware to meet demand.

> I am extremely sorry to inform you of a most unhappy event –
> no less than the shutting up of this house. . . . In the bitterness of
> my vexation and disappointment you must allow me to say that
> either the manufactory has not produced a sufficient quantity of
> these articles, or you have sold them to others in prejudice to us
> your best customers – Seriously – No man reading a letter
> that brought him an account of this loss of half his property by a
> Storm at Sea could be more shocked than I was at finding no
> RP dishes in the Invoice Received to day.[13]

There was an equal demand from visiting merchants from overseas. The days of slack trade seemed to be ending.

The first half of the 1780s, then, saw Wedgwood with new honours and an expanding trade. What was lacking was the old drive for experiment and development. Bentley was sorely missed.

A rather fanciful representation of the sarcophagus where the Portland vase was found. The scroll shows a diagram of the vault, while the inscription gives due acknowledgment to Sir William Hamilton, who brought the vase to England.

Wedgwood's copy of the Portland vase. He regarded this as his greatest single achievement.

Sacred to the Memory of
JOSIAH WEDGWOOD, F.R.S. and S.A.
Of Etruria in this county.
Born, August 1730.   Died January 3rd. 1795.
Who converted a rude and inconsiderable
Manufactory into an elegant Art and
An important part of National Commerce.

[16]

Masters and Slaves

IT had long been Wedgwood's dream that the manufacturers of Britain would combine to speak together with a united voice, a voice too strong for even the unreformed Parliament of rotten boroughs and privilege to ignore. He had been unable to arouse much enthusiasm for his campaign to prevent skilled workers emigrating, but new opportunities arose in 1785 when Pitt put forward his plans for an Irish Commercial Treaty.

Ireland had suffered appallingly from its years of English rule, or rather misrule: absentee landlords, a peasantry living always on the brink of starvation, a corrupt legislature and economic dependence – a sorry catalogue of ills. Some political concessions were made in the 1780s, but the loss of American markets had seriously weakened trade; and it was to relieve the economic plight of the country and to give at least some satisfaction to the voices clamouring for Irish freedom that the treaty was proposed. In effect, it was intended to create free trade between Ireland and the rest of Britain with free access to Empire markets. To the Irish, it was a minimal concession after the years of pillage; to the manufacturers of Britain, it represented a threat, an opening up of their own markets to unfair competition. In the past, Wedgwood had managed to rally support for his schemes among the potters, and this was his chance to extend the same principle to the whole manufacturing interest. He wrote to Matthew Boulton of his plans.

I go to Birmingham as you desired and will endeavour to see

Mr. Garbett and one or two more at the Hotel. I mean to recommend them the measure of a Committee of Delegates from all the main factories and places in England and Scotland, to meet and sit in London all the time the Irish commerical affairs are pending. This strikes me as a measure which may be productive of many beneficial effects, principally informing and cementing a commercial band which may be of great use upon others as well as the present occasion.

If this idea is approved I submit it to you, Gentlemen, who are already on the spot, whether it would not be proper to apply to the various county connections in town for them to write to their friends – perhaps a printed letter from the *delegate already in town* recommending such a measure after stating the necessity etc. might be proper.[1]

Samuel Garbett, mentioned in the letter, a successful manufacturer of chemicals, was to prove a most willing and valuable ally, and it was very largely through his efforts that a General Chamber of Manufacturers of Great Britain came into being. Once formed, it proved a remarkably efficient body and Garbett an effective lobbyist. Given the general lack of scruples in such matters, their co-ordinated efforts were needed if the obvious advantages that lay with government were to be counteracted. Wedgwood put in a great amount of time conducting operations in London during the spring and summer of 1785. He explained to Boulton some of the problems posed by government patronage of their own potential supporters.

The principal glover in this town has a contract under government, so he cannot come.

The button maker makes buttons for his majesty, and so he is tied fast to his Majestie's minister's button hole. In short the Minister has found so many button and loop holes to fasten them to himself, that few of the principal manufacturers are left at liberty to serve their country. . . .[2]

The same letter described a meeting at which Sir Herbert Lackworth – a name surely belonging to a villain in a Restoration comedy rather than to a respectable manufacturer – was elected president to the Chamber. The crucial position of the chairman of the committee, set up to decide which matters should be discussed and acted upon by the Chamber, went to Wedgwood. As at most such meetings, hours were wasted over procedural wrangles – in this case centring on the precise definition of the word "manufacturer". It was guaranteed to strain the patience of a man of good sense. Wedgwood, being a reasonable man, was duly impatient but managed to argue some sense into the meeting.

The Chamber was successful. The unfortunate Bill was so weighed down with amendments and alterations in its passage through the two Houses and an unhappy Irish House that it finally sank without trace. The British manufacturers congratulated themselves, and the Irish were left to their misery and increasing bitterness. Within just a few years this bitterness had grown into disorder, disorder into division and uprising, uprising into repression and slaughter. The rifts in Irish society were deepened, leaving a yawning gash in that country's life that remains open nearly two centuries later. The failure of the treaty brought relief to British manufacturers, but at an appalling price.

It must, however, be said in fairness to Wedgwood that he was not blind to the wider implications of the trade treaty. He favoured a complete political and economic union between Great Britain and Ireland, arguing that if Ireland was to be granted equal benefits, she should equally bear the costs. The view took little account of the degree and nature of Irish poverty, nor did he foresee the terrible consequences of continuing with the old policies. But one must acknowledge that his views were not entirely motivated by self-interest, however mistaken those views may now be seen to have been. It is easy to condemn with the advantages of hindsight, but successful policies for Ireland were no easier to come by in the eighteenth century than they are today.

There was another opportunity for the Chamber to make its presence felt in the following year when negotiations began for a new commercial treaty with France. This time, the manufacturers felt that they had rather less of a fight on their hands as the negotiations were entrusted to an old Parliamentary friend, William Eden. Wedgwood wrote congratulating him on his appointment.

I sincerely congratulate you, or rather my brethren and the

kingdom in general upon your appointment to an office peculiarly important to this commercial nation, and which your very general knowledge of commercial affairs, your distinguished talents, and unwearied application, will enable you to fill with honour to yourself, and advantages to us all. We may now rest assured that our interests, our particular and individual interests, will have every attention paid to them, subordinate only to the general welfare of the nation at large.[3]

Wedgwood was concerned, however, that Pitt might be opposed to the Chamber and its lobbying – a concern which proved justified in the event. In theory, the Chamber took no part in party politics and personalities, being concerned only with particular commercial interests. Wedgwood saw the whole thing in very simplistic terms.

To political knowledge I have no pretensions, nor did I ever aspire to it; but every manufacturer can judge whether particular measures have a tendency to advance or to ruin the interests of his own manufacture, and of course will naturally use his best endeavours for promoting the one and opposing the other. Further than this, I have never intermeddled; and all the merit I am ambitious of is that of having acted, both as an individual and as a delegate, from the fullest conviction of my own mind.[4]

But politics could not be kept out. Eden's agreement to serve under Pitt angered his parliamentary friends among the Whigs, who had always loathed the Prime Minister, and Pitt himself showed an active hostility towards the Chamber. With their friends in Parliament divided by party, supporting either Fox or Pitt, the Chamber compounded the disruption when the members quite failed to reach agreement among themselves. Some, such as Wedgwood and the potters, were well pleased with the terms; others such as the textile manufacturers of the North of England, were opposed. As the whole rationale of the Chamber was that it provided a united voice for the manufacturers, such divisions proved fatal. Wedgwood continued to be an enthusiast for the cause but it simply withered away and died.

During its brief and flourishing life, the Chamber had proved an interesting experiment. The advantages of bodies with a common interest having a formal organization through which to make their views known were amply demonstrated by the early successes. However, industrial growth had been so rapid, and the new industrial masters were such an assorted group, that stability proved to be impossible. Nevertheless, this forerunner of the modern Confederation of British Industries earned its place in the history books and the important role played by Wedgwood in its affairs is an indication of just how far he had risen in the ranks of manufacturers.

Another point that emerges strongly from the treaty negotiations is the importance of overseas trade to Wedgwood. European trade was thriving in the late 1780s as many of the existing business letters testify. There were many offers of trade by the exchange of goods, offers Wedgwood invariably refused, and other proposals from would-be agents which were given more favourable consideration. Even so, by the end of the decade Wedgwood found himself having to turn down many offers, including one from Cadiz: "I find myself already charged with more commissions from correspondants whom I have long been in connection with, than I shall be able to execute in any reasonable time, insomuch that I have been obliged to refuse many new offers to a great amount." American trade too was picking up after the war, though the demand was not always for the type of ware Wedgwood produced. A visitor to Etruria later sent a request for samples for Charleston, South Carolina. He wanted plates, dishes and assorted items including "punch bowls with writing on, for Country People", adding with some accuracy: "It appears to me that the very inferior kind is most liked, to suit that Market at present, and I am somewhat doubtful whether you manufacture any of that sort."[5]

All this busy lobbying over trade terms and meetings of the Chamber brought Wedgwood into contact with other men who had risen to power on the flood tide of the Industrial Revolution, and among these men was Richard Arkwright. It was Arkwright whose mill had been burned in the Chorley riots, but by now his cotton spinning machinery was spread throughout the northern textile areas. In a sense, Arkwright was to textiles what Wedgwood was to pottery, and there is some interest in comparing these two leading figures of the age. Wedgwood was, above all, a man of sense, taste and intelligence; Arkwright made up for a lack of all three of those commodities by energy and a bull-like determination not to be diverted from his chosen path. Like Wedgwood he had trouble with patents, in this case the patent for the spinning machinery for which he claimed the authorship – a dubious claim at best. When the two men met, Arkwright was smouldering after losing that particular battle, and was finding little sympathy. Boulton commented in a letter to Watt: "It is agreed by all who know him that he is a Tyrant and more absolute than a Bashaw, & tis thought that his disappoint-ment will kill him. If he had been a man of sense and reason he would not have lost his patent." Wedgwood, however, found him "a very sensible intelligent man," if somewhat limited in his views. He described his visit to Arkwright at his home in Matlock in September 1785 in a letter to James Watt:

> I have visited Mr. Arkwright several times and find him much more conversible than I expected, and he invited me to come and see him as often as I can, tho he tells me he at present shuns all company as much as possible because it robs him of his time and breaks in upon his plans – And besides he says he is no company for them, for whilst they are talking to him upon one subject he is thinking upon another, and does not know what they say to him.
>
> He is much affected by the ill usage he received at the last trial, particularly from Mr Bearcroft who pointing to him said, *There sits the thief.* He has just now got the trial down translated out of short hand, and I believe means to prosecute some of the evidence for perjury. I do not yet know if he has any thoughts of a new trial. He will be in Birmingham in a few days and I will ask him to call upon you. I told him you were con-sidering the subjects of patents, and you two great genius's may probably strike out some new lights together, which neither of you might think of separately.[6]

Wedgwood also tried to persuade Arkwright to look into the possibility of spinning wool as well as cotton by machines, recom-mending him to take out another patent and introducing him to Sir Joseph Banks, the president of the Royal Society, as a potential ally. Wedgwood continued to press the subject, writing again the following year: "Being myself fully convinced that this is a subject of the first magnitude I should be happy to contribute any thing in

my power towards promoting so great & usefull a work." But the
scheme came to nothing, and Wedgwood had to be content with
selling Arkwright a Queen's ware service instead. It seems odd
that Wedgwood should have been so taken with a man whom
others, including his own business partners, found impossible. It
may perhaps have been their equivalent positions as leaders of
industry that formed the common bond, but it could hardly have
been sensible for Wedgwood to concern himself in Arkwright's
patents, a subject fraught with acrimony and bad feeling. This
involvement with the irascible mill owner seems to have been a
fundamental error, based on a misreading of his character – just
such a misreading as had previously led to trouble with agents and
employees such as Voyez.

Wedgwood, however, soon found other matters demanding
what time and energy he could spare from his business. In 1787 the
Society for the Suppression of the Slave Trade was founded, and
Wedgwood became an enthusiastic member of its committee. His
own special contribution to the movement was a cameo which he
designed himself and which was modelled by Hackwood. It shows
a slave in chains and carries the inscription "Am I not a man
and a brother?" It was an early version of the modern campaign
badge, but designed for the gentry rather than for a mass market.
The cameos were immensely popular. They were set and worn as
jewellery, used in snuff box covers and in short became fashionable,
thus helping to make the cause equally fashionable. Thomas
Clarkson, a clergyman and pamphleteer who did much to promote
the Society, wrote to Wedgwood's agent:

> My friend Mr Wedgwood was so good as to furnish me, during
> the last Session of Parliament, with several Cameos for Distribu-
> tion. Tomorrow I enter upon a Tour through the Southern
> Counties of the Kingdom on the Subject of the Slave-Trade,
> and as some of these will again have their use, I should be
> extremely obliged to you to furnish me with as many as you can
> spare. I should not have taken this Liberty, but that I understand
> Mr Wedgwood is out of Town and that he has always desired
> me to make applications for any if I should want them in the
> Service of the Cause.[7]

Wedgwood personally sent cameos to the more important supporters, including Benjamin Franklin.

> I embrace the opportunity of a packet making up by my friend
> Phillip to inclose for the use of yourself and friends a few Cameos
> on a subject which I am happy to acquaint you is daily more and
> more taking possession of men's minds on this side of the
> Atlantic as well as with you.
>
> It gives me great pleasure to be embarked on this occasion in
> the same great and good cause with you, and I ardently hope
> for the final completion of our wishes. This will be an epoch
> before unknown to the World, and while relief is given to
> millions of our fellow Creatures immediately the object of it,
> the subject of freedom will be more canvassed and better under-
> stood in the enlightened nations.
>
> I labour at the moment under a rheumatic head ache which has
> afflicted me for some months and this obliges me to use the hand
> of an amanuensis and also prevents me from saying more than
> begging to be considered, Sir, among the number of those who
> have the highest veneration for your virtues, and gratitude for
> the benefits you have bestowed on society.[8]

He spent a deal of time soliciting the support of friends. He asked
Anna Seward to supply a poem on the subject but she refused on the
grounds that slavery was "absolutely necessary to maintain our
empire, and other commerce in the Indies". She then proceeded to
recite old tales of slaves who have been treated leniently and had
repaid kindness by attacking their masters. Wedgwood replied in a
long letter refuting her arguments and setting out the case for
abolition.

> You have mentioned the two principal objections to the former
> – that we should sacrifice our West India commerce, and that
> the slaves would only change their masters without being able
> to shake off their bondage.
>
> How mortifying it is to be assured that even the latter, a
> mere change of masters, would be a blessing of no small
> magnitude to these poor wretches! Turn them over to a
> Spanish master, and a ray of hope, unknown to our West

India slaves, breaks in upon their poor benighted minds; for here you put them within the probability of liberty. They have at first two days of the week to themselves: when they have, by their labor on these free days, acquired one fifth of the amount of their first cost, they bring it in their gladdened hands, and can demand another day of liberty, and so on, till they have bought all the five and are as free as their masters.

What labor will not hopes like these enable them to endure, when every exertion brings them nearer and nearer to that state which they must be so earnestly looking after, and of which they must have numberless encouraging examples before them! Contrast this chearing state for a moment with the absolute despair of a West Indian slave, wearing out by immoderate and incessant labor, with *known* and *calculated* certainty, in the course of a few years, and we cannot but confess that a change of masters would, in this instance, be to him a blessing most devoutly to be wished for.

The slaves in the French W. India islands meet with that protection from the *code noir* which ours are utter strangers to, and with respect to that state of slavery in Africa, compared with that in our islands it does not deserve the name, if you will believe those who have long resided upon the spot. You will see what Mr Newton says – page 27. Mr Moore says in his Travels, "that it is thought so extremely wicked to sell a family slave (those which we purchase are generally procured by fraud or violence on purpose for sale) that he never heard of but one person who ever did so, except for such crimes as would have authorised its being done had he been free; that there are many slaves in a family, and that, if one commits a crime, the master cannot sell him without the joint consent of the rest; and that they live so well and easy that it is sometimes difficult to know them from their masters and mistresses." – So that a change (where we shall hide our heads while we confess it!) to any other master, would certainly be a blessing.

I am afraid, Dear Madam, of wounding your feelings too much, and of intruding father than I ought upon your time and patience, if I should go on to relate an hundredth part of what has come to my knowledge of the accumulated distress brought upon millions of our fellow creatures by this unhuman traffic.[9]

He continued by pointing out that there were already sufficient slaves in the West Indies so that little harm would be done to British commerce. In any case, the conditions of slavery would always make abolition a proper course to follow.

Anna Seward produced no poem. Fortunately, a far better poet, William Cowper, obliged instead. *The Negro's Complaint* is a decidedly sentimental work but an effective piece of propaganda. Here by way of example is just one stanza:

> Deem our nation brutes no longer
> Till some reason ye shall find
> Worthier of regard and stronger
> Than the colour of our kind.
> Slaves of gold, whose sordid dealings
> Tarnish all your boasted powers,
> Prove that you have human feelings,
> Ere you proudly question ours!

Modern commentators have pointed out the element of hypocrisy among the anti-slave traders. It was, they argue, a convenient sop to humanitarian feeling for manufacturers to campaign against black slavery abroad, enabling them to ignore the white slavery of mill and factory. It is worth noting that what was being advocated was not the abolition of slavery, but the abolition of the trade in slaves. If Wedgwood's comments were accurate, and there were already sufficient slaves at work, then the element of hypocrisy must be conceded. But even so that is not the whole truth. Even if one admits that the conditions for British workers, especially women and children, were a disgrace that was never condemned by those abolitionists who were in a position to apply direct remedies, it does not alter the fact that there was genuine revulsion at the slave trade. To say Wedgwood did not condemn the exploitation of working children is true; yet the truth remains that he did condemn the slave trade and did work against it with great energy at a time when his health was far from being good. The words put in the mouth of the slave by Josiah Wedgwood "Am I not a man and a brother?" still do not receive the universal answer "yes" in the world of today.

Whatever else he may or may not have done, he stood up when the movement began and was counted in on the side of right and humanity.

There was another touchstone against which political feelings could be measured in 1789 – the French Revolution. Among Wedgwood and his friends in the Lunar Society there was general, if not unanimous, delight. Mary Ann Schimmelpennick wrote: "I have seen the reception of the news of Waterloo, and of the carrying of the Reform Bill, but I never saw joy comparable in its vivid intensity and universality to that occasioned by the early promise of the French Revolution. ... Even with my father's scientific friends, politics became all absorbing." And, indeed, something of that first feeling can be gauged from the letters between the friends. Wedgwood wrote to Darwin, "I know you will rejoice with me in the glorious Revolution which has taken place in France. The politicians tell me that as a manufacturer I shall be ruined if France has her liberty, but I am willing to take my chance in that respect, nor do I yet see that the happiness of one nation includes in it the misery of its next neighbour."[10] And Darwin in turn wrote to Watt: "Do you not congratulate your grandchildren on the dawn of universal liberty? I feel myself becoming all french both in chemistry & politics".[11]

In those early, heady days, few were more enthusiastic than the great chemist himself, Priestley – an enthusiasm for which he was soon to pay a heavy price. Unlike Darwin, however, he showed no inclination to go French in his chemistry. Across the channel, Lavoisier was using the discovery of oxygen to propound a new theory of burning, but Priestley remained obstinately tied to the old. Wedgwood, for one, was delighted: "I cannot forbear expressing my particular satisfaction to find that my old favourite, Phlogistan, is likely to be restored to its former rank in the chemical world."[12] On this occasion, the political radicals proved to be scientific conservatives.

Wedgwood himself was now proving to be a scientific innovator of very considerable stature, even though some of his important work was not published. One example is his research on the development of good optical glass for scientific instruments. Wedgwood, noting that flint glass behaved in many ways like the clay mixtures with which he was so familiar, discovered that flaws could be removed during the heating process. This discovery is usually attributed to Guinard in 1798 but was actually first made several years earlier by Wedgwood. All these activities took him some way from Etruria and business, but it was as a potter that his reputation had been made and in that field he was still to receive further acclamation.

[17]

End of a Career

BY 1790 Josiah Wedgwood had reached his sixtieth birthday, and the elder boys were quite old enough to take an active interest in the concern, especially as they could rely on the help of the increasingly valuable Tom Byerley. It is, however, a fact of life which Wedgwood was not alone in discovering that sons are not as easily moulded as parents might think – or wish. Jack as the eldest was expected to take a lead. He had left school in 1780, spent some time at Priestley's old Warrington Academy and concluded his formal education in Edinburgh. He was then sent to Europe to gain a working knowledge of the overseas markets and to see those relics of antiquity which had been the chief inspiration for so much of his father's work. Unfortunately for the father, the European tour had effects rather different from those intended.

His first trip took him to Paris in 1786, where he was supposed to learn French but found too many distractions to study. He was honest enough to write back to suggest he might learn more in the provinces, but Jack was clearly not his father writ over again. One cannot imagine Josiah ever being similarly distracted. Nevertheless, the next year saw him off on a second trip. Jack was more enthusiastic for the tour in general than for the potter's itinerary laid down by his father. Wedgwood solicited help from friends to make sure that Jack saw the right people and the right places.

My son John having finally determined to pursue the business in which his father has been laboring for many years, I have confirmed to him my promise that he should visit, and see with his own eyes, those invaluable remains of antiquity upon the continent, particularly in Italy, which I have often wished to do but in vain, and of which the copies we have are acknowledged to be very imperfect. He leaves home in a fortnight, and his route will be by way of Paris to Basle, Berne, Geneva, Turin, Genoa, Leghorn, Florence, Rome, Naples. He will return through Bologna, Ferrara, Padua and Venice.

I shall be extremely thankfull to you for the honor of a line to any of your friends on the continent in this route to beg their protection and good offices. I hope he will not give them much trouble, and I depend upon your goodness, and well known liberality, to excuse that which I am now giving to you.[1]

It must have been galling to Wedgwood to see his son setting off with such reluctance to see those ancient ruins which he himself would have so dearly loved to have visited. The sour note in the letter is at least understandable.

The objective of Jack's tour may have been different but the route he took was remarkably similar to that of the Grand Tour of the young noblemen. The similarity seems to have struck Jack, who wrote home from Rome to say that he felt disinclined after all to become a potter. He had, as Wedgwood had once feared, received the education of a gentleman and now had little taste to follow the occupation of a manufacturer. However, when he returned home he was persuaded to take his place at Etruria, though as a less than enthusiastic potter.

Jack Wedgwood was a comfortable character, with none of his father's ambition and drive. He was wealthy enough and happy enough as he was, an attitude to life that bewildered and aggravated Josiah. But if Jack seemed unlikely to prove the natural heir to the Wedgwood business, there were two other sons who could make good the deficiency. Between them, Joss and Tom shared out the main Wedgwood characteristics. It is perhaps a little unfair to divide them too neatly, but in general it could be said that to Joss went the application and ambition, to Tom the brilliance. At least it seemed that between them there was the real possibility that an honourable succession would be assured. On 16 January 1790

Tom Byerley and the three sons were taken into the partnership.

Wedgwood himself was busily occupied with his last great work – the Barberini or Portland vase. The vase had been discovered in the earlier seventeenth century and placed in the Barberini Library. It was at first thought to be stone, but Winckelmann was among those who demonstrated that it was in fact made of glass. When the library was dispersed, the vase was bought by Sir William Hamilton and was then sold to the Duchess of Portland before eventually going to the Duke of Portland for approximately one thousand guineas. Wedgwood knew the piece from engravings, but in 1786 he received his great opportunity and at once passed on the news of his good fortune to Sir William Hamilton.

> You will be pleased, I am sure, to hear what a treasure is just now put into my hands, I mean the exquisite Barberini vase with which you enriched this island, and which, now that we may call it the Portland vase, I hope will never depart from it. His Grace the Duke of Portland being the purchaser, at the sale of his late mother's museum, had generously lent it me to copy, and permitted me to carry it down with me to this place, where I stand in much need of your advice and directions in several particulars. . . .
>
> When I first engaged in this work, and had Montfaucon only to copy, I proceeded with spirit, and sufficient assurance that I should be able to equal, or excell if permitted, that copy of the vase; but now that I can indulge myself with full and repeated examinations of the original work itself, my crest is much fallen, and I should scarcely muster sufficient resolution to proceed if I had not, too precipitately perhaps, pledged my self to many of my friends to attempt it in the best manner I am able. Being so pledged, I must proceed, but shall stop at certain points till I am favored with your kind advice and assistance.
>
> It will be necessary however for you to know something of the powers I am in possession of for this attempt, before you can tell what advice to give. I have several modellers constantly employed in the several branches of that art; and one of them [Webber], who was recommended to me by Sir William Chambers and Sir Josuah Reynolds, is esteemed the first in his

profession in England. I need not add that I shall give myself unwearied attention to the progress of this great work.[2]

The vase was not loaned for nothing. Wedgwood paid £100 for the privilege and the work of copying took four years to complete. Modelling the figures proved difficult and there were more problems over firing the black and white jasper. But in 1790 it was ready. A special exhibition was arranged in London and in the leaflet he wrote as an introduction, Wedgwood passed over to the public the task of judging the work.[3] However, he took care to add a postscript to point them in the right direction. "I have now the pleasure to find that my imitation of this vase, after a strict comparison with the original, has given perfect satisfaction to the most distinguished artists and amateurs in Britain." The authentication was signed by the Duke of Portland, Sir Joseph Banks, President of the Royal Society, the Earl of Leicester, the President of the Society of Antiquities and Sir Joshua Reynolds, President of the Royal Academy – a list impressive enough to satisfy anyone. Equally impressive in content was the list of twenty-four subscribers for copies of the vase, which included the Prince of Wales, the Duke of Marlborough and Lord Auckland.

There is no doubt that Wedgwood regarded the production of the Portland vase as marking the very pinnacle of his career. The technical difficulties in copying an Alexandrian glass vase of *circa* 40 B C were formidable, and to overcome them was indeed a triumph. Artistically, however, it was when all is said and done a copy and not an original work of art. And in terms of effect on the public, the Portland vase was never quite the sensational success that the Russian dinner service had been. True, the Queen came to see the vase and pronounced herself delighted by it, but it did not send the world rushing to Wedgwood's door. This last great work of Josiah Wedgwood's showed as clearly as anything could just what had been lost at the death of Bentley. There can be little doubt that there would have been more of a flutter in London society had Bentley had the managing of the affair. More importantly, there could well have been new interests preoccupying Wedgwood. Bentley would have been looking for the new trend, not working towards providing a culmination to the old.

One unusual medium in which both Wedgwood and his vase received fulsome praise was in poetry. Erasmus Darwin had been labouring hard and long on what he felt certain was to be his greatest work, a lengthy allegorical poem that used the forms and vocabulary of classicism and the ancient world to describe the changes brought by industry to the modern world. It was not entirely a new idea. Dyer had done something similar in *The Fleece*, but Darwin's work, *The Botanic Garden*[4] was on a far greater scale. It is easy to dismiss it as rather absurd – and indeed many did – but it was a brave attempt to explain great changes in such a way that the educated public would both take notice and understand. The poem celebrated the Potteries among the other industrial scenes. The sequence begins with an address to the gnomes who work for the goddess of botany.

> Gnomes! as you now dissect with hammers fine
> The granite-rock, the nodul'd flint calcine;
> Grind with strong arm, the circling chertz betwixt,
> Your pure Ka-O-lins and Pe-tun-tses mixt;
> O'er each red saggars burning cave preside,
> The keen-eyed Fire-Nymphs blazing by your side.
> And pleased on WEDGWOOD ray your partial smile,
> A new Etruria decks Britannia's isle. –
> Charm'd by your touch, the flint liquescent pours
> Through finer sieves, and falls in whiter showers;
> Charm'd by your touch, the kneaded clay refines,
> The biscuit hardens, the enamel shines;
> Each nicer mould a softer feature drinks,
> The bold Cameo speaks, the soft Intaglio thinks.
> To call the pearly drops from Pity's eye,
> Or stay Despair's disanimating sigh,
> Whether, O Friend of art! the gem you mould
> Rich with new taste, with antient virtue bold;
> Form the poor fetter'd SLAVE on bended knee
> From Britain's sons imploring to be free;
> Or with fair HOPE the brightening scenes improve,
> And cheer the dreary wastes at Sydney-cove;[5]
> Or bid Mortality rejoice and mourn
> O'er the fine forms on PORTLAND's mystic urn. –

At least one can say that Darwin managed to make his verse flow and some of the images such as the "saggar's burning cave" hit off their effects very neatly. Wedgwood at any rate was delighted with the work.

The Portland vase was used for prestige promotion all over Europe. In June 1790 Joss and Tom Byerley took a copy with them on a tour that lasted for six months. They made full use of the vase to ensure appropriate aristocratic interest, and in this they were helped by friends such as Lord Auckland who was then ambassador at The Hague. There they put on a display in which one room was set out with assorted ware, another room contained the Portland vase in solitary splendour and two further rooms were put aside for the visitors to have breakfast. The Prince and Princess came and bought some ware but declined to subscribe to the vase.

On their return from Europe, Joss and Byerley were able to relieve Wedgwood of much of the pressure of business. The concern that was being passed over to the next generation had grown mightily in the twenty years that had elapsed since the establishment of the works at Etruria. By 1790 there were about three hundred employees, two-thirds of them in the useful works, the rest in the ornamental. Wages varied enormously, from the apprentices getting 1s or 2s to the élite – overlookers such as Daniel Greatbatch on 21s a week and, at the top of the scale, the modeller Hackwood who was receiving 42s a week.[6] Wedgwood himself gave this estimate of the increase in trade in the potteries.

> With respect to my own business, having examined some of the oldest men in the pottery here near thirty years ago, who knew personally the masters in the pottery, and very nearly the value of the goods they got up fifty years before that; from these data I can pretty nearly ascertain the annual value of the goods made here at that time, which was something under £10,000; but this certainly arises chiefly from the very low state and great simplicity of the manufacture, and the few hands employed at each work. But if I am asked what is the annual value of the goods *now* got up, in order to form a comparison between that time and this, I can only say that I have heard them estimated at £200,000 – some have said 300,000; perhaps the truth may be

near the medium, which compared with the above annual amount about 80 years ago makes the increase in that period 25 fold.[7]

It was a great business over which Wedgwood was gradually relinquishing control. His health was not good, and he frequently complained of "nervous or rheumatic headaches". It was ill health more than anything that persuaded him to share out the rule of his Etruscan empire, though he was very far from passing into an inactive retirement. He continued to take a keen interest in the business and all its affairs; and the letters he received from Joss showed that business was very much as usual. There were the familiar scares over spies in the works, disagreements about wages and the occasional strike. Politics also appeared as an element on the scene, which gave Wedgwood an opportunity to lecture his son. One of the Newcastle candidates, Fletcher, had asked for Wedgwood's support and Wedgwood replied that he wished him well but never interfered in elections. In a covering letter he explained his views:

My dear Jos. will see by the inclosed to Mr Fletcher the line of conduct which I mean to observe – that is, the same which I have hitherto done on all similar occasions, as I do not see any good reason for altering it.

I have no vote for a member of that borough, and have therefore no specific or local reason to interfere; and I do not know any *general principle* which, if valid in this instance, would not hold much farther, and claim from me a like interference throughout the county at least – perhaps far beyond.

Speaking politically, I believe you know my sentiments that so long as we have septennial parliaments 'tis of little consequence who is chosen into them; they will generally, in like circumstances, so long as human nature continues the same, act as they have hitherto done. A real parliamentary reform is therefore what we most stand in need of, and for this I would willingly devote my time, the most precious thing I have to bestow, or any thing else by which I could serve so truly noble a cause.

You will say, perhaps, that to accomplish this end we should chuse independent members of parliament. Alas! It is too certain that this object never will be obtained from parliament in the first instance; so long as parliament remains on its present plan, all little partial struggles is beating the air, and wasting that time and strength which should be employed for better purposes, I mean, to promote a radical cure by reducing the duration of parliaments to their original limits.

Mr Fletcher's political principles are, I believe, in many respects, the same as my own, and I have long had a sincere value for him as a friend and neighbour; but I have for many years past determined to keep clear of electioneering disputes, unless I should perceive it to be more incumbent upon me to involve myself in them than I have yet done.

These are the principles on which I have hthterto acted, but I do not desire you to adopt them merely because they have been mine. Examine for yourself, and then act according to your honest conviction, in this and every other instance, and your conduct, whether it is the same as my own would have been in like circumstances or the contrary, will nevertheless have my approbation.[8]

The dangers of taking part in elections were well illustrated by Joss's accounts of the campaign. "I am afraid we shall suffer much from the contest as I hear the ale houses are to be opened at Newcastle & Trentham hall is so now I believe. No mobs or murders at Newcastle as Mr B. has heard but much drinking & I suppose some fighting – one of our labourers who has got drunk in Trentham hall was so imprudent as to cry Fletcher for ever & in consequence was well thrashed."[9] One labourer was even less fortunate, for he got drunk and then joined the army and had to buy his way out again. The son was clearly seeing father's lessons reinforced in practice.

The fate of the Fletcher supporter gives a glimpse of the violence of the political scene – the following year was to see that violence erupt in a far more dangerous and damaging way. Revolution across the channel had bred reaction in Britain: suggestions for reform were taken as signals for insurrection, dissent in religion was construed as an attack against the established church and thus against the king. Radicals continued to support the aims and achievements of revolutionary France, but they did so at an increasing risk to themselves and their property. In 1791 a dinner was given in Birmingham to celebrate the anniversary of the storming of the Bastille. Though the attendants could hardly have been more respectable, rumours grew and forged lists of revolutionary toasts were circulated in the town. Agitators worked on emotions until a mob was gathered to oppose all the radicals and dissenters. The cry was "Church and King". Perhaps the best known of all the Birmingham dissenters was Joseph Priestley. He had not, in fact, been to the now notorious dinner, but he had never attempted to hide his views, and he was forced to flee as the mob descended on his home. The house was burned to the ground. This was serious enough, but what made it all far worse was the complete destruction of Priestley's books, his scientific papers and notes and all his apparatus.

Wedgwood, who was on holiday in Weymouth at the time, was among the first to write to Priestley with condolences and offers of help.

I do not know where this will find you, but can no longer forbear to ask you how you do after the severe trials you have lately been expos'd to, and to condole with you on the irreparable loss you have sustain'd from the brutality or rather let us hope the temporary insanity of your late neighbours. You will have occasion for all your philosophy, and for all your Christianity too to support your mind under the highly aggravated injuries you have received. If they had arisen merely from the ungovern'd madness of a mob, from the lowest order of our species, one would then lament all its effects like those of a storm or hurricane, but if there is reason to believe the rabble were acted upon and encouraged to such proceedings by those who should be their superiors, one cannot but perceive the too evident spirit of the times or of the place at least by which you and so many of your worthy neighbours have suffered.

Can I be of any use or service to you upon the present occasion? Assure yourself, my good friend, that I most earnestly wish it. Believe this of me – act accordingly, instruct me in the means of doing it & I shall esteem it as one of the strongest instances of your friendship.[10]

Few stood in support of Priestley, many were ready with vituperation, attacking the man who had lost a life's work in one night. Anonymous poems were published:

> Burnt children dread the Fire but the Doctor is untamed
> By fair means or foul means he ne'er can be reclaimed
> The blessings of *Equality* he still must be praising
> Tho the equal *Rights of Man* set his Mansion House a blazing

And there were few who seemed to care of the damage done to the work of the country's leading scientist. "Perhaps, however, the world, wearied with the sound of infidel, Unitarian, seditious, leveling argumentation, will no more lament the loss of future sermons, pamphlets, letters and histories, than of the mistaken and false system of chemistry and natural philosophy already defeated and detected."[11] The more credit then must attach to Wedgwood for standing by both friend and principles in such a violent time.

Priestley, nor surprisingly, received expressions of sympathy and support from the scientific community in France, including that other very great chemist Antoine Lavoisier. Wedgwood was also in correspondence with Lavoisier, though in his case the matter was purely scientific. No greater compliment could perhaps be paid to Wedgwood the scientist than the attention he received from two such chemists. Lavoisier contacted Wedgwood for practical help with his experiments in melting platinum, part of the long business of establishing standard weights and measures. The problem was to find a furnace capable of withstanding the high temperatures needed, a problem that was very much in Wedgwood's line as he himself noted: "It was natural enough for them to apply to me." But it was not an easy problem to solve. However, he sent two of his thermometers to Lavoisier and set about conducting a series of experiments on a "clayie composition for bearing intense fire" as he described it in his commonplace book. It does not perhaps sound especially exciting, but Wedgwood's work in supplying reliable ceramic apparatus to Priestley, Lavoisier and others was of the very greatest importance to them in helping to establish new standards of

A page from the oven book of March 1791, giving a record of each firing, with marginal sketches for identification

accuracy. His leading position as an experimenter in the science as opposed to the art of ceramics was recognized in many ways, not least by his being asked to contribute towards Lavoisier's prestigious *Annales de Chemie*.

But to return to politics. In the flurry of panicky activity that followed the "Church and King" riots, Wedgwood sensibly but very firmly refused to join the general hysteria. He looked with stern disfavour on the various "loyal" associations and their over eager pledgings to defy republicanism and uphold the constitution.

> With respect to the associations, I do not see or know their object, but so far as I can judge, I think them useless, to speak in the most moderate terms, but if they should unhappily set one part of the nation against the other they would be something worse than useless.
>
> It will not be expected that I should upon this occasion make profession of my Loyalty or attachment to our constitution. I shall let my actions speak for me, and continue to perform what appears to me to be my duty to all around me. I shall certainly love my friends, and if I cannot arrive at the perfection of loving my enemies likewise, I will not injure them unless in my own defence.[12]

Wedgwood could become notably prickly in his later years, though often, as here, with some justification.

Other matters, however, offered rather more pleasure. Joss went off for a holiday to Wales and wrote back from Tenby in 1792.

> You will have heard by a letter of mine to Tom that we have had a very gay week at Haverfordwest Assizes. I have not been at Cresselly since, but as I left them all very well I hope to find them so to-morrow. The family at Cresselly is altogether the most charming one I have ever been introduced to, and their society makes no small addition to the pleasure I have received from this excursion. I am very happy to perceive that their spirits are not much affected by their Father's marriage. Our pleasures here are very simple, riding, walking, bathing ,with a little dance twice a week.[13]

Joss obviously found one member of the Allen family of Cresselly particularly charming – Elizabeth, usually known as Bessie. The rest of the family were not always quite so endearing. They had social distinction, but the father had the reputation of being evil-tempered. To this he added, so the family proclaimed when the marriage referred to in the letter took place, gross eccentricity. As his second wife, he chose a coal miner's daughter. This might have been termed boldly unconventional had he not spoiled the effect by never deigning to bring her home to Cresselly to meet her new step-daughters. The faults of the father were less interesting to Joss Wedgwood than the virtues of his daughter, however, and in December 1792 Joss and Bessie Allen were married. They received a wedding present of £3,000 from Wedgwood and in the spring they returned to Staffordshire and moved into Little Etruria, the house originally built for Bentley.

Family affairs took a less happy turn in the same year when Jack finally made the break with the pottery business he had never enjoyed. He was set up as a partner in the London and Middlesex Bank. There was no hiding the disappointment at his eldest son leaving what Wedgwood described, with a note of bitterness, as "a business which has done me no discredit and I hope it would do none of my children". But he had sense enough to accept that where there was so little inclination it was sensible to call a halt; better a successful banker than a failed potter. In spite of his disappointment he could still write to Jack: "I wish you to consult me as a friend and with the utmost freedom, and assure yourself that I do not know of anything in this world that can make me more happy than contributing all in my power to ease, health and welfare of my children."[14]

If Jack did not share his brother Joss's taste for pottery, he soon found he shared his taste for the Allen family. Where Joss had courted Elizabeth, he courted Louisa, the family beauty and its spoiled child. This, at least, was good news for the Wedgwoods and the father was happy to give his blessing.

> I have shewn your letter to your mother and asked her opinion upon the subject and find that we are happy enough to agree in our sentiments respecting the choice you have made of a companion for life. It is no doubt a subject of the first importance

to you both, and you will do well to consider each others tempers and dispositions, whether they are such as are likely to make you mutually happy in each other, for I need not tell you it must be *mutual* or not at all in the married state. Your friends here, not only your mother and myself but your brothers and sisters, wish with sincerity and earnestness for your welfare and happiness, particularly upon your entrance upon so interesting a connection, and I am sure you will do us the justice to believe that the real happiness of the parties weighs more with us than any other consideration whatever, and we have so exquisite a sample before us from the same family of everything that is desirable and lovely in the female character, and hearing besides so excellent a character of the lady of your choice, we do not hesitate to give our free and most cordial assent with our sincerest wishes and prayers for your long continued enjoyment of all the comfort and happiness your intended union can bestow.[15]

They were married the following year, and if at first Louisa did not show quite the "excellent character" her in-laws expected, the pair proved to be well matched and eventually settled into a placid partnership marked by geniality and good humour.

Tom also left the family business, in his case less from choice than from necessity. He suffered from ill health and there was little chance of his being able to sustain the regular work that would have been demanded of him and which he would have demanded of himself. It was in many ways a sadness that Tom was forced to leave, for he was blessed with an inquiring mind, great inventiveness and a powerful imagination. Like his father, he was an avid experimental scientist, and yet many of his friends were drawn from the world of the arts. He was a man of strong humanitarian impulses, and during his brief period in business he began a scheme of providing education for the workmen. The plan was much approved by the London bookseller Samuel Phillips, who in writing in praise of the son inadvertently turned upside down the famous doctrine of the father: "Too many look on their workmen as meer machines & this perhaps is one reason why so many are so little better. Thou art about (I hope) to realise the Torch of Prometheus & by infusing some of the Fire of Science to make *men* of those clay machines – as thy motive is the

improvement of the people thou wilt not be deterred from prosecuting thy plan with a vigour tho' thou shouldst be checked by
stupidity & repaid with ingratitude".[16]

So the family business was carried mainly on the shoulders of
Joss and Tom Byerley, and broad shoulders they proved to be. It
was well that they were so, for Josiah Wedgwood after fifty years
of work that would have strained any man, let alone one so constantly plagued by ill health, was more than ready for a rest. He
was still active in his experiments, constantly striving to make yet
further improvements in the ware. As late as 1793 he was beginning
a new experiment book which contains ample proof of a vigorous
mind attacking and solving a variety of problems. Here are some
of his notes on a typical series of experiments, numbers 6002–6:

> Some experiments for bringing our black ware to its former
> state of excellence. Its faults are, blistering, and where it is not
> blistered, a rough harsh, pinholy surface. The causes of these
> imperfections appear to be, the burnt carr, or pitchers, or
> manganese, not being ground, or washed, or sifted sufficiently
> fine and the ware having too hot and hasty a fire. In proof of
> this, compare the specimens of No. 6005, which are fragments
> from a piece of our present raw ware, with 6006, which are
> part of the same piece ground finer, & fired in the same sagar –
> which shew decidedly, that the badness of the ware proceeds
> from want of fineness & sufficient mixing.

In 1794 he was again busy with public affairs including the active
promotion of a parliamentary bill for uniting the parishes of Stoke,
Burslem and Woolstanton. But increasingly it was among his
family and friends that he spent his time. He could look now on two
married sons and in that year he had the pleasure of seeing the first
grandchild, Sarah Elizabeth, the daughter of Joss and Bessie. It was
among the growing family that he spent Christmas of 1794, but his
health had deteriorated badly. In the first week of January Tom
Byerley sent the sad news to Samuel Boardman, Bentley's old
partner.

> I have the extreme unhappiness to announce to you the decease
> of our revered and ever to be lamented Mr Wedgwood. This

awesomeful event happened on Saturday last after an illness of about three weeks in which he was perfectly sensible till near the fatal and melancholy period, and to the great consolation of his friends was without much pain the last two or three days of his existence.

Poor Mrs Wedgwood supports herself under the heavy affliction with all that fortitude which her friends would expect and we hope is tolerably well, tho' its much to be feared this separation will long prey upon her spirits – My poor Uncle had the comfort in this his last illness to be attended only by his children, who nursed him with an anxious care and constancy that has not been surpassed. This long watchfulness and anxiety of mind has been too much for the tender frame of Miss Wedgwood who has been in a poor state of health for some time, and she has suffered extremely but is now much better. The rest of the family are as well as can be expected.

The agitation of my own mind upon this dreadful chasm in our society has been so great as to cause me to be inattentive to what I owe my friends, and I have been longer than I ought to have been before I acquainted you with this truly sorrowful event, and I beg you will pardon me.[17]

So it was that on 3 January 1795, in the house he had built within sight of the great pottery of Etruria, surrounded by the family he loved, Josiah Wedgwood died.

[18]

The Dynasty and its Founder

THE death of Josiah Wedgwood did not signal the end of Wedgwoods, manufacturers of pottery, nor did it signal an end to achievement in the family. His widow, Sally, lived on quietly but in poor health until 1815. The children and the grandchildren made their own distinctive marks in the world. Of these, Jack's place was the most modest. His career in banking was not entirely covered in glory. Indeed, for a man as bad at handling finance as he was, banking was probably the last career at which he could have expected success. When the London and Middlesex was rescued from bankruptcy by Coutts, Jack left business and the city for a good-humoured, cheerfully placid life as a country gentleman in Dorset. The only highlight in that uneventful existence came when he chaired a meeting at which the Royal Horticultural Society was formed, and there is every reason to believe that that was achievement enough to satisfy John Wedgwood.

The brilliant Tom had a sadly brief career. He died at the age of thirty-four after a long and painful illness. In that short career, he worked hard at his chemical experiments and was one of the first men ever to produce a satisfactory photographic image. Although he was unable to find a fixative that would keep the image on the plate, he ranks as one of the first pioneers of modern photography. In the arts he was both friend and benefactor to Coleridge, and made a strong impression even in the highly talented and emotional group of which Coleridge was a member. Wordsworth wrote of him: "His calm and dignified manner, united with his tall person and beautiful face, produced in me an impression of a sublimity beyond what I ever experienced from the appearance of any other human being."

Joss was a very different character – a man more revered than loved, described as "silent and removed, so as to be a rather awful man". But unlike as he and Tom were, there was a strong bond between them and Tom's death affected him deeply. He was to prove a stolid custodian of the family business, but was to see it decline during his life time as taste moved away from the clarity of classicism towards the clutter and ostentation that marked the taste of mid-Victorian Britain.

Of the rest, Sukey deserves special mention. In 1796 she married Robert Darwin, the son of Wedgwood's old friend Erasmus. Their child, Charles, was to become the most famous scientist of the age. It is fascinating to see how the close web of intermarriage that had characterized the Wedgwoods and the close connections between the different family groups continued on into another generation. When Charles Darwin was offered a post on HMS *Beagle* he found his father strongly opposed to the idea, and it was only due to the intervention of "Uncle Jos" that Darwin ever took that momentous voyage. And the family connection went on, for when he returned it was his cousin Emma Wedgwood, Josiah's daughter, whom he married. Grandfather Josiah would surely have approved as much as Uncle Josiah did.

So the Wedgwood children continued to bring honour to the family. But this book is the story of the first Josiah Wedgwood and not that of the children. In attempting to assess the achievements of his life, there are some that can easily be measured. The boy who lived in a modest house and who had to set out to work as an apprentice at the age of nine with a legacy from his father of £20 (unpaid) ended his days in a home where the staff was listed as butler, under butler, footman, groom, coachman, postillion, gardener and female servants too numerous and inconsequential to mention.[1] That was one form of achievement, but it was not a unique achievement in an age where the revolutions in industry could bring sudden wealth to a few enterprising or forceful men. Another achievement not quite so easy to measure was the personal enrichment that saw the boy who left school before his tenth birthday grow up to become a patron of the arts, a notable bibliophile and a Fellow of the Royal Society.

Ultimately, however, it was the changes he wrought in the Staffordshire pottery industry that have ensured the continuing fame of the Wedgwood name. Again his special achievement is not easy to isolate, for it had so many facets. Many of the changes he made were changes that others had already been considering or had even begun to put into practice. What makes him unique in the history of pottery, and of industry as a whole, is that he managed to combine so many different aspects of industrial development within his own work. It was Wedgwood who appreciated the need for industry to be based on a sound foundation of scientifically conducted experiments. It was Wedgwood, with the very considerable help of Bentley, who saw that his own particular industry was also an art and who kept abreast of the latest thinking among artists and their patrons. It was Wedgwood and Bentley together who formed a partnership that changed the whole concept of entrepreneurship in a way that could only be matched by their good friends Boulton and Watt. It was Wedgwood who took a local craft and, for good or ill, turned it into a highly organized national industry. It was Wedgwood who was among the first and most important promoters of the new canals, the transport system that helped to make the Industrial Revolution possible. Add his active involvement in such issues as the Irish treaty and the abolition of the slave trade and one has a portrait of an astonishingly impressive man. And Josiah Wedgwood was impressive. Looking back on his career, one can have reservations about the way in which the changes in industrial organization were pushed through with very little regard for the feelings of the workmen of the time. Josiah Wedgwood made a fortune from those changes, yet the wages of the workmen he employed showed very little change from the wage book of 1762 to the lists of 1790. But for all this, one can say that Josiah Wedgwood, if little better than the vast majority of his contemporaries, was at least no worse.

Wedgwood was buried in Stoke and a memorial duly erected, but his true memorial is not a marble tablet but the pots that he made. His epitaph can be read in the form, texture and colour of his Queen's ware, basalt, jasper and the rest. In the introduction to his first experiment book Wedgwood wrote of the rewards to be had by one who laboured diligently in the potter's field. Wedgwood did more than labour diligently, he changed the whole pattern and structure of that wide field. The story of that great upheaval which we now call the Industrial Revolution is, when we come to look at the Potteries, also the story of Josiah Wedgwood.

Notes

Unless otherwise stated, the documents quoted below are from the collection currently housed in the Wedgwood archives of Keele University, Staffordshire and at Wedgwood's, Barlaston, Staffordshire.

I THE POTTER'S FIELD

1 Simeon Shaw, *History of the Staffordshire Potteries*, 1829
2 Lorna Weatherill, *The Pottery Trade and North Staffordshire 1660–1760*, 1971
3 Eliza Meteyard, *The Life and Works of Wedgwood*, 1865

2 THE EARLY YEARS

1 Manuscript notes by Sir John Leslie, tutor to the Wedgwood family in the 1790s. They are annotated with notes by the family
2 Introduction to Experiment Book 1

3 MR WEDGWOOD'S WORKS

1 Manuscript notes by Sir John Leslie
2 Meteyard, op. cit.
3 Wedgwood to Thomas Bentley, 6 July 1767

4 BENTLEY

1 Quoted in John Towill Rutt, *Life and Correspondence of Joseph Priestley*, 1831
2 Wedgwood to Bentley, 15 May 1762
3 ibid., 26 October 1762
4 Cox to Wedgwood, 18 June 1763
5 Wedgwood to Bentley, 31 March 1763
6 ibid., 6 January 1764
7 ibid., 23 January 1764
8 ibid., 28 May 1764
9 Wedgwood to John Wedgwood, 1 February 1765
10 Wedgwood to Sir William Meredith, 2 March 1765
11 Wedgwood to John Wedgwood, 17 June 1765
12 ibid., 6 July 1765
13 ibid., 25 July 1765
14 ibid., 7 August 1765
15 ibid., 2 August 1765

5 THE GRAND TRUNK
1 Wedgwood to John Wedgwood, 11 March 1765
2 Maria Edgeworth, *Memoirs of Richard Lovell Edgeworth*, 1820
3 Quoted in Hesketh Pearson, *Doctor Darwin*, 1930
4 Wedgwood to Bentley, 15 October 1765
5 ibid., 2 January 1765
6 *Seasonal Considerations on a Navigable Canal Intended to be cut from the River Trent . . . to the River Mersey*, April 1766
7 Wedgwood to Bentley, 14 January 1766
8 ibid., November 1765
9 Wedgwood to John Wedgwood, 4 June 1766

6 EXPANSION
1 Wedgwood to Bentley, 11 April 1766
2 ibid., 31 December 1767
3 ibid., 26 May 1766
4 ibid., 26 June 1766
5 ibid., 15 September 1766
6 ibid., 14 February 1767
7 ibid., 12 March 1767
8 ibid., 8 November 1767
9 ibid., 20 May 1768
10 ibid., 16 February 1767
11 ibid., 20 May 1767
12 ibid., 27 May 1767
13 ibid., 23 May 1767
14 ibid., 5 August 1767
15 ibid., 2 October 1767
16 ibid., 9 October 1766
17 ibid., 2 March 1767
18 Wedgwood to Griffiths, 21 December 1767
19 Wedgwood to Bentley, 8 September 1767

7 ARTES ETRURIAE RENASCUNTUR
1 Wedgwood to Bentley, 3 January 1768
2 ibid., 10 April 1768
3 ibid., 22 February 1768
4 ibid., 24 March 1768
5 ibid., June 1768
6 ibid., 15 March 1768
7 ibid., 30 August 1768; Wedgwood to Cox, 31 August 1768
8 Wedgwood to Bentley, 21 November 1768
9 Wedgwood to Sarah Wedgwood, 15 February 1769

10   ibid., 23 February 1769
11   Wedgwood to Bentley, 17 September 1769
12   ibid., 27 September 1769
13   ibid., 1 October 1769
14   ibid., October 1769
15   ibid., December 1768
16   ibid., 9 April 1769
17   Bentley to Cox, 7 December 1768
18   Wedgwood to Bentley, 11 November 1769

8 OUR HUMBLE FRIENDS
 1   Wedgwood to Bentley, 20 June 1768
 2   ibid., 28 December 1769
 3   ibid., 10 January 1770
 4   ibid., 9 April 1769
 5   ibid., 19 November 1769
 6   ibid., 5 March 1768
 7   ibid., 25 June 1769
 8   ibid., 9 April 1769
 9   ibid., 13 September 1769
10   ibid., 12 May 1770
11   ibid., 28 December 1769
12   ibid., 17 September 1769
13   ibid., 9 May 1770
14   ibid., 23 May 1770
15   Bentley to Boardman, 4 November 1769; quoted in James Boardman,
       Bentleyana, 1851
16   Wedgwood to Bentley, July 1769
17   ibid., 19 November 1769
18   Cox to Wedgwood, 9 May 1769
19   Order from Cox, 7 October 1769
20   Wedgwood to Bentley, 30 September 1769
21   ibid., 28 February 1769
22   Cox to Sarah Wedgwood, 19 September 1769
23   Wedgwood to Bentley, 2 January 1770
24   ibid., 15 January 1770
25   ibid., 3 February 1770
26   ibid., 10 February 1770

9 DEVELOPING THEMES
 1   Wedgwood to Bentley, 24 July 1770
 2   ibid., 13 October 1770
 3   ibid., 2 August 1770
 4   Bentley to Boardman, 15 December 1770; quoted in Boardman, op. cit.
 5   Wedgwood to Bentley, 24 December 1770

6 Matthew Boulton to James Watt, 7 February 1769
7 Duc de Holstein to Wedgwood, 4 July 1772
8 Wedgwood to Bentley, 11 May 1771
9 ibid., 7 September 1771
10 Henry Lubridge to Wedgwood, 30 August 1771
11 Wedgwood to Bentley, 23 August 1772
12 ibid., 27 October 1772
13 ibid.

10 DOMESTIC INTERLUDE
1 Wedgwood to Bentley, January 1769
2 ibid., 17 February 1772
3 ibid., February 1771
4 ibid., 15 May 1771
5 ibid., 6 June 1772
6 ibid., 10 September 1772
7 ibid., 4 October 1772
8 ibid., 26 December 1772
9 Wedgwood's Commonplace Book I, letter dated 1774
10 ibid., letter dated 4 October 1774
11 Wedgwood to Bentley, 24–26 December 1770
12 ibid., 28 September 1772
13 Darwin to Boulton, 5 April 1778
14 Account with Cadell's, January to June 1774

11 RUSSIA AND JASPER
1 Wedgwood to Bentley, 23 March 1773
2 ibid., 30 July 1773
3 John Wood to Swift, 11 April 1774
4 A catalogue was sent on 19 September 1774
5 Wedgwood to Bentley, 5 March 1774
6 John Wood to Swift, 14 April 1774 and 19 April 1774
7 Wedgwood to Bentley, 21 July 1774
8 ibid., 14 January 1775
9 ibid., 30 November 1774
10 John Wood to Wedgwood, 10 October 1774
11 ibid., 24 October 1774
12 Wedgwood to Bentley, 6 February 1775
13 ibid., April 1778

12 CORNWALL
1 Thomas Hyde to Wedgwood, May 1773
2 Commonplace Book I
3 Wedgwood to John Wedgwood, 19 October 1775
4 Susannah Wedgwood to Wedgwood, 3 December 1775

5 Wedgwood to Bentley, 13 February 1776
6 ibid., 10 April, 1777
7 James Boardman, *Bentleyana*, 1851
8 Commonplace Book I

13 THE CHILDREN
1 Wedgwood to Bentley, 29 December 1777
2 ibid., 6 October 1778
3 ibid., 3 October 1779
4 ibid., 9 October 1779
5 ibid., 13 October 1779
6 The Leyden jar, which could deliver an electric shock, had recently been
     discovered and put to a number of bizarre uses – from the antics of Louis of
     France, who made a brigade of guards jump in unison, to medical treatment.
7 Wedgwood to Bentley, 8 November 1779
8 Wedgwood to Catherine Wedgwood, 27 March 1780; letter copied into
     Commonplace Book I
9 Commonplace Book I
10 ibid.

14 END OF A PARTNERSHIP
1 Wedgwood to Bentley, 3 March 1778
2 Sir William Hamilton to Wedgwood, 22 June 1779
3 A full account of the Stubbs–Wedgwood collaboration can be found in the
     catalogue of the Tate Gallery exhibition of 1974: Bruce Tattersall, *Stubbs
     and Wedgwood*, 1974
4 Wedgwood to Bentley, 4 November 1777
5 ibid., 8 March 1779
6 ibid., 18 April 1778
7 Tom Byerley to Swift, 22 January 1779
8 Wedgwood to Bentley, 18 August 1780
9 ibid., 25 May 1780
10 ibid., 9 September 1780
11 ibid., 12 November 1780

15 WEDGWOOD WITHOUT BENTLEY
1 Anna Seward to Lady Marianne Carnagy, 21 March 1785
2 Priestley to Wedgwood, 30 November 1780
3 Josiah Wedgwood, *Description and Use of a Thermometer for Measuring the
     Higher Degrees of Heat*, 1784
4 Wedgwood to James Watt, 15 May 1782
5 Pitt to Lord Gower, 11 November 1784
6 Evans of Long Acre to Wedgwood, 16 May 1782
7 Josiah Wedgwood II to Wedgwood, 7 March 1783
8 Tom Wedgwood to Wedgwood, 11 March 1783

9   Josiah Wedgwood, *An Address to the Young Inhabitants of the Pottery*, 27 March 1783
10 Wedgwood to Wright, 29 April 1784
11 Wright to Wedgwood, 3 May 1784
12 Draft of a letter to Lady Templetown dated 27 June 1783
13 Tom Byerley to Thomas Wedgwood, 13 May 1782

16 MASTERS AND SLAVES
1   Wedgwood to Matthew Boulton (copy), 21 February 1785
2   ibid., 1 January 1785
3   Wedgwood to William Eden, 13 December 1785
4   Wedgwood to Richard Lovell Edgeworth, 13 February 1786
5   Letter to Wedgwood dated 27 August 1788
6   Wedgwood to James Watt, 17 September 1785
7   Letter from Thomas Clarkson dated 27 August 1788
8   Wedgwood to Benjamin Franklin, 29 February 1788
9   Wedgwood to Anna Seward, February 1788
10 Wedgwood to Erasmus Darwin, July 1789
11 Darwin to James Watt, 19 January 1790
12 Wedgwood to Priestley, 19 October 1788

17 END OF A CAREER
1   Wedgwood to Sir Joseph Banks, 28 June 1787
2   Wedgwood to Sir William Hamilton, 24 January 1786
3   Josiah Wedgwood, *Description of the Portland Vase*, 1790
4   Erasmus Darwin, *The Botanic Garden* (1791 ed)
5   Refers to a medallion struck to commemorate the first British colony in Australia
6   Alexander Chisholm's Commonplace Book II
7   "A Report on the Present State of the Potteries", sent to Lord Auckland on 28 January 1792
8   Wedgwood to Josiah Wedgwood II, 17 May 1790
9   Josiah Wedgwood II to Wedgwood, 25 May 1790
10 Draft of undated letter quoted in Henry Callington Bolton, *Scientific Correspondence of Joseph Priestley*, 1892
11 Letter in *Gentlemen's Magazine*, July 1791
12 Wedgwood to Byerley, 14 December 1792
13 Quoted in Emma Darwin, *A Century of Family Letters 1792–1896*, 1904
14 Wedgwood to John Wedgwood, 17 June 1793
15 ibid., 16 September 1793
16 Samuel Phillips to Thomas Wedgwood, 13 July 1790
17 Byerley to Samuel Boardman, 8 January 1795

18 THE DYNASTY AND ITS FOUNDER
1   Listing of male servants, May 1794

Select Bibliography

Works dealing with Wedgwood ware are legion. Similarly, there are vast numbers of books dealing with the Industrial Revolution that refer to Wedgwood and the Potteries. Both categories have been excluded from this list, which is limited to those books that are more directly concerned with the lives of Wedgwood, his family and his friends.

Bentley, R., *Thomas Bentley 1730-1780*, 1927
Boardman, James, *Bentleyana*, 1851
Bolton, Henry Callington, *Scientific Correspondence of Joseph Priestley*, 1892
Burton, William, *Josiah Wedgwood and his Pottery*, 1922
Darwin, Emma, *A Century of Family Letters 1792-1896*, 1915
Edgeworth, Maria, *Memoirs of Richard Lovell Edgeworth*, 1820
Farrer, Katherine, *Letters of Josiah Wedgwood* (3 vols), 1903-9
Finer, Anne, and Savage, George, *The Selected Letters of Josiah Wedgwood*, 1965
Flaxman, John, *Lectures in Sculpture*, 1829 (contains an anonymous biography)
Litchfield, R. B., *Tom Wedgwood*, 1903
Mankowitz, Wolf, *Wedgwood*, 1953
Meteyard, Eliza, *The Life and Works of Wedgwood* (2 vols), 1865
Meteyard, Eliza, *The Wedgwood Handbook*, 1875
Pearson, Hesketh, *Dr. Darwin*, 1930
Rutt, John Towill, *Life and Correspondence of Joseph Priestley*, 1831
Schofield, Robert E, *The Lunar Society of Birmingham*, 1963
Seward, Anna, *Letters*, 1811
Shaw, Simeon, *History of the Staffordshire Potteries*, 1829
Smiles, Samuel, *Josiah Wedgwood*, 1894
Tattersall, Bruce, *Stubbs and Wedgwood*, 1974
Weatherill, Lorna, *The Pottery Trade and North Staffordshire 1660-1760*, 1971
Wedgwood, Josiah C., *A History of the Wedgwood Family*, 1908
Williamson, George C., *The Imperial Russian Dinner Service*, 1909

Index